## Advance Praise

"Reading *Those Who Dare* was li[...] of inspiration and encouragement I needed! I felt my own courage soar with each page and realized that courage comes in many shapes and sizes. I can't wait to share this book with others who are starting out on new adventures, facing old fears, and seeking opportunities for growth and ways to overcome life's varied challenges."

— Lisa Hammond, author of *Dream Big* and founder of Femail Creations

"Katherine Martin has written a brilliant, inspiring, and very real tribute to the remarkable in all of us. Her clear, captivating, and honest storytelling of the bold and raw courage of both extraordinary people in extreme situations and the everyday challenges of living a bold and courageous life is masterful and potent. Her own insight into courage reveals a deep wisdom, and she writes with both great care and riveting clarity."

— Lynne Twist, author of *The Soul of Money*

## Praise for *Women of Courage*

"This is a humbling and inspiring book that will make you want to grab hold of life and live it more loudly. These women will change you. Every man should read this book!"

— Deepak Chopra, author of *The Seven Spiritual Laws of Success*

"The women in this book push against the grain, defy complacency, and reach for their dreams. That alone is remarkable, but more remarkable still is that they do it for the good of others. In that, they inspire us all to speak and live from our hearts."

— Sharon Stone, actress

"A groundbreaking, courageous testimony to the power of women's voices to speak out, to risk, to break barriers, to find truth. But this book isn't just about women. It's about everyone who refuses to be small or to accept anything less for themselves than absolute spiritual and personal freedom."

— Judith Orloff, MD,
author of *Dr. Judith Orloff's Guide to Intuitive Healing*

"I want this book for my daughters."

— Stephen Simon, producer of *What Dreams May Come*
and author of *The Force Is With You*

"These stories will capture your heart. . . . Be ready to be changed and to live life more richly for having been in the company of these women."

— Marci Shimoff, coauthor of *Chicken Soup for the Woman's Soul*

"*Women of Courage* is a book every man and woman should read. Katherine Martin beautifully tells the stories of real women confronted with real choices that challenge their souls to the utmost. Their experiences give us many new definitions for the word *courage*. Beautifully written, this book inspires and encourages all of us to walk in courage."

— Mary Manin Morrissey, senior minister, Living Enrichment Center

"Filled with wisdom and gratitude like a Thanksgiving banquet with cherished friends, it inspires me to remember that it takes courage and humility to love and to be loved — which is a generous meal indeed."

— Barnett Bain, producer of *The Celestine Prophecy*
and *Homeless to Harvard*

# Praise for *Women of Spirit*

"My kind of women!"

— Gert Boyle, chairman, Columbia Sportswear Company

"Virginia Woolf once declared that women need to develop the habit of freedom. We are not in the habit of making the connection between self-esteem and dignity, activism, or personal freedom. For that, we need the fire of inspiration. But it's right there, in the common experiences we share, in our common desire to act as if everything we do matters. And it's right here in the pages of *Women of Spirit*. Maybe you'll recognize the woman you are; maybe you'll find the woman you want to be. Either way, these stories will inspire you."

— Anita Roddick, OBE, founder, The Body Shop

"These stories reveal the way the world has always been made better — by individuals who courageously follow their heart's inner wisdom. At a moment in history when the tide of events seems determined by faceless governments and corporations, we need these examples of individual action more than ever."

— Larry Dossey, MD, author of *Healing Beyond the Body* and *Healing Words*

"Right in front of each of us is the power to make a difference for ourselves and for others — that's the lesson you learn from these brave women. Their revealing stories tell about the life journeys they took and share the valuable lessons they learned. From ordinary to extraordinary, from politicians and activists to grandmothers, authors, and doctors, they are indeed women of spirit."

— Ellen Pack, founder, www.women.com

THOSE WHO

# THOSE WHO

# DARE

## Real People, Real Courage

*...and what we learn from them*

# KATHERINE MARTIN

NEW WORLD LIBRARY
NOVATO, CALIFORNIA

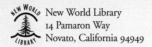 New World Library
14 Pamaron Way
Novato, California 94949

Cover design by Mary Ann Casler
Text design and typography by Bill Mifsud

Excerpt from "Welcome to Holland" on pages 177–78 used by permission of the author, Emily Perl Kingsley.

Quotes from *Hate Is My Neighbor* by Tom Alibrandi with Bill Wassmuth used by permission of the authors.

Quotes from the iVillage.com community board, "Life Coach: Expert Advice from Katherine Martin," Relationship Channel, used by permission. All names have been changed.

The stories in this book are told to the individuals' best recollection, and details cannot always be confirmed.

Library of Congress Cataloging-in-Publication Data
Martin, Katherine.
   Those who dare : real people, real courage / Katherine Martin.— 1st ed.
      p.   cm.
   ISBN 1-57731-453-0 (pbk. : alk. paper)
1.  Social reformers—United States—Biography. 2.  Courage—Case studies.
3.  Risk-taking (Psychology)—Case studies. 4.  Social action—Case studies.
I. Title.
   HN57.M269 2004
   303.48'4'0922—dc22                                                                            2004010357

First printing, November 2004
ISBN 1-57731-453-0
Printed in Canada on partially recycled, acid-free paper

New World Library is dedicated to preserving the earth and its resources. We are now printing 50 percent of our new titles on 100 percent chlorine-free postconsumer waste recycled paper. As members of the Green Press Initiative (www.recycledproducts.org/gpi/), our goal is to use 100 percent recycled paper for all our titles by 2007.

Distributed to the trade by Publishers Group West

10   9   8   7   6   5   4   3   2   1

⊙

*To my father,*

*Stuart Lane,*
*who has always believed in me:*

*from my heart,*
*thank you.*

◉

*To dare is to lose one's footing momentarily.*
*To not dare is to lose oneself.*

*— Søren Kierkegaard*

# Contents

Part III | Loving beyond All Measure

# Acknowledgments

First and always, I want to thank my best friend and husband, Franc Sloan, for his wisdom, humor, nurturance, great spirit, courage, love, and unwavering support of my work. He has been an inspiration to me for thirty years. And our son, Benjamin, love of our lives, an unfolding wonder to me, intelligent, funny, insightful, kind, and pushing the envelope of his life in ways that make me unabashedly proud.

To every person in this book, thank you for being who you are, for lighting us up with the possibilities of life, for reminding us of the difference we can make. Thank you for your generosity of time and spirit, for your enduring patience, for your sustained enthusiasm, and for your keen attention to detail. I am so honored to know you.

Thanks to Kellie Gould, editor-in-chief of iVillage.com, for bringing the courage material to one of the leading women's online sites, to senior producer of the relationships channel Charity Curley, and to incomparable community board host Karen, as well as to Lisa, Kim, Nicole, and all the others who made the courage board an intimate, fun, and thought-provoking place to talk and share and inspire one another.

To A. T. Birmingham, who while at the Giraffe Project faithfully put me in touch with their awardees and plied me with materials.

To the Goldman Environmental Foundation in San Francisco, which for fifteen years has recognized people like Dr. Paul Cox. The Goldman Environmental Prize is the world's largest prize program, annually honoring six grassroots environmental heroes from each of six continental regions: Africa, Asia, Europe, Island Nations, North America, and South and Central America. The combined work of past recipients has benefited an estimated 102 million people worldwide.

To the Cavallo Foundation, which honored Debbie Williams with an award for moral courage. To Dan Wichmer, who believed in her when others didn't and put heart and soul into her lawsuit. To Clark Cunningham, today the W. Lee Burge Professor of Law and Ethics at the Georgia State University College of Law, who knew she was telling the truth and stood by her.

To Mary Frances, wife and great love of Bill Wassmuth.

To Lynne Twist for her generous support of my work and for opening doors to Jim Garrison and John Perkins. To Sandi Bain, sweet friend, for introducing me to Karen Murray. And to my beautiful friend Manuela Dunn for taking me to Kathy Eldon.

To Juanita Howard, for her enthusiasm and friendship, and for bringing Nichelle Nichols to a *Women of Courage* theater event. To Gail McCormick, without whom I might never have met Karen Gaffney. To Stephen Ericksen-Roddy of Adonal Foyle Enterprises, who graciously fit me into Adonal's busy schedule. And to Dean Acosta, press secretary to

Dr. Fred Gregory, deputy administrator of NASA, who helped with factual accuracy and arranged my interview with Dr. Gregory.

I first came to know some of the people in this book because of writers. I am grateful to Benjamin Brink, who wrote and photographed a thrilling feature story about Mark Nyberg for the *Oregonian;* to Scott Hammers of the *Lake Oswego Review,* who wrote an in-depth feature about Shannon Meehan; to David Steele, who profiled Adonal Foyle for the *San Francisco Chronicle;* and to Alison Osius for her wonderful book, *Second Ascent: The Story of Hugh Herr.* A few people's compelling books greatly informed my own writing: Nichelle Nichols's *Beyond Uhura;* John Perkins's *The World Is As You Dream It;* Dr. Paul Cox's *Nafanua: Saving the Samoan Rain Forest;* Tom Alibrandi and Bill Wassmuth's *Hate Is My Neighbor;* and *The Journey Is the Destination: The Journals of Dan Eldon.* I am also grateful to *Seattle Times* reporter Florangela Davila for her stories about Bill Wassmuth.

Several people steadfastly sustain me with their love, and I cannot thank them enough: my beautiful and wise mother, Virginia Lane, from whom I inherited an indomitable will and optimism; my sister and lifelong hero Nancy Mackenzie, who as friend, single mother of three extraordinary girls, and assistant dean of admissions at Macalester College always inspires me with her intelligence, integrity, and compassion; my ever-curious, ever-social, ever-innovative father, Stuart Lane, who is so widely loved by many; my mother-in-law, Joan Hixon Martin, kindred spirit and seeker of the deep meanings of life, whose presence is healing and whose support is an anchor; and my sister Karin Arsan, whose faith and generosity are unfaltering. And my cherished friends of twenty-five years Lawrence Stoller and Sunni Kerwin, and Marcy Basel, who have always been the wind at my back. And beloved friends Vicky Davies and Jim Joyce, Courtney Price, Carolyn and Louis Kickhofel, Marilyn Arnett and David Siegler, Elizabeth Schoultz of the Eagle People, and Robin Damore. And thanks to Robin again for being champion and mentor and for giving generously of her time and substantial talent in photographing the women and men in this book and in the courage theater events, creating stunning theater posters with David Friedman of Fried Art Studio in Portland. And again to Vicky for her creative eye in designing the "Courage" T-shirt and to both her and Jim, whose Gourmet Productions in Lake Oswego, Oregon, is daily sustenance for me when I'm on writing retreats.

Many people have contributed to my work with their unwavering belief in its power to make a difference, with the risks they've taken on behalf of it, and with the generosity of their time and talents. To Ricka Fisher, who in addition to being friend and cohort tenaciously championed the courage work with heart, soul, and smarts, and who directed the courage theater piece at the Marlborough School, at the Mark Taper Auditorium in Los Angeles, and at the 2004 *Fortune* Summit for the Most Powerful Women. To Albert Fisher, who has given enormously of his time and talent to the theater events and has been a trusty wind behind our backs.

To Rita Wilson, Andrea Martin, Juanita Jennings, Lauren Tom, and Ari Graynor for their generous portrayals of women in the *Women of Courage* show at the Mark Taper Auditorium. For featuring the show during their Los Angeles exhibit, my thanks to Facing History and Ourselves, which reaches some million and a half students every year with lessons about diversity, prejudice, and tolerance in promoting the development of a more humane and informed citizenry.

To Laurie Howlett and Carrie Welch of *Fortune* and FSB Fortune Small

Business for infusing courage and soul into the Summit for the Most Powerful Women and for believing in the *Women of Courage* show. To Sandy
Suran of the Suran Group for seeing the potential in my work and for her
business guidance in creating People Who Dare, LLC. To Cindy Thompson
of Cindy Thompson Event Productions, who is creating courage benefit
performances in unique and innovative ways. To my pal Karla Ekdahl, who
put her smart, elegant passion behind the courage theater evolution; and
to Frances Wilkinson and Blanche Hawkins for their encouragement
and support.

For ongoing inspiration in the art of personal reinvention, *hola* to
Cynthia Price in San Miguel Allende. For his generosity in designing the look
of People Who Dare, LLC, Loren Weeks, founder of the ad agency BLW &
Associates in Portland, Oregon. To Pat Rutan, who created a powerful show
of the women and men of courage for me to use whenever I speak. And to
Karen Kimsey-House, coach extraordinaire, for being midwife of the first
book and for creating the Coaches Training Institute, for believing in what's
good and true and beautiful in people, and for asking the right questions to
draw up knowledge and wisdom from the deep well within us.

Thanks to all who have guided me spiritually. And to my wonderful
editor and champion Georgia Hughes, editorial director of New World
Library, to marketing maven Munro Magruder, to publicist Monique
Muhlenkamp, and to my New World Library family for continuing to
believe in my work and the power of courage to make the difference. To
everyone at Publishers Group West who champions this book. To every
bookseller who gives it light. To every media person who gives it wing. To
you, dear reader, who gives it breath.

# Prologue
*Starting out in one place, ending up in another*

Ten years ago, when I started writing *Women of Courage,* the first book in what came to be my People Who Dare series, I had no idea it would bring me here. I was a writer looking for inspiration, a woman trying to get my own life moving. I thought I could jump-start it by spending time with people who lived on the edge, restless and bold people who took on big challenges fearlessly. I wanted to be like them. I wanted to "draft" in their courage.

I was commuting between Portland, Oregon, and Los Angeles, writing screenplays and in the middle of a sulfurous shift from the world of magazines and books. Hollywood can be seductive, and I'd signed on for a ride unlike anything I'd ever experienced as a writer. Years later, I'd find humor in referring to Mike Rich when I spoke about this period in my life. A radio news anchor in Portland, Mike wrote the movie *Finding Forrester,* and his experience in Hollywood appeared to be the stuff of fairy tales, with his first feature film starring Sean Connery and snowballing into a second, *The Rookie,* and a third, *Radio.*

My *Finding Forrester* became *Losing Katherine.*

I'd been a writer all my life, and inevitably, I guess, the day came when I thought, *I want to write a screenplay,* because even a lowly writing assignment to cover county fairs could spin across my mind like a movie. Imagine, then, the flurry of images that possessed me in the world of figure skating, where I dwelt with some regularity for several years, profiling the top skaters and going to the national championships. In the bowels of the stadium, I'd slip past the security guards as though I belonged there and into the dressing room where the girls were getting ready to go on the ice. Hanging out with them and their moms, I heard all the dirt about this lovely sport with a distinct underbelly. My imagination whirred with story possibilities. I would set my first script in this environment. I would call it *The Cutting Edge.* Don't get too excited.

Out I went to sell it. I had no agent — just me scratching at leads and green at the gills. Six months later, I was beginning to wonder if I'd made a mistake. After another six months, I thought I must be the worst wannabe screenwriter on the face of the earth.

Tenacity, I would come to appreciate, is elemental to courage. And so, at times, is naïveté. I kept at it, and the day came when the phone rang with the right call. The script was purchased. I was on my way. Off I flew to do script notes with my producer, who was on location shooting a film in Canada. There I was, hanging out with movie stars for the first time in my life, with the hair on the back of my neck standing up every time the director called, "Annnnd . . . action!"

When I returned home, I asked my husband, Franc, what he thought about moving to Los Angeles. Even as we started talking about the idea, I faltered: *How can I ask him to do this?* Our son, Benjamin, was young, and we were living outside San Francisco in a place where we had rooted tenderly. Even my producer thought I was nuts: "You have the perfect life. Why on earth would you move to L.A.?"

The City of Angels didn't top Franc's list of places he'd love to live in. That he even entertained the idea speaks volumes about him. We mulled it over; we debated. If I really wanted to make a go of this thing, this screen-writing, wasn't it critical to move to the epicenter of the film industry?

*And just who do you think you are?* Hand on hip, my inner critic had a field day. *Wannabe screenwriters are a dime a dozen in Hollywood. And you think you're going to be different? You're a nobody.* The tone of this nagging voice grew ominous, because to go and fail would be to pull my family away from paradise for nothing.

Let's do it, said Franc.

Before we left, an acquaintance who worked in the film industry told me, "You are either really naive or really stupid or really brave." I laughed — nervously.

Three years later, I was caught in what one journalist called the "Holly-wood undertow," what I would come to call the Big Wait. I didn't know that it could take years — eight, twelve, twenty! — to get a movie off the ground and onto the big screen. I didn't know that a film called *The Cutting Edge* with an oddly similar story line could get made by a producer I didn't know. Being myopic and willful, I continued to write what I thought were socially relevant screenplays with strong characters, certain that they would be made into wonderful movies.

Was I frustrated? Oh, yes. Between script and screen lies a great distance, and the development process is slow and fraught with false starts. A producer would tell me how "brilliant" my script was. The flurry of negotiations between agents would create a buzz. Names of stars would be tossed about, celebrities who might attach to the project. All the while, time would pass...and pass...and keep on passing. Even the script that won a Blockbuster/McKnight Film Award and was optioned by Demi Moore's film company got close to being made but wasn't. The highs were high and the lows were awful.

Little by little, my confidence eroded, and I grew increasingly anxious and insecure, fitting right in with a culture where job security was an oxymoron. And yet I continued to be easily seduced by every new possibility of a hot deal or a star interested in one of my scripts. I had not only gone to Hollywood. I had gone Hollywood.

I didn't notice how I had changed until the idea of doing a book about courageous women came up, and it was not I but Franc who saw the value in it. "This would be good for you," said he, who knew me better than anyone on the planet, having rooted around with me for twenty years at that time. Ah, but I was busy, "doing lunch" and "taking meetings" and generally "doing" Hollywood. "This is good work," he persisted. But I was too busy; I had characters to develop, dialogue, plot points. *Don't bother me.* But he kept bringing it up because he saw that what really mattered to me was getting lost and that this book could bring me back. Watching me flounder in Hollywood wasn't easy for him. It was painful. In fact, it sucked.

Facing the truth wasn't pretty. I was chasing a dream that had become an elusive fantasy — always within reach but never in hand. I was close, on the brink, always with a perfectly sound reason why the movie wasn't getting made ... not quite yet ... but it will ... just as soon as ...

I was losing Katherine.

As our son grew toward adolescence, Franc and I decided it was time to leave Los Angeles. We headed to the Pacific Northwest for some wholesome living, clean air, and good company. But a part of me stayed in Los Angeles. Insecure and afraid to let go all the way, I kept an efficiency apartment there, because in Hollywood your footprints close up quickly. Still locked into my identity as a screenwriter, I commuted to do lunch and take meetings about my scripts.

Living between Portland and Los Angeles, I felt stymied, stuck, caught between. I felt like I had failed, and I had nowhere to go to shake that feeling, no pretense to hide behind, no new gig that would disguise the feeling: *All that time in Hollywood.* For what? First came the anger at all the people who had said no to my dream, then the blame, the self-pity, the feeling of being unappreciated as an artist. Then came the remorse, which ran deep and roiled across my soul: all the lost time with my family, the lost opportunities to do meaningful work. Why hadn't I listened to Franc earlier?

Remorse is uncomfortable. Part of me wanted to skip right over it, to push off my mistakes and hurry into the next chapter. But remorse will not be denied. Had I not paid attention, it would have come back, infecting my health or my marriage or my future work. I knew that unless I dealt with it right then and there, unless I forgave myself, I wouldn't be able to move forward unencumbered.

One of the most courageous things we can do is to change. I say that regularly in reference to other people. Now I felt it happening in me. I was significantly changing, my identity shifting, and I felt out of control. My image had gotten so tightly wound around Hollywood that I wondered who I was now.

Letting go was scary. Horrible for a tenacious person. Simply anathema. Courage, I discovered, is not only about persisting, but at times about letting go. The more I let go of the old dream, the more room became available for what really mattered to me, meaningful work with a tangible impact. The more space I made where that elusive fantasy had been, the more authentic I became. I plunged into writing *Women of Courage,* and doors opened. Horizons expanded in front of me.

That was ten years ago, and I haven't stopped writing about courage since. I didn't see it back then, but I had placed my feet on the path of a long work that would lead me to speak at conferences, special events, and schools; that would inspire the creation of a courage theater piece, a second book, *Women of Spirit,* and now *Those Who Dare;* and that would give rise to the formation of a company, People Who Dare, LLC, where more dreams are brewing.

Not only was that first book a good idea, but it was healing medicine for me.

*Those Who Dare* continues my query into the lives of people who make a difference, whether in bold and clamorous ways or in the unheralded quiet of everyday courage. I've interviewed eighteen women and men to capture moments when their lives took a turn because of their integrity, their adherence to principles, their convictions, and their commitment to living a life that matters.

As with *Women of Courage* and *Women of Spirit,* my focus is the emotional context of a story. I want you to feel as though you're inside the skin of the people in this book, so I tell much of their stories in the first person, with the goal of speaking authentically in their voices. Unlike in the earlier books, I have also brought my own voice to the page, bringing you with me as I go to an interview or as I talk with people who are in the heat of a courageous moment. Often our courage is a collaboration, and I want you to know the people who were supportive, who also put themselves at risk, who persevered alongside the stories' subjects. In addition to Adonal Foyle, I want you to meet the courageous couple, Joan and Jay Mandle, who made possible his transformation from a kid in the Caribbean to NBA basketball player. In addition to Karen Gaffney, it's essential for you to know her remarkable mother, Barb. This broadening is reflected in the Resources and Links section at the back of the book, which includes contact information not only for people, but also for organizations relevant to the stories.

In *Those Who Dare,* I also do something I haven't done before. I talk about lessons I've learned over the span of these many years, principles of courage, how it works, misconceptions, tools for crafting a courageous life. Courage is like a muscle, and we can strengthen it in ourselves. In the final part of the book, I set out Cornerstones of Courage and Keys to a Daring Life.

Putting so much of my voice into this book was challenging. I had spent a decade setting it aside; I had "disappeared" myself in order to authentically capture the voices of others. Now it was time to bring mine forward and come out from behind other people's stories. My inner critics had a field day, as you'll read about in the last chapter.

You'll also find this book to be different from *Women of Courage* and *Women of Spirit* because of my choice of people to include. Whereas the earlier books included stories from interviews with famous women like Isabel Allende, Dana Reeve, Judith Orloff, Sarah Weddington, Faith Popcorn, Marianne Williamson, Geraldine Ferraro, Judy Collins, Joan Borysenko, Julia Butterfly Hill, and others, *Those Who Dare* is intentionally focused on people you may not have heard of — with the exceptions of Nichelle Nichols, the eternally famous Lieutenant Uhura of *Star Trek,* and Adonal Foyle. I wanted you to experience being with folks who might live next door, because we so easily associate the word *courage* with superheroes and forget that it lives in all of us.

⊙

Where I am now on this courage quest is light years away from where I began. Over these ten years, I've seen the deep desire in people to make their lives matter. I've witnessed the profound power of the individual to make a difference.

"But why?" you may ask. "Why should I bother reading a book about courage? The last thing I need is another challenge in my life." And yet here you are. Something in you responds to the call of courage — maybe something you've longed to do but have been too afraid to do, maybe something that you know to be right but that puts you at risk. Here you are, piqued by the thought of daring to go ahead, taking the risk, becoming more truly you.

At the end of the day, as we assess our lives, we see that what we've done that is honest and true to who we are, the times when we've dared to push the envelope, to leave the reasoned path, to love beyond all measure, to live replete, and to stand up for what's right, these are what bring us peace. "Yes," we will say, "I have used this life well. I have left a strong courage legacy."

# ONE

## Pushing the Envelope

When you do common things in life in an uncommon way, you will command the attention of the world.

— *George Washington Carver*

When I started writing about courage, I thought I knew all about it.

Researching the first book, I set out to find people who had risked everything to do the seemingly impossible, putting themselves in great physical jeopardy. I was looking for the big courage of those who had conquered challenges against all odds. Legends. Heroes, the grand explorers, people who had dared to do things that no one else had done, who had gone to the ends of the world and back, or people who had broken down cultural barriers, stood up against injustice at great personal risk. I was looking for headliner stuff that was dramatic and wildly public.

That courage could arise from a grand exploration of the heart did not occur to me.

In pursuit of that big courage, I met people like Fanchon Blake, who was the first woman to sue the Los Angeles Police Department for sex discrimination, the first to break a scary code of silence. Her lawsuit lasted for seven years, and at one point she had to be put under federal protection. Because she stayed the course and dared to speak out when no one else would, some seventeen hundred women in Los Angeles have jobs on the force.

I found that big courage in young women like Heather O'Brien, who as a budding journalist at the age of nineteen went to Cambodia and traveled the border with Thailand, gaining entry to refugee camps and bringing out stories from the people inside. As she set out for the last camp, the one that had been the hardest to secure passage to, she couldn't have known that she would take a wrong turn on a remote road and come upon a secret Khmer Rouge camp where she would be taken prisoner.

Into the domain of these courageous people I traveled, feeling the utter magnitude of their stories, breathless with the dramatic turns in their lives and how they stepped up to meet those turns with wills of iron: "I will not back down." They embodied the best in us, they lived large. I wanted to be like them. I wanted to be fearless, confident, gregarious, willful, undaunted.

I had a great distance to go. I was a woman regularly visited by unsubstantiated fear. I was shy. I did not cotton to making mistakes and would do just about anything to avoid them. This was not the profile of a woman on her way to courage.

And then along came Ann Bancroft.

Ann Bancroft was the first woman to cross the ice to both the North and South Poles. She was the only female member of the Steger International Polar Expedition in 1986, dogsledding a thousand miles from the Northwest Territories in Canada to the North Pole. She had nearly died falling through an ice shelf into the Arctic Ocean. Seven years later, in spite of seemingly insurmountable odds, she organized and led the American Women's Expedition, the first women's expedition to the South Pole. She would make history again by traversing the entire continent of Antarctica with fellow explorer Liv Arnesen, from Norway. But that was later. When I interviewed her, she had recently been inducted into the Women's Hall of Fame. She was a legend in her own time. An icon of courage — perfect.

A riveting interview generates heat, and this one was a scorcher. But when we finished, in the space between climactic ending and wrapping up our interview, Ann leaned in and said, "Katherine, I really have to be honest with you..."

*Ah, the story deepens,* I thought, leaning forward.

"...that wasn't courageous."

I didn't quite catch her words. *Say again?*

"It wasn't courageous, not for me."

*Hold on. She's just told me about a sixty-seven-day journey on skis (no dogs and sleds and "mush, mush" for these women), pulling a two-hundred-pound sled against seventy-five mile-an-hour winds in subzero temperatures, and that's not courageous?*

"Put me in those wild, open places and that's where I'm at home. That's where I find myself, where I'm at peace."

*But, but, but...*

"But let me tell you about being dyslexic."

At a time when there wasn't much known about dyslexia, Ann was in college and struggling with her classes, hanging on tightly to her dream of becoming an elementary school teacher. Although a great athlete, she was far from a stellar student, and she knew that getting into the required teaching practicum would be a challenge. But when her college counselor suggested she get her B.A. and go on with her life, Ann was stunned. Give up her dream?

"I'd never had an adult tell me to quit: *Here, take the easy way out, just get your diploma.* I think she saw me as one of those athletes who aren't very serious about education and thought that unless I was willing to devote more time to getting the grades I needed, I should just take the diploma and run."

The woman unfortunately sat on the committee that heard petitions from students who had failed to get into the practicum and were trying again. She had authority. She was intimidating. And to Ann Bancroft — legend, icon, Hall-of-Famer — this ordinary moment in time became her defining moment of courage. Standing up to her counselor, she said, "You don't understand. The B.A. means nothing to me if I can't teach." When her counselor tried to convince her to give up field hockey and to buckle down, to hit the books, Ann could have relented. But she didn't. She stood her ground: "I won't give up sports, because it's the one place where I get the confidence to face how hard it is for me academically."

In the end, Ann got her teaching credential and became an elementary school teacher. "My graduation was a pretty big deal," she told me. "My entire family came to the ceremony. I was our first college graduate. And, as it turns out, my learning disability and my struggle to get through school were great training that I would use later on when I needed perseverance. Ten years later, standing in the bitter cold at the North Pole, I had the distinct thought, *This is no worse than school.* When I was having a bad day on the Arctic ice, that's what I would dredge up in my mind to keep myself going: *School was harder.*"

Ever the passionate teacher, Ann would create a curriculum and an online site so kids could follow her polar expeditions. More than three million people worldwide tracked her as she and Liv Arnesen traversed Antarctica, calling in reports from the South Pole on the satellite phone.

Talking with Ann was a turning point in my understanding of courage. Here was a woman whose true courage had nothing to do with the expeditions that turned her into a public heroine. Hers was much more personal and universal and, as such, more perfect than I had realized. I doubt that many of us can relate to being dropped at the edge of the continent of Antarctica, facing three months of nothing but white and ice, with howling winds that make it impossible to hear the person next to us, in subzero temperatures, all the while pulling a two-hundred-pound sled. However, all of us can relate to standing up to an intimidating person who's trying to tell us what we should do or who we should be or that our dream will never come true.

After that interview, my understanding of courage began to shift significantly, and I started to go deeper, to look beyond the obvious, to see the unexpected. Ann showed me that one of the most courageous things we can do is to know ourselves, down to the bone where it really counts, and then to be true to that, to take a stand for who we really are, to walk our innermost talk. And we do this not just for ourselves, but for those we love and because of the impact we have on our communities and the world at large when we show up fully for our lives.

With everyday practical courage, we can craft more meaningful and authentic lives, not waiting to do something dramatically courageous but doing it daily, awake to what really matters and making a difference.

Nichelle Nichols

# Lieutenant Uhura and a Different Kind of Trek
### Challenging the Status Quo and Changing Minds

Presence.

The people I interview have lots of it. They walk into a room, and something in the air shifts. People around them take notice. Who is *that?* Presence is the true and most authentic *you* coming forward fully into the moment. It's magical.

The first time I saw Nichelle Nichols, she was sitting on a bench at a reception. *Who is that?* I wondered. The people around her had that look that comes over one in the company of celebrity. I could see from a distance how much they admired her.

Celebrity presence can be different from the kind of presence I'm talking about. On the surface, celebrity presence is all about persona and very little about authenticity. But not always.

At just that moment, Nichelle looked over and smiled at me. Her warmth, her genuine presence washed my way. Honestly, I didn't know who she was; I'm not a "Trekkie." But to her millions of fans, this woman will always be Lieutenant Uhura, communications officer of the *Starship Enterprise* on *Star Trek,* a role model and inspiration worldwide. Nichelle was captivating, and I wanted to know more about her. Believe me, there was much to know about this woman who was raised in Chicago, a place she still calls home even though she lives in Los Angeles.

Dr. Martin Luther King Jr. let his children watch *Star Trek* because of her. As a "kid from the projects," Whoopi Goldberg saw Lieutenant Uhura as "the only vision of black people in the future," not knowing that one day she would join the cast of *Star Trek: The Next Generation.* Dr. Mae Jemison became the first African American astronaut because of her and began her shifts in space by speaking Lieutenant Uhura's words: "Hailing frequencies open...." When the first space shuttle, *Enterprise,* was christened at Cape Canaveral, Nichelle was there.

Before all the glitter and glitz of Hollywood, Nichelle was discovered at the age of fifteen by Duke Ellington when she created and performed a ballet for one of his musical suites. While touring with Ellington, she stepped in for the lead singer, who had become ill. She performed all over the United States, Canada, and Europe, including a guest stint with Lionel Hampton.

But well before all the dancing and singing, theater and film, the seeds of indomitable definition were planted in Nichelle. Her lineage traces back to the renegade son of a Welshman who made a fortune on his southern plantation with "four hundred head of slaves." That renegade son became her grandfather, enraging his family by marrying a woman of Moorish-Spanish and African American heritage. Disinherited by his father, he moved north with his bride to a small town thirty miles southwest of

Chicago, one of four towns in the country that were entirely governed by African Americans.

Here is where Nichelle would meet the world and begin a life informed by the commitment of her parents, Samuel and Lishla, to always doing what was right and refusing to compromise their principles. In Robbins, Illinois, in the house where he was raised, her father became magistrate and then mayor while working as a chemist for Hydrox Chemical Company on the north side of Chicago. Her mother, half Cherokee and half African, had the gift of seeing into the unknown; she was psychic.

I guess all that accumulated history was coming through when I first met her. Nichelle is strong, intelligent, unabashed. She's warm and funny. She laughs often, a gusty laugh. She's sensuous and clearly loves being a woman.

Lieutenant Uhura had been in her life for more than three decades and wasn't about to leave any time soon. Recognizing her lasting impact on people, Nichelle has a great respect for her. "Any time you develop a character that's so strong, it follows you through the rest of your life," she told me. Uhura continues to give people, women and minorities especially, a sense that they can do what they think impossible, that they can take hold of dreams and live them. For Nichelle, it was an honor to create and embody her — her history and lineage, her dignity, humor, integrity, and talent (like Nichelle, Uhura has a three-and-a-half-octave voice, and is coaxed by crew members on three occasions to sing).

But had it not been for Martin Luther King Jr., the gift of hope that Uhura gave people around the world would have lasted only one season. Nichelle was at a NAACP fund-raising event when a man came up to her and said, "There's someone who would like to meet you. He's a big fan." She turned and was stunned to see Dr. Martin Luther King Jr.

"I was absolutely speechless," said Nichelle, who at first didn't grasp that King was that fan. He told her that his children faithfully watched *Star Trek* and were devoted to Uhura. "You can imagine how I felt." Fumbling for words, she thanked him when he told her how proud he was of her. "I said I was really going to miss the crew of the *Starship Enterprise.*"

"What do you mean?" asked Dr. King.

Just the day before, she had told producer Gene Roddenberry that she'd be returning to the stage at the end of *Star Trek*'s first season. Roddenberry, who had created the show, was understandably upset because he had worked hard to bring together what he often called "this special crew," the first interracial all-star ensemble cast on television. He had fought for the role of Uhura, who was a vital member. But although the crew and cast and production company of *Star Trek* were "like a family," says Nichelle, she was worn down by the studio racism, subtle and not so subtle. And for the sake of her career, she felt she had to return to the theater, to her music and dance. She had never intended to be a television star. Nichelle and Gene were also close friends, so the decision was especially difficult.

With unassailable clarity and authority, Dr. King looked her square in the eyes and said, "You cannot do that. You must not." He went on about Uhura's impact: "Don't you realize how important your presence is? You have the first nonstereotypical role on television, male or female. You've broken ground. Everyone can identify with you, men, women, of all colors and races and religions."

"But it's just a role on a television show."

"No. It's unprecedented. It's not Beulah or Amos and Andy. For the first time, the world sees us as we should be seen, beautiful, talented people, intelligent, qualified people of dignity and grace. You've changed the face of television forever. You've opened a door, and you cannot let that door close. It's important for black children to see you in that role, but it's also important for people who don't look like us to see you. You must not leave."

Nichelle was stunned. "I didn't know what to think. That entire weekend, I was obsessed by what Dr. King had said. On Monday, I went to Gene's office. 'If you want me to stay, I'll stay.' A six-foot-three, hatchet-faced strong man, an ex–motorcycle cop and a World War II fighter pilot hero, Gene just sat there and looked at me, and a tear fell down his cheek. I stayed and never looked back. Lieutenant Uhura was, in fact, more than a role, *Star Trek* more than just a television series. Throughout the years, letters I continue to receive prove Dr. King to be right."

Nichelle could have turned to many places in her life to find a defining moment of courage. Talking with Dr. King was unequivocally one such moment. But for a defining moment of courage, she chose something that, years later, brought vivid memories and emotions that caught in her throat because of the significant difference she had made in the face of controversy. No, it wasn't as Uhura, although the twenty-third-century lieutenant was indelibly present.

It's January 1977. I'm in Washington, D.C., to give a speech at a conference about saving our space program.

Because of my interest in space research and exploration, I've already written and produced for the Smithsonian Air and Space Museum a film called *Space: What's in It for Me?* I've had the privilege of flying an eight-hour mission aboard the Kuiper C-141 Astronomy Observatory and being present at the Jet Propulsion Laboratory when the *Viking Lander* touched down on Mars. I've toured the Marshall Space Flight Center and the Alabama Space Rocket Center. Recently, I've been appointed to the board of directors of the National Space Institute. Attending space conferences, I periodically give speeches. This one is "New Opportunities for the Humanization of Space."

In the audience is the head of NASA's Office of Manned Space Flight, John Yardley. Apparently, he's impressed with what I have to say. He comes up at the end and asks me to meet with some people at NASA headquarters. I know him to be a man of integrity. Yes, what has he got in mind?

At the NASA meeting, John says, "Nichelle, we want you to help us with a problem we're having." He goes on to explain that they're six months into a yearlong astronaut recruitment campaign, and they're utterly baffled by the dearth of female and minority applicants.

Now, I know about NASA's other national campaigns to recruit astronauts. "Why would you be baffled?" I ask. "You've had five recruitment drives before this, and each time you've said that you're looking forward to having women and minorities become astronauts. And yet, even though you've had many fine applications from qualified minorities and women, you've said that none were as qualified as the all-white male astronaut corps. Not one person of color? Not one woman on the entire planet qualifies? You've sent a message: Don't bother to apply."

"She's quite right," says John, and a couple of other people in the room agree. "What should we do about it, Nichelle? We have only five months left, and we mean business this time."

I like this man's honesty. But still, I wonder, "How is this time different from the others?"

"Before, we needed pilots, people with jet training. With the shuttle, we need a new kind of astronaut, we need doctors, engineers, and scientists. The qualifications are different. Size isn't a factor. Eyesight isn't a factor, as long as it can be corrected with glasses."

Dr. Harriett Jenkins, one of NASA's first black female administrators, says that they've got to find a way to get their message across. "How would you correct this, Nichelle?"

"Well, qualified people are out there, they just don't trust NASA."

"We need somebody to make them trust us," says John. "What do you think?"

I still don't grasp that he's asking me for anything other than my opinion. "I think you've got to get somebody with great visibility and credibility to do a major media blitz with television, newspapers, radio. Someone to make speeches, public service announcements, commercials. Someone who will get out there and identify qualified people. Someone who will convince them and the public that NASA is serious, that this is a new era. You need someone who will change people's minds and convince them that this isn't just some public relations ploy."

"Like who?"

"John Denver is one of the most famous people on the planet right now. He's highly respected for his humanitarian work, people adore him, and he has a huge interest in space exploration. I've seen him at several of the space research centers around the country. He'd have great credibility with both men and women. Maybe he'd even write a song for you. Or ask Bill Cosby, he's the father figure to the nation. Or Coretta King; certainly women and African Americans have a high regard for her, and I think she'd do it if she were convinced that NASA is serious this time."

Yardley looks at me. "What about Lieutenant Uhura?"

I burst out laughing.

He raises an eyebrow.

"No, no, no . . . you don't want me. The first thing people will say is that it's a gimmick, and that NASA got a Hollywood astronaut as a publicity stunt. They'd never take me seriously."

"They hear you speak for five minutes, and they'll take you seriously. I've never been so moved and challenged."

In the speech I gave the night before, I challenged NASA to come down from its ivory tower and make a sincere outreach to women and people of color.

Before I know it, the people in the room are convincing me that I'm the right person for the job, and I'm getting increasingly nervous (nearly thirty years later, I still feel the heat of that nervousness as though it were yesterday). How can I, with no governmental experience, even begin to consider doing such a monumental, groundbreaking job?

"Okay, but I have some conditions. It has to be more than a media blitz. I want to go out and identify qualified applicants. I don't want any token women or minorities. Second, I want to work as a NASA contractor. I'll report to you, but to get this done in the time left, I need to be free to formulate it, organize it, carry it out through my own company. And last, doing this will require significant time away from my career." *Here I go, just as my music career is taking off again.* I've made a couple of records and am talking with a record company about a third. I've been singing all over the world. "I know I can do this. I know..." *Actually, I don't know at all.* "...that the people are out there." But would I be able to convince anybody to come down from a six-figure job to take a thirty- to fifty-thousand-dollar-a-year government job, an incredibly risky job to boot? "I'll be going after America's best men and women, not some college graduate who thinks it's a whiz of an idea, and I have to convince them that this is more than a nice notion."

John understands what I'm saying. "We know. And if anyone can convince them, it's you."

*Here I go....*

"All right, here's my final condition. If I put my name and reputation on the line for NASA and I find qualified women and minorities to apply, and a year from now I see a lily-white, all-male astronaut corps, I'm going to file a class-action lawsuit against you. And I won't stop with the publicity against NASA. You will be my dedicated target."

John Yardley doesn't blink an eye. "Done."

Before I know it, I'm on a plane to the Johnson Space Center in Houston to undergo modified astronaut training and briefing, to tour the facilities and mission control, and to be briefed on the Space Shuttle Orbiter Simulator. I go to the Kennedy Space Center at Cape Canaveral, where I visit the environmental chamber and am tested at the medical checkup facilities. Thankfully, I do the simulation of the space shuttle without crashing it!

From the start of the recruitment campaign, I fear that people are going to laugh me out of the hall, if I can even get into a hall. Lieutenant Uhura? People are going to break up when they see me on television: Boy, NASA must really be hard up; they've got a fake astronaut plugging the space program. I fear that black people are going to roast me over the coals and that women are going to castigate me.

A few years earlier, I'd created a company, Women in Motion, to produce educational and motivational films and plays to encourage women and young people to think bigger, broader, and not let obstacles stop them. Now Women in Motion contracts with NASA, and I'm the one who needs to think bigger, broader, and not let obstacles stop me.

The first thing I do is to make several public service announcements for television. Instead of the slogan "Uncle Sam needs a few good men," I use "Uncle Sam needs a few good men...and women." We do a mass mailing to women telling them what I'm doing and why. We send out press releases to the media to let them know that I'm looking for women and minorities, not just African Americans but Hispanics and Asians. With Alan Bean, *Apollo XII* astronaut, I produce a film at Cape Canaveral focused on the theme "space is for everyone."

Traveling the country and going to every major city, I visit universities with strong physics and engineering departments and speak to professional organizations, technology-oriented corporations, any place where I might find a potential applicant. As expected, I encounter some distrust. Many times, my contact at a university or organization forewarns, "They've heard all this before from NASA, and they're not going to believe it now." Not all my appearances are met with enthusiasm.

Some of the questions are hostile, and I don't always break through the cynicism.

By a stroke of good timing, many professional organizations of physicists, engineers, and scientists have their annual conventions in March and April. Women in Motion contacts them, requesting that they invite me to speak. "You won't have to fly her in," says my fine staff. "We'll send her to you under the NASA Recruitment Contract. All you need to do is treat her with dignity and give her a respectful place on your program."

Well, most of them are Trekkies and enthusiastic to have me. They probably figure, "Hell, if NASA's paying for it, let her come on ahead. We get a free speaker and a Hollywood star, too." Onstage, I give my impassioned speech and take questions at the end, and, lo and behold, the audience is practically at my feet. Not only do they take me seriously, they say, "Wow, you really know your stuff. Where did you get your degree?"

"I didn't."

"But . . . but you know so much, you must have."

One of the industries I target is aerospace. They themselves are just crossing the color and gender lines, and understandably, they don't want me stealing their scientists and engineers. "But think about it," I urge the top executives at Rockwell, Lockheed, and Boeing. "If one of your people becomes an astronaut, you'll always be able to say that you gave your finest to our space program." They soften and set up meetings where I can speak and, yes, recruit.

At Rockwell International, the company that builds the space shuttle orbiters, the corporate vice president of research and engineering is Jim Meechan, a renowned solid-state physicist. He inaugurated an Engineer of the Year program and riled folks up by nominating B. Dunbar, who won before the committee realized who they were choosing. When some on the committee balked, Jim simply told them, "You don't want to fight me on this." And they didn't. B. Dunbar is Bonnie Dunbar, who later became an astronaut.

By now the media is starting to pay attention, and our biggest breakthrough comes when *Good Morning America* sends a crew to Cape Canaveral with me to do a major story about the campaign. The other big shows follow, and national magazines like *Newsweek* and *People* run articles about my involvement in the recruitment drive. The major daily newspapers of every town I visit put journalists on the story.

When I approach Latino and Asian newspapers about covering the campaign, the reaction is a bit different at first. Some of them hesitate. "Why come to us?"

"Look, I'm not here as a black person, I'm here as an American, and this is an American program. We've got to change the face of this astronaut corps."

"Oh! Yes! You're right!"

Those are the wonderful moments.

The women are harder, much harder, some with good reason. The most difficult moment of the entire campaign is having one of them tell me, in essence, that I'm being used, that I'm not going to change a damn thing, and that she resents my being part of this duplicity.

That stings.

How easy it would be to walk away. But instead, I stand my ground, as I do whenever a highly qualified potential applicant — male or female

— comes at me with a cynical attitude. If nothing changes, I point out, they'll be part of the reason. "Here you are, one of the most qualified people, and you refuse to apply because you want to tell NASA to go to hell. That's what I'm fighting, that's why I'm out here. I've put my career on the line for this, and I'm calling on you to help me."

With the advent of the Space Shuttle Program, the astronaut corps will conduct medical and scientific experiments that can be done only in space, experiments that are vital to humankind here on earth. "We are the mothers of the future," I tell an audience of women, "and we need to think about our children, because someday there's going to be a *Spaceship Enterprise*." The audience usually smiles at the thought. Little do I know that, as a result of a million letters pouring into the White House, the first space shuttle — originally named *Columbia* — will be renamed *Enterprise* in honor of our *Star Trek* ship. "I'm here for a selfish purpose," I go on. "I'm looking out for my great-great-great-great-great-granddaughter, whose name is Nyota Uhura. Who are you looking out for?" That brings a hush over folks.

Of all the newspaper articles about the campaign, only one takes a stand against me, and it's in a southern black newspaper. The interview takes place when I'm about three months into the recruitment drive, and I'm compelled to ask the reporter, "Why are you being so hostile to me?"

He finally comes out with it. "Why are you being an Aunt Tom for NASA?"

Good Lord. I look him square in the eyes and say, "I'm going to change the face of the astronaut corps. What are you going to do?"

He gets up and walks out and writes a seething, absolutely scathing article. It's a small paper in a small southern town, but it's enough to get NASA's dander up, and the public affairs people call. They fly me out to Washington for an update meeting, but clearly what they want to talk about is the article. They've decided to attach a NASA person to me. I respectfully decline. "You're not going to monitor me and have me jumping through NASA's hoops. My credibility will be out the window, along with all my good work. No." Fortunately, John Yardley is behind me all the way.

Taking on the NASA recruitment campaign is daunting, yes, but it's also rewarding and sometimes funny. I'm flying from Los Angeles to speak at a science conference one day well into the campaign, with my PSA airing all across the country and in prime time preceding *Star Trek* reruns. Because my NASA budget is modest and the travel expenses are significant, I travel coach so I can cover as much territory as possible. A stewardess recognizes me. "Ms. Nichols," she says, "what are you doing back here?" I explain about my NASA contract. "Well, we're not full," she says, "and we miss you up front. Won't you and your assistant come and join us?" I'm touched and stand up to follow her, and the whole airplane bursts into applause. As I pass, a woman says, "Great work, lady!"

Before I began the campaign, John Yardley, who understood the risk I was taking, asked me why I chose to do it. How often, I thought, do we have the chance to do something for God and country that makes a differ-ence? "Martin Luther King said I changed the face of television forever," I answered John. "I'm going to change the face of the astronaut corps, and children everywhere will be able to look at that crew and, as they did on *Star Trek,* see themselves."

That was why I did it.

There it was, the most defining moment of courage in my life. Because it truly made a difference. Dr. Mae Jemison might never have gone into space. Fred Gregory might not have gone. The astronaut corps would not look like it does today. The word *astronaut* is derived from the Greek, meaning "star sailor." Today, all of us, looking at our star sailors, can see ourselves. And all our hopes and dreams for the future ride with them.

⊙

That remarkable year in Nichelle's life built bridges and chased prejudices. As she recalls it in her book *Beyond Uhura,* the recruitment campaign brought a significant change in the number of minority and female applicants: When she started, NASA had received sixteen hundred applications, fewer than a hundred from women and thirty-five from minority candidates. "Of these, NASA told me, none of the women or minority applicants qualified." By the time she had finished, "just four months after we assumed our task, 8,400 applications were in, including 1,649 from women and an astounding 1,000 from minorities."

Today the deputy administrator of NASA, Dr. Fred Gregory, who was one of those accepted, recalls the moment when he saw Nichelle on television, wearing a blue flying suit and standing on a runway with a Boeing 747 behind her. "She looked straight at me, pointed, and said, 'I want you to join the astronaut program.'" An Air Force test pilot for several years, Gregory was ready for a change: "If I had had any doubts in my mind about applying to NASA, they were all cancelled at that point. I attribute the spirit I needed to pursue it to Nichelle. She's an absolutely beautiful woman, inside and out, and she had a significant influence on me."

Having been to NORAD (the North American Aerospace Defense Command), having testified before Congress about the space program, having spent more and more time in the company of scientists and physicists and businesspeople dedicated to the program, Nichelle was tempted to stay in that world. "I had garnered a lot of attention and was being inundated with more government contract offers. I was suddenly in Washington, D.C., more than I was in Hollywood."

She returned to her career as a singer and actress, but not without a new business partner — Jim Meechan, the Rockwell vice president who had caused a brouhaha when Bonnie Dunbar was named Engineer of the Year. Nichelle discovered that he was also a musician, a brilliant composer and lyricist, and they began working together on many projects, including a one-woman show for Nichelle. Shortly after her star was installed in the Hollywood Walk of Fame, *Reflections* opened in Los Angeles at the Westwood Playhouse — now the Geffen Playhouse. It garnered tremendous reviews and traveled to the Bayview Playhouse in Toronto for a two-month run as a prelude to a national tour. The interest of Broadway producers came just as Paramount called Nichelle with another *Star Trek* movie. And it seemed like every time she got revved up to do *Reflections* again, another *Trek* movie was going into production. In addition to the movies, she and Jim were busy outlining the books for a science-fiction trilogy she conceived, *The Adventures of Saturna*. She wrote the first, *Saturn's Child*, with science-fiction writer Margaret Warnder Bonanno and the second, *Saturna's Quest*, with Jim.

At last, in 2003 Nichelle and Jim prepared to remount the show, in which Nichelle becomes twelve legendary entertainers, among them Mahalia Jackson, Sara Vaughan, Leontyne Price, Josephine Baker, and Ella Fitzgerald. "I do them all in their different styles and voices, so it takes the audience from the drama of Billie Holiday to the comedy of Pearl Bailey to the very sensuous Lena Horne and Eartha Kitt, which is a highlight of the show. Most of them were highly influential in my career; most of them I had met. I wanted to be like all of them. *Reflections* is my homage to these great women."

I wondered if it was daunting for her to return now to the stage in a one-woman show. She laughed that gusty laugh. "My whole life is daunting."

Many years ago, Nichelle received NASA's coveted Public Service Award. Fittingly, Judy Resnik did the honors in the Rose Garden at the White House. "I shook when she pinned me," Nichelle recalled. "This was Judy Resnik, one of my first six women astronauts, who was standing there saying, 'If it were not for you, I would not be doing this.' I'm shaking just thinking about it again. We laughed and talked, and she was fabulous." Judy was on the fateful voyage of the *Challenger*. "I almost died with them," Nichelle murmurs.

Like those in the NASA family, she felt the devastation of the *Challenger* tragedy at a deep and personal level. "Three of my astronaut recruits were onboard, Judy, Ron McNair, and Ellison Onizuka. That was tough. Truly devastating. As was the last one, the *Columbia*...ironically, I was in Houston when it happened."

This is difficult for her to talk about, and her thoughts hang, ragged. "I was staying with Mae Jemison, and we just held onto each other."

Nichelle is not a woman to shy away from emotion, but she doesn't want to stay in this memory too long. "It was really tough," she repeats and pushes away from the pain.

Did she ever have a desire to be in one of those space shuttles when it rocketed out into deep space? "In a New York minute," she says without hesitation.

We are finished, but Nichelle lingers. "I want to thank you for resurrecting something so wonderfully important to me. I didn't know just how much I still cared."

*Star Trek* became the first television series to be honored with an exhibit in the Smithsonian Air and Space Museum, where an eleven-foot model of the U.S.S. *Enterprise* is exhibited on the same floor as the Wright brothers' original airplane and Lindbergh's *Spirit of St. Louis*.

## Hugh Herr

# A Climber's Defining Ascent

*Limitations Are Illusions*

Courage is fluid, ever changing and ever changing us. What is daring to us today may be a walk in the park tomorrow. And what is courageous to one person may no big deal to another.

If I'd asked Hugh Herr about courage years ago, his answer would have been much different from what it is today. Undoubtedly lots of people looked up to Hugh as a hero when he was just a kid. He was a child prodigy on the vertical face of a mountain, called a wall in the climbing world. He started when he was eight. He did things that would make the hair on the back of your neck stand up, and, boy, did it take guts.

Climbing was a family thing in the Mennonite household of the Herrs. Hugh would go with his two older brothers, his father, who was a chemist and builder, his mother, who was president of the local literacy council, and sometimes his two sisters. "I loved climbing," he told me. "I'm not sure why." Maybe he wanted to be like his oldest brother, Tony, who was the best climber in the family? "It was something else that I just can't explain."

Over time, he would outclimb Tony, drawn almost reverently to the face of a mountain, a spirit quest in a way. Before a climb, he'd get very still, meditating on the sheer rock in front of him, almost seeing through to the very soul of the mountain, feeling every intricate placement of fingers and feet.

His life's ambition was to be the best climber in the world.

By the age of eleven, he was climbing every day, sometimes even leading groups. By fourteen, he did dangerous climbs, sometimes without ropes. "It was more challenging, and, in the climbing world, it was considered pure to climb without ropes." By fifteen, he was up Bugaboo Spires in British Columbia without a rope. Bugaboo is at eight thousand feet and rises straight up out of a glacier, a two-thousand-foot, almost vertical rise to the top. He was one of the youngest people up there at the time. By sixteen, he was on climbs that no one had done before, not just no one his age but, as far as he knew, no one, period.

"In the climbing community at that time, the elite thing to do was to cheat death. If you climbed a huge and difficult wall without a rope and came back alive, that was considered cool and noble. The absolutely worst thing was having to be rescued. To not be self-sufficient, to rely on and put other climbers in harm's way to bring you out, was the worst thing you could do. As a teenager deeply steeped in this culture, the idea of making such a mistake was horrific."

By the time he was seventeen, the climbing world had watched and predicted that Hugh would be one of the best ever. He was at the top of his game, and going higher. If I had asked him back then, "Does this climbing straight up a mountain, with no safety harness, only you and God and the impossible surface of rock, does this thing take courage?" I don't know how he would have answered. I doubt that he would have thought it was courageous. It was more like the embrace of love, something inexplicable, ineffable, something he just had to do.

But there was a moment in his life when Hugh knew real courage, when he knew fear and anger and shame and willed himself not to buckle under them. Maybe he had become overly confident, maybe reckless. Maybe he felt too invincible. Maybe fear would have been his best friend that day as he and his climbing partner, Jeff Batzer, then twenty years old, headed off to New Hampshire's White Mountains and the challenge of a winter climb on Mount Washington, notorious for its wild weather.

The reputation of Mount Washington merits a website called "Surviving Mount Washington." At 6,288 feet, it's the Northeast's highest peak. But height isn't its claim to infamy. Three major storm tracks converge over the mountain, bringing wild and turbulent weather: The average year-round temperature is twenty-six degrees; winds average thirty-five miles an hour; fog often limits visibility to a hundred feet or less; the average annual precipitation is eighty-six inches, including twenty-one feet of snow. The world's highest surface wind speed, two hundred and thirty-one miles an hour, belongs to Mount Washington. As does the moniker "Home of the World's Worst Weather." The website warns, "There is no room for poor judgment and carelessness in this unforgiving mountain environment" that has taken the lives of a hundred and twenty-four people by avalanche, falling ice, drowning, and hypothermia. Climbers are encouraged not to be ashamed to turn back: " 'Bagging' another summit is never worth the cost of a life."

The challenge, of course, was reason enough for Hugh to go. It was late January, and he was still on top of the world.

⊙

All my life, climbing was the thing I hung my identity on, even when I was a kid. It made me think I had control over my life.

Mount Washington changed all that.

One bad decision, a few seconds in the making, and so many lives altered. It nearly killed me. But that's not the worst of it.

Leaving Lancaster, Pennsylvania, Jeff and I set out for a weekend climb on Washington and a hike up to a cabin at the base of Huntington's Ravine to spend the night. The next morning, we awaken to an unexpected brew of weather. It's snowing. But the winds aren't too extreme, and we decide to attempt our climb anyway. Because the avalanche danger is severe that day, we decide to leave our backpacks at the base so we can move quickly through the snow.

We start up Odell's Ice Gully, about a fifty-degree climb on very hard ice. By the time we get to the top of the ravine, the wind is really screaming, and we can't hear each other unless we crouch down to create a pocket for our voices. *Should we still attempt the summit?* We decide to go on for another ten minutes and, if things get worse, turn around. As we keep climbing, the winds whip more ferociously so that, standing five feet apart, we can't see each other. We decide to get out.

Between the snow and the whiteout, we can't see where we've come from, and the wind, which is constantly changing direction, provides no clues. *Wasn't it at our backs on the way up?* We turn into the wind. When we hit a gully that looks like the one adjacent to Odell's, we head down, relieved to know where we are and to be close to where we started. It isn't until we get to the tree line that we realize how wrong we are: This isn't where we came from; nothing looks familiar.

We are dead lost.

It's getting dark, and we know that if we turn around and go back to find Odell's Gully, we will most likely die on the mountain. We have to continue in the direction we're going and pray it will take us down before nightfall. We walk until three in the morning. Exhausted and unable to go any further, we find a big outcrop boulder and dig the snow away from its base on one side. We lay branches from spruce trees on the ground to keep our bodies off the snow, take off our wet clothing, and hold onto each other to share body heat.

I am scared to death.

Miraculously, we survive the night. The morning breaks at minus twenty degrees. The wind is howling and hurling snow across the mountain. We put our wet clothes back on, already starting to shake. And step out into the weather.

We are on the wilderness side of Mount Washington, a place where people rarely go, especially at this time of year. It's very dense, the snow so deep that tree limbs plunge right into it. We can't tunnel through; we'll have to follow the river.

At times, we can't tell when we're on thin ice covered with snow, and we break through, soaking our feet and stumbling to safety. Being wet in such severe weather conditions is agonizing and dangerous. When I break through and sink to my waist, I think I'm gone. I can hear the river rushing beneath my legs and I brace myself for the ice to break up all around me, to be swept under and gone in a split second. Jeff grabs for me and carefully, slowly, he pulls me out. The icy water, the snow, the wind all begin to freeze my legs.

I start to become delirious.

We make maybe a mile that day. Night falls, and we dig in again and hold onto each other to conserve our body heat. *We'll make it, we'll get out of here. We will.* The second day, we make another mile. I'm becoming increasingly delirious. I see things — bridges and trails that I'm sure will lead us to safety but in fact aren't there. By the third day, I can barely move. I walk three steps and fall over. My lower legs are numb. It's the strangest sensation not to have any sensory feedback — I'm falling before I know that I'm falling.

As night descends, any hope we have of surviving drains away. We burrow into the snow. But this time we leave on our wet clothes. We sit apart. We stop trying to survive. It's too painful. The sooner it's over, the better. The feeling of final defeat periodically swings to a sudden and extreme grasp for survival: We have to get up! We have to get out! We have to get going! Desperate, we crawl out of our cave, get up, and fall over.

Unable to go on, we crawl back into the cave. Hours pass as we lie in the snow, hypothermic, and finally we no longer grasp at surviving. I find out later that my core body temperature is dropping into the eighties and my liver is closing down. I let go and sink into unconsciousness.

When I hear a rustling in the trees, it seems far away at first. But I haven't slipped so far beyond consciousness that I don't connect with it, and it doesn't subside. I open my eyes. A woman in her twenties is standing there. Delirious, I think, *She's not real.* Jeff and I start shouting, expecting her to vanish into thin air.

She shouts back.

Melissa Bradshaw is out snowshoeing on her day off from work. She saw our footprints, noticed that they were kind of chaotic and staggering, and decided to follow them, knowing that a search-and-rescue team was on the other side of the mountain looking for two lost boys. We don't know any of that yet. All she says as she crouches down is "Are you guys from Odell's?"

She gives us water and food, a vest and wool shirt. I barely remember it. Seeing that we're immobile, she promises to be back and leaves to get help. She doesn't tell us how far we are from Pinkham Notch, the main entrance to Mount Washington. She doesn't say anything about being five hours from a search-and-rescue effort. It will be dark by the time she can get help. She's not sure we'll make it.

On her way off the mountain, a mile and a half down, she comes upon two men who rush up to help, following her footprints. Using a foam sleeping bag pad like a stretcher, they drag us out of the cave and put us in sleeping bags. As they try to give me water, I drift back into oblivion.

Hours later, the helicopters are overhead, and we're pulled off the mountain. I cannot begin to describe the feeling of knowing, with certainty, that I'm going to die and then realizing, with absolute clarity, that I'm going to live. It simply defies language.

We're taken to Littleton Hospital and treated for hypothermia and frostbite. My skin is dyed blue from my clothes, and warm water bottles lie all over my body when my parents rush into the emergency room.

The extreme contrast of sitting next to death one moment and being pulled into the modern world the next is surreal. The media swarms in from all over the country. High from the sheer adrenaline of surviving, Jeff is effusive, giving interviews, talking a mile a minute. I can barely string two words together. As grateful as I am to be alive, I feel deeply ashamed that we had to be rescued. When I hear that a rescue team was sent out to search for us, my shame deepens. And when I learn that twenty-seven-year-old Albert Dow was killed in an avalanche trying to find us, I weep. I sink into a dark depression. This is far more horrible than being lost on the mountain. I withdraw into myself.

Jeff and I both have severe frostbite. Jeff loses a thumb, parts of four fingers, five toes, and his left foot. Probably because I fell in the river, my legs are the worst. With all the publicity surrounding our rescue, a well-known surgeon hears about my condition and contacts my parents. He has a treatment for frostbite that he wants to try in an effort to save my legs. It will be his gift to us. My parents agree, and I fly out to Philadelphia, while Jeff remains in New Hampshire.

For weeks, the doctor tries his best. Between the two surgeries a week, medics clean my lower legs and remove dead tissue. My legs don't look like legs anymore; you can see my anklebones, which is helpful psychologically, because at a certain point, I want to get rid of these things that are making me so sick. I think the reason the doctor waits so long to amputate is partly because of this gradual acclimation. For a climber to lose his legs is unspeakable. For a climber whose sole identity rests on the feats those legs perform, it is dangerous. He wants me to make the decision. And, watching the gangrene slowly climb up my legs, I finally can.

On March 10, they amputate. Six inches below the knee. Both legs.

I feel a lot of things during this time, but mostly anger. Anger at myself for getting in a situation where we had to be rescued, where people put their lives at risk looking for us. In my mind, I had grabbed a gun and pulled the trigger on Albert Dow. The hate letters from people blaming me for his death are nothing. I already hate myself enough for it.

What drives me to climb again comes from that anger, that belief that I screwed up in the worst way possible, causing someone to die. I will climb again because to not climb again would be a disgrace to him, to his family. I will climb again to honor him.

Thankfully, my parents don't discourage me. Knowing how much I love to climb, they reason that it's good therapy for me. It will be a way for me to heal. But even as I begin mentally to make plans, I know what a big risk it is, because I'll be vulnerable to getting hurt, and being in another accident is too much to imagine, for me and for my family.

After the amputation, I stay in the hospital for a few weeks, and then I return home to the 130-acre farm outside Lancaster where I was raised. A month later, at a rehabilitation center in Philadelphia, I'm fitted with prosthetic limbs. The first time I try to walk, I'm up for maybe a second before sitting back down again. The pain is excruciating. I feel pathetic.

My rehabilitation doctor tells me I'll never climb again. Walk with canes, yes. Drive with hand controls, yes. Ride a bicycle, maybe. Climb, no. I can barely hear him, I'm so upset. A day later it occurs to me that the doctor has never climbed a day in his life. So, I reason, his judgment is questionable.

Typically, rehab patients are allowed to go home on weekends. The first few times, I go without my legs. I'm in a wheelchair. The third weekend, I go home with temporary plaster legs. Although I can barely walk, hobbling along after Tony like an old man on crutches, I convince him to take me climbing.

Tony is probably a little concerned about taking me, but he doesn't say so. I shuffle over to a cliff and sort of crawl along to the base while he strings up a safety rope. I grab hold of it and pull myself onto the rock. I'm shockingly weak. I shake the entire way up. But I climb a forty-foot cliff that I'd climbed countless times when I was younger. I make it to the top on my plaster legs.

Tony is elated. I don't tell him how nervous I am about failing. I don't tell him even as he's bragging about me when we get home. I'm still so angry inside, so full of shame about what happened on Mount Washington, that I feel no celebration now.

That year, I miss most of my senior year of high school and begin to loathe being the object of people's pity. *I'm so sorry, I'm so sorry, I'm so sorry.* I can't hear it one more time. Eventually, I leave the rehab center and start studying at home with a tutor. And climbing every day. I have to climb. I need to throw myself back into this thing that caused me to hate myself, I need to find myself in it again. I can take people's hate due to Albert Dow's death. I cannot take people's pity.

As I regain strength and work to recover my climbing skills, the frustration at not being able to do old, familiar climbs overwhelms me at times. I have temper tantrums, I throw things. But over time, I begin to realize something startling: I can manipulate my prostheses to help me climb better than I could when I had legs. My mother helps me with some of the changes; some of the adjustments I make on my own; some I ask my artificial limb maker to construct. Slowly, my climbing feet morph from replicas of human feet to something altogether different. Gradually, I change to prostheses that are optimized for function, not cosmetics. For example, very short feet — the size of a child's — are lighter and give me more flexibility. Also, by bonding sticky climbing rubber to the bottom of my artificial feet, I do away with climbing shoes. And one day, I realize that I don't need a heel; it's extra weight, so I cut it off. My legs and feet become more and more optimal for climbing, lightweight and shaped for maximum scaling. My climbing improves. I get physically stronger and healthier.

Six months after my surgery, I'm climbing not quite as well as I had before Mount Washington, but pretty close. I start going to world-famous climbing areas. On a difficult climb with a partner, I hear people below who have stopped and are staring up at us. "Who's that?"

My partner yells down, "Hugh Herr."

"That can't be Hugh Herr; his legs were just amputated."

I start to gain a lot of notoriety for my quick recovery. At some point, I'm climbing better than I had before the accident. And I'm doing more difficult climbs. That's when I start to really heal emotionally. I'm being made whole again.

A common fear when a person is injured the way I was, especially as a teenager or a young man, is that no one of the opposite sex will be attracted to you again.

You do absolutely everything possible to hide the fact that you have prosthetic limbs. You feel ugly. And you feel angry about feeling ugly. A former girlfriend told me that when I was in *People* magazine, she went to the library to check out the issue, and as she was signing it out, she mentioned to the young woman behind the desk that she used to date me. With a look of horror, the young woman gasped, "You actually slept with him?" People would say to my parents, "It's a good thing he isn't married." That outcasting really hurt.

In part it was the pain of being outcast that drove me to climb, to climb not just well enough but better than I had before my accident. To climb better *because* I had artificial legs. I would use the fact that my legs and feet were artificial to my advantage. I would shave and cut and trim and redesign them so that they fit better in the cracks and crevices of a mountain face. I engineered a foot with a bladelike front for cracks and another type for ice. I experimented with leg extensions; with an Allen wrench, I could add an inch or two.

Amputation is, to a large degree, considered a failure in the world of surgery. All attempts are made to "save the leg." So, as an amputee, you begin this painful transition as a failed experiment. Years ago, you'd get legs that didn't work worth shit but looked good, with toes and veins. Largely, the message from the medical community was *This is the state of the art in legs; you must accept your disability.*

My doctor's telling me what I could and couldn't do was typical. He didn't say, "Try to figure out how to solve the damn problem." He wasn't malicious, he just didn't want to get my hopes up, but the impact of this kind of "realism" can be tragic. If I had taken my doctor's advice and really believed I couldn't climb again, I don't know where I'd be today.

I've come to believe that there's no such thing as a physically disabled person; there are only physically disabled technologies. No one should accept a limitation. Everyone should strive toward better technology that rehabilitates. Now when I climb, I carry a sack with a file, wrenches, and feet of different shapes. With a file, I can alter the shape of my feet on the spot. With a wrench, I can simply put on a different pair of feet to match the terrain.

As an advocate of technical solutions to physical disabilities, I have a mantra: Limitations are illusions. It's what I learned from surviving Mount

Washington and the black hole I sank into following our rescue. It's what I learned from losing the one thing that had given me a sense of identity and finding it again in a way I never could have imagined. Do not accept what you can change. If there's a problem, you can solve it. You can. You may have to look in an unexpected place, do an unexpected thing. But no one benefits from the quitter; you gain nothing, you give nothing, by giving up.

Studying at the Massachusetts Institute of Technology and later working there, Hugh was known to climb the side of the campus chapel, spidering up the wet bricks on his stilt-shaped limbs in the rain. Below him, people cupped under umbrellas stopped dead in their tracks. When he descended to terra firma, he'd take off his "climber legs," put on his "civilian legs," and go about his business unperturbed.

"The guy has pulled off an absolute first," Michael Kennedy, then editor of *Climbing Magazine,* told the *Boston Globe.* "He came away from his accident determined to climb with the best in the sport, not simply the best among the disabled." Hugh was awarded a Partners for Disabled Youth Award at the Kennedy Library for serving as a role model in overcoming limitations.

Over the years, he has dedicated himself to creating more efficient and less expensive prosthetic limbs. "During my rehabilitation, I was in a lot of physical pain; it's especially difficult when you first get an artificial leg. Coming out of surgery, your leg is swollen and, as soon as you put external pressure on it, liquid escapes, causing shrinkage. So if your prosthesis fits well and is comfortable, two days later everything changes. My first year was uncomfortable and nearly every four days I had to get an adjustment. Because of that pain, I knew I wasn't going to be a construction worker — or do any kind of work that required me to be on my feet. I decided to go back to school."

He studied computer science and mathematics but eventually turned to physics because he was fed up with being in so much pain and wanted to design a better prosthesis. He wrote his first patent on a prosthetic socket with adjustable fluid "bladders" in an attempt to make the artificial limb more comfortable. Then he went for a master's degree in mechanical engineering at M.I.T. and on to a PhD in biophysics from Harvard. In the end, he returned to work in the Biomechatronics Group, a robotics lab at the Media Laboratory at M.I.T., where he is director. Prior to joining the Media Lab, he was an assistant professor of physical medicine and rehabilitation at Harvard Medical School.

Inevitably, Professor Herr created a foundation to bring together an elite team of engineers to design inexpensive and efficient limbs. At the Herr Institute for Human Rehabilitation in Cambridge, that team works to develop the technology for more affordable prostheses for the Third World. Later, he founded a for-profit corporation, Intelligent Prosthetics and Orthotics, iP&O, to develop high-tech, smart, computer-controlled artificial limbs that automatically measure and adapt resistance as a person walks. Their first design, a computer-controlled prosthetic knee four years in the making, will come to the marketplace in 2004. "It's more stable, so people fall less frequently. They're able to walk with lowered metabolic cost, so walking is easier and safer."

Not surprisingly, Hugh earned a spot in *Who's Who of American Inventors*.

"It's a remarkable time in the world of physical disability. People are breaking down the devastating stigma of being disabled. In my world, the look of artificial legs is drastically changing. It used to be that the focus was on cosmetics. Now, the focus is more on function: legs often don't look human; they look beautiful, artificial, like something out of science fiction. Young men and women are out there wearing shorts with legs that look high-tech and colorful, and they exude this wonderful energy."

Amid all the work and research and groundbreaking designs, perhaps the most wonderful things in the life of Professor Hugh Herr are the woman he met at Harvard, Patricia Ellis, who became his wife, and their daughter, Alexandra, born in January 2003.

Shannon Meehan

# Refugee Work in the Heat of Chaos
*Taking Risks for Freedom*

The day Shannon Meehan and I met was a quintessential summer day, with doors and windows flung open and birds singing so loudly that they became the background music on our taped interview. We were sitting at the kitchen table in the home of her good friend where she'd been staying, having recently returned from Iraq. Shannon is a refugee worker and spends more time close to desperate, sometimes dangerous situations than to singing birds and budding gardens. As we sat down by the window that looked out over the busy feeders, I wondered what it felt like when she came home, how she adjusted to ordinary life after the intensity of doing humanitarian work.

The day before, the United Nations headquarters in Baghdad had been bombed, which weighed heavily on Shannon. "I knew a lot of those people," she said, at once angry and saddened by the loss of Sergio Vieira de Mello, special U.N. envoy to Iraq, a man known for his near-miraculous ability to bring mortal enemies to the table to reconcile. Twenty-one others had died when a truck bomb loaded with fifteen hundred pounds of explosives detonated next to the Canal Hotel right under de Mello's offices. "I'd met with Sergio a few times and regularly emailed his chief of staff. Someone I knew who worked for UNICEF was in the building and another woman I knew... all died in the bombing."

Working with refugee organizations, Shannon has been not only in Iraq, but in Kosovo, Guinea, Liberia, Senegal, and Ivory Coast. She was eager to tell me about the courageous people she'd met, like the fourteen-year-old girl enslaved by Liberian rebels, raped and made a house slave, and then one day dropped off in a refugee camp, where Shannon met her. And the five-year-old boy who was fluent in French and wouldn't stop following her around one of the camps, a particularly sweet memory. "We fell in love," she smiles. "His name was Bonaventure, which means good adventure."

Others came quickly to mind. "But how about you; what's been courageous for you?" She sat back in her chair with an easy laugh now. "You're talking about my daily life. I'm always coming up against things that are scary or that I know could be if they took a turn."

When things take a turn, Shannon Meehan is someone you want near at hand. She told me about one of her trips from the port city of Monrovia, the capital of Liberia on the Atlantic Ocean, to Conakry, the capital of Guinea, an hour-and-a-half flight, "no big deal." About forty-five people were on the flight — the Guinean soccer team, businessmen, four other humanitarian workers. "We're in an old, creaky Russian plane with no cushions to speak of, the seats all bent metal. We're circling Conakry when the pilot comes on and says that our landing gear isn't working. No one on the plane reacts. I'm chatting in French with the Lebanese man next to me, and we continue talking."

Then the pilot comes on again, and this time he gets their attention. "We're getting close to running out of fuel. We have to land, but we're not sure our landing gear will lock, so you have to prepare for a crash landing." Shannon's instinctive reaction was to turn to the man sitting next to her and say, "I don't know about you, but I've had a great life. I've seen a lot of the world and had a really good time doing that." Both of them remained calm. *"Moi aussi,"* he said. Me too.

The landing gear locked.

"Many of my staff and people I've worked with have told me, 'You're the one I want to be around if the shit hits the fan, because you don't lose it.' In urgent situations, I naturally tend to keep things steady and work through crises in a systematic manner. Things move forward."

At thirty-six, Shannon has put that calm under fire to good use in her refugee work. Once, though, she was pushed close enough to an ugly ending that she wanted out. She was in Liberia, and Charles Taylor was still in power. Liberia is on the western coast of Africa and surrounded by Sierra Leone and Guinea to the west and north and Ivory Coast to the east. Civil wars have plagued much of the area for years. Rebels swept through, and refugees fled across borders looking for shelter and safety. In Liberia, Taylor's militias committed atrocities that would lead to his indictment for war crimes and crimes against humanity.

I'm in Liberia to assess the refugee situation for Refugees International. I want to get into an area called Grand Jedeh County and its capital, Zwedru, which is deep inland, close to the border of Ivory Coast. To get clearance and transport, I go to the U.N. High Commissioner for Refugees and ask to travel out with them. Sure, they say, they'd love for me to go, but it's the most dangerous area, and they're concerned about security. I press the point that aid workers have reported on just about every other area of Liberia except this one. "Let me go with you. I'll stay a week and come back."

Finally they agree, and we leave Monrovia and head inland.

In Grand Jedeh, I visit refugee transit centers, and it's in Toetown Transit Center that I meet Bonaventure, a lively kid with a big smile and beautiful face whose father is an assistant to a Catholic priest, which explains why his children are well educated and have access to French books.

Traveling to the border of Ivory Coast, where most of the fighting is taking place, we come across fifteen hundred refugees in a village of seven hundred people. A massive influx of Ivorians fleeing civil war in their country has completely overwhelmed the village. We check the food situation, the health situation, and bring back five of the most urgent medical cases.

Throughout the week, the tension in the refugee camps is palpable. At the end of every day, I go to the UNHCR quarters and tell them, "This place could spin on a dime. Any second, it could blow." At night, rebels invade the camps, and the refugees flee. During the day, they see rebels who destroyed their villages in Ivory Coast, and obviously they're scared. I'm not alone in my concern; several internationals are worried that this could whip either way. The Liberian militia of Charles Taylor could get frustrated with the chaos and start in with their atrocities.

At the end of the week, the head of UNHCR, Moses Okello, arrives to check on the food situation and the relocation of refugee camps. I arrange to make the ten-hour drive back to Monrovia with his convoy. As we set out, Mr. Okello and his driver are in the lead vehicle. Behind are people from two Liberian organizations working with the U.N. I'm in the fourth and last vehicle with some of the local U.N. staff.

Our return trip is uneventful until we're about an hour away from Monrovia, at a place called Checkpoint 15. All of a sudden, fifteen militiamen heavily armed with AK-47s and M-16s and sidearms surround us. I can see that they're high on drugs, completely loaded. They look to be anywhere from twelve years old to fifty-five. Getting stopped in a U.N. vehicle is unusual. Normally you go right through the checkpoint because you're in a white vehicle with the big, blue U.N. letters. If you're going to get stopped, it's when you're in a quirky NGO vehicle that's not easily identifiable.

The soldiers order us out of our vehicles. Charles Taylor has decreed that no U.S. diplomat may go beyond the airport, which is maybe twenty miles outside Monrovia, and they're whipped up because they think we're in violation. In a nice and even way, Mr. Okello tries to explain that he's a U.N. diplomat, not a U.S. diplomat.

I've been through so many checkpoints in so many different countries that I've learned when to be assertive and when not to be. At some checkpoints, if I'm stopped, I yell at the person like they don't have any right to hold me up. But in Liberia, you wait it out, because with heavily armed guys, some just kids, who are loaded on drugs, you never know which way it's going to flip.

As the soldiers continue to detain us, I get very quiet. Mr. Okello and

I are the only internationals, and I'm the only female international. Mr. Okello is trying to negotiate with the soldiers. They want to go through our bags, and you just don't do that with a diplomat, especially a corps diplomat, one of the highest-ranking U.N. officials in the country. I feel bad for him. Finally, he relents: "Fine, you're just going to find dirty underwear."

After going through his bags, the soldiers start coming toward my vehicle, and I think, *Oh, God, there goes my computer, there goes all my cash for temporary staff and food and lodging, there goes the digital camera, the SAT phone, the mobile phone. . . .*

The only other woman in our convoy is Liberian, and luckily, she knows how to play these guys. "Sure, you can look at my stuff," she says, starting to pour out everything.

They don't expect that. "No, wait."

"You want to see this . . . ?"

"No, no."

"You wanna see the rest of the bags, I'll just empty 'em all."

"That's okay." They back off.

One of them turns to me and says, "I need to see your passport."

Just the night before, my colleague in Monrovia called to warn me not to show anyone my passport, because the person who handled our arrival at the airport bungled our entry into the country. You were supposed to check in with the police within forty-eight hours or get arrested. That was seven days ago.

"I need to see your passport," the soldier repeats.

"Suuuurrrre. . . ." I get it out and, without letting go of it, flip it open to the picture so he can see that it matches me. He reaches out, looks at it, takes hold of it. I hang on, making sure he doesn't see the stamped page. He looks closer, still holding onto it. I can see Mr. Okello in the background watching; he'll tell me later that he was afraid for me, afraid the soldiers suspected me of being an American diplomat.

The soldier leans closer, squints at the picture. I've still got a grip on the passport. He stares at my face. Can he see fear? What is he thinking? Why is he taking so long? He grunts, "Okay" and turns away.

An hour and a half pass. The longer a situation like this drags on, the greater the chances are that it will end poorly. I approach Mr. Okello. "Is there anything in particular that we should be doing?"

"No, I'm just happy that we're all pretty low-key and quiet and outside."

Finally, they allow us to use a telephone so Mr. Okello can contact UNHCR headquarters in Monrovia to assure the soldiers that he's a U.N. diplomat and to verify with Charles Taylor's office that he's legitimate. The phone isn't working properly, which adds to the already mounting frustration.

Another thirty minutes pass. Mr. Okello approaches me. "They're starting to get agitated, and I'm nervous that there may be shooting. I'm the one they're detaining. They don't seem to be focused on holding you; why don't you go on ahead?"

As much as I want to get out, I know it's the wrong idea. Three of the soldiers seem to be vying for authority, and the last thing we want to do is frustrate them and add to their edginess by making a move like this. "I think that picking a vehicle to leave and sending me out might push the tension. Why don't we just stick it out together?"

Two hours have passed. It's hot. It's late at night. With the three soldiers maneuvering more forcefully to be in charge and the phone still not working properly, the situation starts to get chaotic, which is not where you want things to go with a group of soldiers loaded on who knows what.

Another half hour passes.

And then, with no explanation, it ends. They let us go.

Within thirty seconds, we're all back in our vehicles and on the road. By the time I get to my colleague in Monrovia, the full force of emotion has hit: *I want to get the fuck out of here! I hate this place! It can flip on a dime, and we shouldn't be here!* I start crying: *I almost didn't make it today.*

$\odot$

The incident in Liberia was one of the scariest of Shannon's humanitarian career. Yet she told me, "To be honest, what really stands out for me is the everyday courage." Creating a program to help commercial sex workers didn't put her in physical danger, but it was a radical idea that might have ended badly.

She was in Guinea working for the American Refugee Committee as an income generation coordinator, with a revolving loan fund for Liberian refugees. Having arrived at the tail end of a flood of refugees, she was in Macenta, in the forest region. At the height of the refugee crisis, from 1990 to 1996, Guinea hosted more a million Liberian refugees. And Macenta had around a third of them.

$\odot$

As an income generation coordinator, I oversee projects that allow refugees to be self-sufficient. For example, five women might join together to make and sell soap, which is always a good moneymaker and also helpful with hygiene. It's an easy business because the women don't have to pay much for supplies, since much of it occurs naturally.

My staff is made up of Liberians, Sierra Leoneans, and Guineans. As they get to know me over a two-month period, they decide that I'm ready to have an unusual idea thrown at me: They want to help the prostitutes. It's not uncommon for women in dire straits in a refugee situation to survive by becoming commercial sex workers. Helping them, my staff points out, fits our mandate to reach out to the most vulnerable and critically in need.

"How do you want to help them?" I ask, knowing that religion could be motivating them. Many Guineans are Muslim. Liberians and Sierra Leoneans are evangelical, Baptist, Christian. "Some of you are Muslim, some of you are Christian; is that your driving force?" Thankfully, they say no. "They're probably sick," says one of my staff. "Some of them are sure to have AIDS. The driving force is the health of the women and their families."

"Good. Do you want to change their lifestyle? Do you think you'll get them out of prostitution?"

Some of the men say yes, we must. Some of the women say probably not. "But is there a way we can make their lives safer?"

Maybe I'm wrong, but I think we can.

We start developing a plan that will include international health agencies in Macenta. Then we ask local people for advice: How should we go about getting commercial sex workers to trust the staff and to self-identify? When trying to help people, even though *you* know what the problem is, even though you have an idea about the solution, both have to be identified first by the population in need. They need to recognize, "Yes, I have this problem."

Assembling our team, we decide on two core principles. One, we aren't out to change the lifestyle of the women except regarding AIDS prevention and health. We'll succeed if they know their bodies better and know how to prevent sexually transmitted diseases, but we won't judge them if they decide to continue being prostitutes. Second, if they do want to change, we'll have programs ready to help them become self-sufficient, business ideas like the soap making or educational ideas like the local first aid nursing school.

When we're ready, the women on staff — who are mostly refugees themselves — start going out in the evenings, frequenting the bars where the prostitutes work, having drinks, buying them food, and befriending them. Two weeks pass, and none of the prostitutes come forward. We remain patient, because the process will work only if they initiate the contact.

Another two weeks pass. Was I wrong in thinking this would work?

After one month, one of the prostitutes asks the right question. Sitting with a woman named Koo, she says, "I've seen you here twice a week, we talk, we're becoming friends, you've seen what I do for a living, and still you come. Why?" That's the opening we've been waiting for, and Koo says, "I'd like to invite you to a social gathering where you can meet other women who do what you do. I'm a refugee too, and we can talk about what it's like to be a woman and a refugee."

Twelve women agree to come to a gathering. We feed them and show them the film *Pretty Woman*. Everybody thinks I'm crazy. *Pretty Woman?* But I'm betting that three key things in the movie will speak to these women. One, Julia Roberts talks about all the different types of sex that prostitutes have; she fans some condoms and blurts out something about safe sex. Two, she gets smacked. Many of the refugee women may get a dollar for sexual favors, but they also get viciously beaten. Three, the message at the end is, if you want to change, you can change. But if you don't, it's okay; Julia Roberts's friend remains a prostitute. The film sparks a conversation about safe sex, violence against women, and the choice to do things differently. It does what I was hoping it would do.

At this first gathering, I meet Thelma. She has an awful cut down her leg, a three-inch open wound. At the second gathering, I see that the wound isn't healing, and I say to her, "We need to look at that." I get my first aid kit.

"You're willing to do that?" She's stunned.

The cut is beyond first aid, so we take her to the missionary hospital, where the people are especially nice and very skilled. They clean out the wound and put her on antibiotics, and, over the coming weeks, it finally heals. I grow to love Thelma. She's a refugee three or four times over, fleeing whenever the rebels infiltrate or other circumstances force her to move again.

We run a six-week course with the women coming in twice a week, and they learn about basic women's health: what a period is, what it is to have a baby, female and male anatomy, how it all works, what it all means. Knowledge is extremely powerful. It can change a person's life in a big way. And that's what I'm hoping will happen.

But at the end of our course, my staff and I can't figure out whether we've done any good, whether the program has helped or not. We decide to take it one step further. I meet with a female ob-gyn, a Swedish doctor, at the missionary hospital and explain what we're doing. "Would you be willing to do a full gynecological checkup on the women and then keep them as patients for regular checkups?"

Without hesitating, she agrees.

My staff and I each take a woman to her checkup, and the experience is nothing short of amazing. "Nobody has ever cared about me," says Thelma, one of the most vocal. "Nobody every thought to do anything for me. I was a nobody."

But she's not a nobody to us.

The time comes when the missionary hospital gets the sophisticated AIDS test, along with a counseling program. We urgently want our women to get tested, but the people at the hospital caution us. "Be careful how you go about this; it has to be the woman's choice to be tested." Half the women decide to take the AIDS test, and half of them test positive. It is an emotional time and yet also freeing. Never before have the women been treated with such respect and care, never before have they received such personal attention without judgment.

I often think about the women in that initial program, their impact on us and ours on them. A couple of years later, I see Thelma in another city. She yells out, "Shannon! How ya doing?" We stop and hug each other. "I'm still here," she says, "and I'm okay." She's working with the commercial sex worker program as it moves into different areas of Guinea, hired to guide it and ensure that it keeps to its original themes and motives. Her life is not perfect by any means, but she's given up prostitution and committed herself to reaching out to other women like her.

⊙

The commercial sex worker program still operates in Guinea and was nominated for a Hilton Humanitarian Award, globally the largest humanitarian award given to those who make extraordinary contributions to alleviating human suffering. As I listened to Shannon talk about the program with modesty and yet deep and lasting satisfaction, I wondered what it was like for her to return to everyday life at home. "When I left Guinea, I was tired. I needed a sabbatical. I just hung out with friends back home and planned on taking off for four months." Before leaving on a cruise to Mexico with a friend, she got a call from Refugees International asking her to go into Liberia, Guinea, and, if possible, Ivory Coast because it was spinning out of control in a civil war.

"How long is the assignment?" she asked. "I'm trying to rest."

"It's only four weeks."

Her love of West Africa pulled on her. Because the regional U.N. offices of Ivory Coast had been forced to evacuate to Dakar, she would be going through Senegal, where she had first felt the adrenaline of international aid work as a Peace Corps volunteer, the only American in a Senegalese village. She took the assignment.

In Dakar, she met with the regional "bigwigs" and worked her way down to Guinea, Liberia, and Ivory Coast with her colleague, Sayre Nyce. "It was like going home," she remembers. "We hit all the areas we needed to hit, I interviewed a lot of refugees, did the reports, and Sayre left for Washington, D.C., to do advocacy on the Hill. I went home and was there when Refugees International called again to ask if I would go into Iraq." That was in April 2003.

Because of her high regard for Refugees International, Shannon took the assignment in Iraq, knowing she'd be able to work outside a political agenda. "Refugees International doesn't get government or U.N. funding, so they're completely independent and able to evaluate and say exactly what they see. I'd be able to go in with a clean slate, be their eyes and ears, send back notes focused on the refugee situation, issues relative to internally displaced persons, and the humanitarian conditions of the people. Together we would review my reports and draw conclusions about what we were seeing and about what should be the priority of our advocacy in D.C."

A few weeks after Baghdad fell, she went to Basra. She was in south central Iraq until May 15, and because no mass movement of people had resulted from the war, the living conditions of the people became her first priority. She assessed health issues, the water, employment, economics, transportation, and security. After traveling to Kuwait for a couple of days, she went to Baghdad and stayed there until mid-June.

"Baghdad was like a trap; once you were in, it was hard to get out. With the vacuum of leadership, the frustration, the five million people who live there, it was overwhelming in many ways, an ocean of issues to look at and assess."

She leans forward on her elbows, places her hands on the oak table, stares at them for a moment. She looks up. "Freedom is a difficult thing to manage."

As I was writing Shannon's story, questions arose in the backdraft of the interview, as so often happens. I emailed her, expecting to find her still staying with her friend, post-Iraq, and getting ready for a move to

Washington, D.C., where she'd been hired by Creative Associates International to be their field operations manager and to standardize their administration, finance, logistics, and human resources policies worldwide

I wondered how she would fare being confined in an office building for extended periods. Would the pull of foreign cultures begin to distract her? Would she feel stifled, boxed in? "Many of us who work in international relief complain when we're overseas — I gotta get back, I gotta be in the States, I want some security and routine. And then, once we're home, we get the itch to be with other cultures. Things are so homogeneous here."

Shannon answered all my questions — from Baghdad.

She had gone back. Over the course of a month, we emailed back and forth, with periodic apologies like "Sorry, I am very, very busy — eighteen-hour days, sometimes twenty — see my answer below." She was the interim director on a sixty-five-million-dollar educational project run by Creative Associates. A gap in staffing had taken her there unexpectedly and would keep her there, not for three weeks as she had anticipated, but for three months. "Fixing a few problems," she wrote. For Shannon Meehan, that seemed perfect.

She was overseeing a secondary school contract with several components such as teacher training, administration, and school materials, including some two hundred thousand desks and a million and a half student kits. "The project is a huge logistical undertaking, and my job is to make sure everything moves forward, which would be impossible without a great team."

At the end of her email, she signed off, "It is very unsafe here."

By the turn of the year, she was back in the States and had settled into her new job in D.C., having made the rather large psychological move of buying a brownstone and putting down roots. Her bed had just arrived — "I don't have to sleep on the floor tonight!" — but to what avail, when one can't sleep or is haunted by nightmares when finally consciousness dissolves?

Iraq was still with her.

"It's hard to articulate the ever-present fear of danger," she told me. "Everything was unpredictable. You never knew when you might get hit. You never knew if your vehicle was going to get ambushed, never knew if you were going to be in the wrong place at the wrong time, in a market when someone decided to blow up a car bomb. By November, it really started spinning that way; every moment was unpredictable. Cars would drive by our compound and slow down, and I'd wonder, 'Is this it? Is this a car bomb?' I'd be working late at my computer and hear shooting, and I wouldn't know whether it was a wedding or whether somebody had been hit."

The stress was relentless. "I was always on alert to every noise, every innu-endo of a staff member. I paid closer attention to complaints to make sure not to incite anger, because I didn't know which way someone might go."

One day a house just down the street from Shannon's compound was hit by two rocket-propelled grenades. "Boom! It went off. I was in the office and I thought, *This is it, this is the day I have to face being hit.* I was sure one of our houses had been hit, it was that loud. I ran out, and our security guys yelled, 'It isn't us, get everybody inside, turn off the lights, stay locked down until we have more information.'"

Because she was working with a for-profit corporation, the security was unlike anything she'd ever experienced. Their operation was set up in three houses in a residential district on the same side of the river as the former palace and main U.S. government offices. "We had heavy-duty security, armed protection all the time, static guards around our compound. Whenever I moved in a vehicle, I had secret service people with me. Understand, this is not my style, it felt like 'the president's moving!' but it was just me. Our philosophy was low-key in that we rode in taxis whenever possible, and weapons were always concealed or in backpacks, but still, people knew that all the internationals had security; local people had security when they felt they needed it."

The stress of all that security compounded the stress of delivering on their contract. Often simply moving from one point to another was difficult. "I couldn't just get in the car and go. To simply attend a meeting, I had to have guards and make sure to change my route. And we're supposed to deliver on two hundred thousand desks?"

Mission accomplished, she returned to the States, an especially odd return this time. "I was coming from a place of poverty and destitution where the Red Cross had been bombed, students and little kids killed, forty people dead. I walked off the plane and went to the mall to buy a sweater because I didn't have any warm clothes. It was surreal."

She was glad to be home but a little ambivalent about adjusting to corporate culture and not being in the field. "My colleagues are still in Baghdad, still risking their lives. That's hard to reconcile. I feel good to be back and, at the same time, guilty." Maybe the conflict will always be there. She's tired of not being around the people she most loves. And yet the field calls, always. Which is why Shannon left Creative Associates and is now an international consultant as an independent agent, free to use her expertise in a variety of ways, able to pick up and go on a moment's notice.

Throughout our conversations and email exchanges, I often wondered why someone is drawn to work that is filled with so much pain and tragedy, filled with rewards but so much struggle. Shannon's answer was quick: "My mom was a generous person and taught her children well." We sat with that for a moment before she added, "We all have the responsibility of helping our neighbors in some way. Not that everyone should do international charity work, but we all must reach out to people in need."

Mark Nyberg

## The Cowboy Missionary
### *An Excruciatingly Conscious Choice*

I first learned about Mark Nyberg the morning my husband handed me the "Living" section of our local newspaper, the *Oregonian*. "Take a look at this," he said. Covering three full pages were the photographs and story of staff reporter and photographer Benjamin Brink, who had been in Albania with Mark. The photos were compelling, especially the one of Mark in jeans and sweater sitting at a desk, a gun in one hand and the phone in another as he spoke to his wife, Lola, who had been evacuated home to the States. The irony in the picture is everywhere. Mark is a missionary in the middle of anarchy, his life literally on the line as Albania erupts in national violence. He's telling Lola not to worry, that everything is fine, and hoping she doesn't hear the gunfire in the background.

Mark went nowhere without a pistol tucked at the small of his back during the first seven months of 1997. He slept with a rifle and a hundred rounds of ammunition in clips. Every morning, he reached for his razor in a medicine chest next to a cabinet housing hand grenades. In the utter chaos that gripped Albania, he stood guard at the Vlora orphanage, protecting the sixty-five children inside. As far as he knew, he was the only foreigner who didn't take an embassy airlift to safety. He wasn't about to leave those children.

In the photo, he looked like a real cowboy.

Say the word *missionary*, and my mind fills with images. Mark definitely didn't fit the prototype. When I met him, he was on an interim stateside visit. Periodically he'd return, bringing photos of the kids and making the rounds of churches that supported his work. Later, during another visit, I went to a presentation he gave at a small local church. You could feel the air in the sanctuary darn near sizzle with his passion for his work, and the folks in the congregation were mesmerized. By this time, several American families had adopted children from the orphanage, including a boy named Mirelli.

On an afternoon not occupied by the raising of money for the orphanage or the commitments of his mission, we sat at my kitchen table and talked. Mark did not come easily to this work. He'd been on a pretty scary path before waking up to the fact that he had put his wife and children, and his own soul, in jeopardy. By then, Lola had sought refuge in her Sundays at a local church. Praise the Lord, you might say, that he followed her. Together, they became missionaries.

⊙

When we first arrived at the orphanage in Vlora, Albania, it was the middle of the night, the dead of winter. Most of the windows were broken out, and snow was blowing in. The building had no heat. The sinks were broken, the fixtures were broken, pipes were broken. Water seeped through the walls, ran down, and pooled across the floors. Lola and I looked at each other: *What had we gotten ourselves into?*

Albania was only our second mission. When Lola and I finished our missionary training, I quit my job as a machinist for a company that makes industrial refrigeration equipment just outside Portland, Oregon, and we sold everything except what would fit in our suitcases, took our two kids out of high school, and set out for a village so primitive that, only fifteen years earlier, the tribespeople had been cannibals and head hunters. For three years, we lived in the jungles of Papua New Guinea with this remote tribe who had rarely seen white people. In New Guinea, we lived in a thatched hut along with snakes and lizards and rats. The Albania orphanage, we were soon to discover, wasn't even fit for animals.

Through the dark building, we were led to a small room with a leaky sink, broken windows, and a bed. Our children were on their own now; it was just Lola and me on this, my first night as the new co-director of the orphanage.

The following morning, a sparse staff showed me around the three-story building, which was built in the 1940s as barracks for Russian troops. The heat had been out for five years. All the wiring was bad. If you plugged in a heater, the wires would literally sizzle. The Turkish toilets, no more than holes in the floor, drained into the basement, which was a foot deep in raw sewage. A nauseating stench permeated the place. Dirty diapers were put in a big bathtub of cold water and stirred with a stick. There was no soap, no hot water. Hepatitis was rampant. The kitchen consisted of a cookstove with two burners and no oven. The kids ate plain rice one day, plain macaroni the next. That was it. Many of them were malnourished. Some were dying.

I was utterly overwhelmed.

Forty children, newborn to age six, lived in the orphanage. Most of them had been badly neglected by the staff; some had been beaten, with black eyes and sores over their bodies. I'd reach down to pick up kids, and they'd throw up their hands in front of their faces as though they expected to be hit. One girl ran and hid in the corner whenever she saw anyone coming.

On the third floor were the special-needs kids. When I opened the door, the stench that rolled out of the small room nearly knocked me over. In a playpen made of raw, unfinished wood with no blankets and no mattress were five kids banging their heads on the side. In an eerily quiet room were the babies, tied to their cribs with strips of cloth. Some of the children had been left in broken-down metal beds for years. One, Mirelli, had been confined for three and a half years. He couldn't walk, he couldn't talk, he couldn't even sit up by himself. He simply moved one hand lazily in front of his face.

I'm not one to show emotion, but standing in the middle of the room, I started to cry. *God, I can't do this. We've got no heat, no food, no medicine, no windows. We've got a basement used as a septic tank. No kitchen, not even a laundry. The kids are beaten and abused, and I haven't got a clue what to do with them. Send me home, God. I don't know what to do.*

Five years later, I would risk my life to defend these kids.

It was a complex, emotional journey. To understand it is to try to make sense of Albania, a difficult task at best. It is the most backward, underdeveloped country in all Europe. During my time there, I had more threats on my life than I can count, simply for standing up for what's right.

For forty years, Albania was ruled by Enver Hoxha, a ruthless Communist dictator who cut the country off from the rest of the world. Very few people got in, very few got out. Because only the elite had televisions, and, even then, the programming was entirely state run, the vast majority of people were ignorant of global affairs. Hoxha told them that Albania was the best country in the world, that foreigners were jealous and would try to take it away from them, and they believed him, thinking this was Utopia, paradise, the greatest place on earth. In truth, it was a hellhole.

When Communism fell in 1991 and the country finally opened up, it was fifty years behind the times. With no economy, it was declared clinically dead by the World Bank. The first time I was in Albania, shops were boarded up. Horses, donkeys, and carts were the main means of transport. Under Communism, no one had been allowed to own a car. Men were imprisoned for having beards. No one was allowed to whistle. Mention Christ, and you could be executed.

With the economy in ruins, the government didn't have the resources to run their hospitals, schools, nursing homes, clinics, orphanages. So they turned to private organizations, and people began arriving from other countries to assess what could be done. Our nondenominational ministry decided to do something about the orphanage in Vlora, a city of a hundred thousand people just across the Adriatic Sea from Italy. Lola and I were sent to rebuild and run the orphanage.

Most of the children, abandoned at birth, came from hospitals. Over the coming months, babies would be left at the front door and others found lying in the street. Some neighborhood kids discovered a baby buried up to its neck on the top of a garbage pile. These were children born out of wedlock, the "illegals." Under Hoxha's rule, they were taken immediately from their mothers and put in orphanages. They were taboo.

An Albanian home isn't made up of simply a mom and dad and two kids; it's a clan. If an unmarried woman gets pregnant, the male members of the clan come down hard on her. They'll throw her out of the house if she tries to bring the baby home. Pride is everything, and whether you're a good family or a bad one, appearance is everything. Having a child out of wedlock is a deep disgrace. Often, they'll take the daughter to another city to have the baby and leave it in the hospital.

Mirelli was born out of wedlock, but his mother tried to keep him. When the grandmother said, "No, it's too big a shame on the family," she didn't listen. In the end, the grandmother hanged herself. Mirelli showed up at the orphanage shortly afterward.

For Mirelli, the stigma of being an "illegal" was just the beginning. He was, according to the staff, *boudala*, which means mentally retarded. The way the staff determined a child to be *boudala* could be completely irrational. "Ah," someone might say, "this one, he's got a left ear bigger than the right, this one is *boudala*." Then, because he'd been labeled *boudala*, the staff wouldn't pick him up or hold him or pay any attention to him. As the months passed, he wouldn't develop like the other kids. And they'd say, "Ah, see, I told you, he's got mental problems." And they'd keep pushing him back and pushing him back.

And that's what they did to Mirelli for three and a half years. They never brought him down from his room, not even for "circle time," a daily event when the staff would arrange small wooden chairs in a half-circle and make the kids sit there for hours without talking, without making a sound, so that the staff could relax in the back of the room, drink coffee, and talk. The kitchen staff would send food up to Mirelli, but if he didn't eat right away, it would be taken away. No one cared if he lived or died.

Lola started carrying Mirelli around on her hip all day, talking to him, singing to him, teaching him slowly how to walk, how to talk, how to eat on his own. When we moved into a house in town, Mirelli came to stay with us. Gradually, he gained weight, took his first steps; he came back to life, became a normal, healthy child. The change was startling. We grew to love Mirelli like a son and even started talking about adopting him. It was very emotional, very hard, because we were becoming so deeply connected to the kids.

Our first year, we worked like dogs. I didn't mind the work, but the mentality of the Albanian people wore me down so much that I often felt like I couldn't take it any more. In the beginning, our orphanage didn't have a wall around it, and people from the neighborhood randomly swarmed in and took things. It got so bad that we nailed scraps of wood over the windows and barricaded doors with old broken beds. And still they came, breaking out holes just big enough to accommodate the long hooks they made to reach in and grab blankets and clothes. When they started running up and stripping the coats and shoes off the kids as they played outside, I'd had it. The next time, I grabbed a stick and ran after them, yelling, "Go on, get outta here!" I ran around the building, where even more people were scurrying away. Thirty minutes later, they were back, like locusts. They stripped our cars, taking the windows, batteries, tires, seats, wipers, mirrors, and radios. Once, when Lola was alone, they stormed the orphanage, forced their way in, and began going through our storeroom.

I kept the stick to chase them off, but it ran contrary to everything I thought a good missionary should do. *Lord, I came here to help these people, and I'm chasing them off with a stick.* After a full year, I was so strung out that I didn't know how long I could stay. Lola had been back and forth to the States a couple of times, but I'd been in Albania the entire year.

It was January again. A truck had just arrived from Germany; people from all over the world were sending supplies. A crowd had gathered this day, as they always did when supplies arrived. We'd built a wall around the orphanage, and they were on the other side of the gate, leaning against the iron bars. The Germans were unloading, and I was inside, working in my office, when I heard a commotion. I kept working, and it kept getting louder and louder. *What's going on here?* I went outside and saw about thirty men rocking the gate. Every time the Germans brought something out of the truck, they climbed over and stole it. One of the Germans turned to me in disbelief. "They've stolen all our clothes, our cameras." Something in me snapped. I grabbed a big piece of pipe and charged the gate, yelling and screaming as I beat on it. When they scattered, I stopped, my throat on fire, my body wound tight with anger. I looked down at the pipe in my hand. *I'm gonna kill someone. I gotta go home.*

As soon as the Germans left, I called our home organization. "Put me on the next plane. I'm taking a month off." I was out of there in two days' time and spent a month in the States just trying to regroup.

Over a period of four years, Lola and I rebuilt the orphanage with the help of people from all over the world. A stainless steel sink came from

Germany. Beds, mattresses, and cabinets from Greece. Counters from the British, who also sent volunteers to paint the interior. Brazilians installed bathroom tiles. Norwegians laid new floors, Japanese painted wall murals. Greeks put in the plumbing. Old doors came from a Portland, Oregon, high school. It was a great success. Attitudes were changing, and we saw the Albanian staff develop a sincere love of and concern for the children. With staff training, with food and medicine, and with love and care, the children grew healthy and happy. The orphanage was filled with their laughter.

And then, overnight, it all comes apart.

It's 1997, and the country implodes with the collapse of massive investment scams into which people have sunk their entire life savings. Started by the Mafia, phony organizations were set up to launder dirty money, and people were enticed to invest in them with the promise of 30 percent interest a month. The government was in on the scam and took its cut to finance politicians. This went on for five years, and nearly every family in the country was invested. Toward the end, people were selling their homes to get in on it; farmers were selling their farms.

Finally, the United States and the World Bank put pressure on the Albanian government to close them down, because the Mafia are laundering billions of dollars of drug money. The top men flee with their money, sucking the country dry. Overnight, people lose everything. Some of our staff members lose their homes. Folks suddenly have no money for food and turn to the government to make good on their investments.

"This is going to get really ugly," I tell Lola.

Seemingly from one day to the next, the government abdicates, people take to the streets, first by the hundreds and then the thousands, rioting, burning, looting. They attack military barracks and steal guns, pistols, Kalashnikov assault rifles, carbine sniper rifles, hand grenades, land mines, bazookas, antitank rockets, surface-to-air missiles, tanks. They steal chemical weapons and even Navy ships. It's absolutely staggering. Albania had three million guns in weapons storehouses. Three million people are suddenly armed and enraged.

We are in pure anarchy. And the hotbed of violence is Vlora.

Most of the phony companies were headquartered in Vlora, right in the heart of Mafia territory. Mobs of people swarm through office and government buildings. The police try to stop them, but three hundred policemen don't stand a chance against thousands of viciously angry people. The things they do to the police are unspeakable. They chase them down, torture them, mutilate them, beat them, stone them, shoot them, pour gas on them, and burn them alive in the streets. They burn all the government buildings, from the library to the presidential villas to the city hall and everything in between. Finally, the police abandon the city.

It happens so fast that the embassies scramble to get their people out of the country. Other missionaries come by to tell us they're getting out, and I know that Lola has to go with them. We've heard about an American who sent his wife and kids out and, a couple of nights later, armed men wearing masks came to his house. He ran out the back door and disappeared, and no one heard from him. Later, I learn that he made his way across country on foot to Tiranë.

Lola fights the idea of going, determined to stay with me. But it's too dangerous. *The violence will only last a few weeks,* I assure her. Just for now, she must go. She'll be back soon enough when it's over. We set a rendezvous with the missionaries who are leaving, and in a matter of a few harried moments, I'm waving good-bye and watching her go.

Over the following chaotic days, I help organize evacuations and stay in touch with the American embassy, but I can't leave. I have an orphanage full of kids I love, and they'll be helpless against the looters who will come and take the shoes off their feet, the food off their plates. I can't go because I've seen the rioters strip buildings down to the bricks, taking window and door frames, ripping out the wiring. I can't go because of all the people from all the countries who have put heart and soul into this place. I can't let everything we've worked so hard to build be destroyed.

I know that the orphanage is vulnerable because the media has splashed our success all over television, newspapers, magazines. Everyone in town knows that we have new washing machines, dryers, stoves. We have food and clothing. Our warehouse is stocked with equipment, supplies, surplus food. When the looters come, and they will come, my own staff won't stop them. That's just the Albanian way. They'll open the gates and start carrying things out themselves. And the moment the neighbors see that first bag go out the door, they'll swarm and loot everything. Already people have swept through other orphanages and taken the beds right out from under the kids. They've pillaged nursing homes, putting the old people on the cement floors and taking the beds and blankets.

Sure enough, I hear from neighbors that the word on the street is that our warehouse, which is in a different part of town, is going to be looted that night. That's our food, medicine, blankets, toys, cleaning supplies, building materials. I have no gun with which to stop them. I consider moving supplies and food to the orphanage but know it will only draw the looters there. I have to step aside.

The next morning, one of our staff knocks on my door at seven in the morning and says, "It's all gone."

Things go quickly from bad to worse. I leave the house that Lola and I had rented and move into the orphanage. The rioting that I thought would last only a few weeks grows into a civil war that stretches on for seven months and, during that time, we have no police, no government, no law other than the law of the gun. Everybody in the city is armed. Massive gun fights break out in the streets, with rocket launchers blowing up cars, hand grenades tossed around like rocks, gunfire day and night, twenty-four hours a day. Thousands are killed.

I buy a gun and some hand grenades and pray that God will understand.

With our food supplies gone, I have to try to get to Greece, a four-hour cross-country trip on dangerous roads. Driving our minibus, I leave at five in the morning, thinking the thugs will still be sleeping. But they're already out, and at one point, I can see a roadblock up ahead where masked men are robbing a car. Later, I'll run barricades, but I haven't reached that point of willful personal abandon yet. Five cars pile up behind the one being robbed. Suddenly, one of the masked men gets angry with the backlog and waves us through impatiently. This happens two more times before I get to the border. I expect to encounter guards there but find the border station burned out, now a mass of rubble. On the Greek side are machine gun nests, lined up to keep out the Albanians.

Once inside Greece, I'm able to buy food, but I know I'll never make it back. I call the orphanage and arrange for men with Kalashnikovs to meet me at the border. On the way back to Vlora, I have an escort of eight men, a car in front of me, everybody armed, so that I can get the food safely to the orphanage.

As the weeks pass and our food supply dwindles again, we grind up rice and eat more soup than I ever want to see again. Finally, the Red Cross is able to get in. But they have no baby food, only U.N. crackers. So we grind up crackers for the babies. With the arrival of the Italian military — a questionable U.N. peacekeeping force that secures the port — we have ferry service and I'm able to get to Italy for food. Always, I'm cautious about how much I bring back, because I don't want word to spread that the orphanage has a lot of food.

I go regularly to check on our rented house about three miles from the orphanage, in a rough area of downtown Vlora. Several times I find it broken into and looted, but the phone still works, and when the lines to the orphanage are cut, it's my only connection to Lola. I try not to worry her with the severity of our situation. *Everything is fine,* I tell her, but she hears the explosions and gunfire in the background. *Ah, that's nothing, no big deal, it's okay.* I can tell she's strung out but trying to be strong. *No, you mustn't worry, we're all safe.* When I hang up, I look down at the gun cocked in my hand. How surreal. Hand grenades sit on the desk next to the phone that I just used to call Lola to tell her, *Things are getting better, no problem.*

When I come out of the house, a dozen punks are hanging around in the driveway, playing with their guns. I know them; most of them are eighteen-year-old kids, some older, who have been harassing us since we got here. They threatened to rape Lola, they threw rocks at our windows, they're the ones who broke in and ransacked the place. It isn't just us, they've terrorized the whole neighborhood. No one stands up to them, because to do so would invite the wrath not only of the punks but of their entire families. A clan never forgets an offense against one of their own. It may be a month later, it may be five years or fifty, but they'll exact their revenge. Consequently, in Albania, nobody sees anything, nobody hears anything, nobody says anything.

Well, not me. I spoke up when I saw people getting hurt, and that set these punks against me right from the start. I tried to rally the neighborhood to take a stand, getting people together and saying, "How long are you gonna let these punks terrorize you?"

"Yes, yes, you're right, you're right," they'd say, but as soon as I left, they were quiet again.

So these guys have had it in for me for a long time. And now they're hanging around, laughing, as I come out of the house. I might have ignored them, but I'm having a really bad day. I'm fed up with them. I've had it. I barrel down on them, yelling, "What's the deal here? What d'you think you're doing?" This is really stupid because they're all armed and don't mind using their guns. But I'm not thinking smart or stupid, I'm thinking, *I've had it with these punks.* "You guys come in here, you break into my house, you think I don't know you're the ones breaking into my house?"

"Ah, Mark, we respect you."

"Don't give me that, I know what you did!"

Suddenly, one of them reaches into his pocket and pulls out a pistol. I'm standing maybe eight feet from him, and he shoots at the ground, right next to my foot, sending asphalt spraying up my leg. He expects me to run. But I'm real hot myself, thinking, *Look at this punk, here he goes again.* I don't remember exactly what I say to him, but it's not real polite, and I don't back off. I start screaming at him. And then he aims straight at me, dead on, and pulls the trigger. In that instant, one of the other guys jumps him and the bullet screams by me and explodes through the window of my truck. As his buddies wrestle him on the ground, I finally have enough sense to get out of there.

It doesn't hit me until I'm driving away how stupid that was, how close I'd just come to getting killed. Fear breaks loose in me.

Around a bend, I see a new roadblock up ahead, set up to keep out thugs. I'm trapped. I can take off on foot, but they'll burn my truck, and I need it to bring in food. I have to turn around and drive through them.

I'm coming back around the bend when I see them, not just a dozen now, but a strong thirty and armed with AK-47s. They must not know about the blockade, because they aren't coming after me, they're shooting up my house with rifles and Kalashnikovs. There is no right or wrong here, just the power of the clan. I've offended a member, and now I have to deal with all of them. As I get closer, one of them sees me, and for a split second, I think of Lola, of Mirelli, of my children who are now grown. Hadn't I missed my own daughter's wedding to stay here, how many years ago?

An AK-47 fully automatic holds about thirty-two rounds.

I hit reverse just as they open up on me. The truck careens back to the blockade, where a group of gypsies have gathered, wondering what's going on. I fly out of the cab and start yelling, "I'm the only American who stayed! I stayed for the kids at the orphanage! And what do I get for it? These punks down the road are shooting up my house. I gotta get out of here!" Ten of them run to the blockade and roll it aside.

Even though I get back safely to the orphanage, I know it isn't over. I'm marked. I talk with one of the Albanian men on staff. Agron is a little guy, not macho, not cocky. He does his best to avoid trouble, but if it comes his way, he confronts it, regardless of the consequences. He's been with the orphanage since we first arrived and is one of the few people I trust. He goes to the family of the kid who tried to shoot me and tells them that I want a meeting. They pick a time and a place.

We meet, all the men, the father and brothers and cousins and uncles, everybody but the kid with the gun. I take Agron and four other Albanian men who work at the orphanage with me. "Look, I don't want any trouble," I start. "You know me, you guys have been after me for so many years, and I'm just not going to take it anymore. If you want a war, we'll have a war. If you want a big shoot-out, we'll have a big shoot-out. I don't want that, but I'm done. We gotta lay all this behind us and make peace."

"Okay, we want peace."

"Where's the kid with the gun?"

"He said he wouldn't come. He's gonna kill you. We can't talk to him, he's out there now looking for you."

"You'd better reel this guy in."

"There's nothing we can do. He's gonna get you."

In a roundabout way, it comes out that the reason they're not afraid of me is that I don't have any family in Vlora. If they break into an Albanian's house, they'll have a whole clan coming after them. But me, I'm a lone American. They can kill me because I don't have any protection.

I return to the orphanage, knowing this kid is out looking for me and that I'm a sitting duck. Agron is tough and will lay his life down for me, but I have no one else to stand by me. The other four Albanian men who work for the orphanage are loyal, but I don't know how far their loyalty will go in the face of a fight.

Agron puts the word out on the street that I can make certain "arrangements." "After all, he's American." They think Americans have all the money in the world. "He can go to Fier," a town thirty kilometers away, "and he can hire one of the gangs. They'll come over here and kill you. And Mark, he'll be on the next plane out of here. He can kill you a whole lot easier than you can kill him. Is that what you want? Now, if you want peace, you'd better come over and we'd better make peace. But if you want a fight, that's what you'll get."

That same day, the kid comes to the orphanage and sits down with me. We make peace, and he assures me, "You'll have no more problems in your neighborhood, and no one will bother you." And no one does.

That's what you have to do to survive in Albania. It's not the right way, but in this case, it's the only way.

We're a couple of months into anarchy when Tom Brokaw, reporters from the BBC, and several other media people come to do a piece on the orphanage and this stupid American who is still here. I tell them all, "Don't mention the guns. You can film the orphanage all you want, but I don't want any mention of the guns. I have nothing to gain by people knowing that we're sitting on AK-47s." *What are my supporters back home going to say? They send a missionary to Albania, and he takes up arms against the people.*

More months pass, with too many narrow escapes and close calls. Not only am I shot at, but our driver is confronted at gunpoint several times and once comes back to the orphanage with a bomb planted in the dashboard of the car. Kidnappings and extortion are escalating, and the word on the street is that I've been put on the list. Now Agron stops me from going across the street to the little bar where I normally get a Coke. "As soon as you step outside the gate, someone is going to grab you," he says. "You think you know the neighbors, you think you know the people here, but any one of them will take you."

I close the door to my room and sit on the edge of the bed. For what seems like an eternity, I sit there, thinking about my commitment to stay. I can get out at any time. Even with the fighting and the bandits on the road, I know I can get to the airport and be out of here in a day. It's a pivotal moment for me because the decision is excruciatingly conscious. It's one thing to think, *Oh, yeah, yeah, I'll take it to the end, I'll stay no matter what,* but will I? I have to tell myself the truth. No heroics. Once I cross this line, there will be no turning back, no matter what happens. I ask myself, *How far will you go, Mark, to protect the children and women on the staff?* In my heart of hearts, I know that I'll give my life for them. If anyone comes in and tries to take one of the women or one of the kids, it will be over my dead body. Even if I don't have a gun, I won't stand there and let it happen. Even if I'm shot, in cold blood, dead.

*I want to call my wife and my kids and tell them I love them one last time.* I don't expect to get out of Albania alive.

Early the next morning, before sunrise and under cover of dark, I steal out to our house, praying the phone line hasn't been cut. I might be shot, I might be killed, I might be kidnapped, but I won't bend to terrorists. I call the American embassy and explain that I don't want anybody negotiating for my release. "If they get me, we don't pay ransom." I call our missionary organization and tell them, "No ransom." I tell our accountant, "If they want only ten dollars, we give absolutely nothing."

And then I call Lola. Now I have to tell her the truth about the danger I'm in. And I have to tell her that she can't allow anyone to pay ransom if I'm kidnapped.

Vlora is a Mafia fiefdom.

It's the closest point to Italy, fifty miles across the Adriatic Sea, so the Mafia uses it as a conduit for refugees and drugs into Western Europe from the East. The Albanian Mafia is connected with the Italian Mafia, the Greek Mafia, the Turkish Mafia, and the Russian Mafia. They keep speedboats lined up along the shore for smuggling.

Even in "normal" times, a large ring of white sex slavery is run out of Vlora. They steal girls off the streets, drug them, put them in boats, and send them to Italy, where they're sold for sex, and no one ever hears from them again. Now they're not only grabbing girls off the streets, they're going into homes at night, taking them out of their beds and sometimes shooting their parents. And they're kidnapping children to sell to pedophiles. An Italian journalist who is writing an article about it comes through the orphanage, and I ask her how many children have been stolen.

Thousands, she says.

When our neighbors in the bar across the street tell us that the Mafia have come around asking how many children live in the orphanage, how old they are, what kinds of guns we have, how many men are guarding the place, Agron and the four other Albanian men on staff move in so we can keep a twenty-four-hour watch. Blessedly, when it comes to the children, they're not about to step aside. I call the U.N. peacekeeping force from Italy to ask for help. At first they say no, don't call. "But they've threatened to take our kids." All right then, they say, call.

The first time, the Mafia come with hand grenades, demanding that we send out the young women who work for us. We refuse. The next time, they come with AK-47s, again demanding the young women. Again we refuse. Shortly after that, one of the staff comes to me and says, "I was out with an old school friend last night and he warned me not to be in the orphanage tonight because the Mafia are going to attack it."

I call the U.N. peacekeeping force. *Now, come now!*

Hurrying, we drag all our weapons up onto the flat roof of the orphanage. A short wall runs around the edge, giving us minimal cover. Downstairs, the doors are bolted, the staff are on watch, the children are quiet. Night comes. We wait, watching as the dark thickens, cut only by a few sparse lights below.

Ten o'clock. Four heavily armed men appear at the front corner. At the back, two men with guns take up positions. At the opposite corner, two others. My heart starts to drum in my ears. Suddenly, I see a shadow going over the wall. It's Agron, his Kalashnikov strapped on his back. *What's he doing?* He storms over to one of the Mafia guys, yelling, "What're you doing here? What do you want?"

The guy falters, "It doesn't concern you, it has nothing to do with you."

Agron looks up at me. He wants to let them know we're not afraid of them. He slips back over the wall and disappears into the orphanage. We are all alone: me and Agron and the four other men. The Italians aren't coming, I'm pretty sure about that. A machine gun goes up on the roof of the building across the street. *So. This is it. I won't be alive in the morning.* What a strange, what a surreal feeling.

Through the night, we wait for it to begin.

The standoff with the Mafia that night pushed me closer to my mortality than I had ever been. I still can't explain why, but they never attacked, and, by morning, they had slipped away and disappeared.

Seven months after it erupted, Albania grasped a fragile peace.

Lola returned.

The police came back.

The open warfare stopped.

And yet, three million guns remain in the hands of people on the streets, and we hear gunfire almost every day. You never know when someone is going to go home and get a gun. You never know when they're going to get drunk and pull out a pistol, claiming, "You offended me," because you looked at them wrong. In the past, that might have ended in something no more serious than an argument, but today it ends in death. The Albanian people killed thousands of their own and walked away. Nobody investigated, nobody did anything. And even though the warring is over, people know that they can kill and get away with it, and they still have the guns to do it.

The orphanage and all of us survived. I believe deep in my soul that it was the prayers said for us by people all over the world that got us through. Another orphanage in town called us when things first exploded and asked for our help because they had no guns, no men, no protection. I got one of the churches in town to send over some of their men, and they guarded that orphanage for seven months. When the whole thing was over, every institution in the city had been attacked, the hospitals, the children's clinics, psychiatric wards, everything but the two orphanages.

My staying in Albania wasn't so much an act of courage as an act of love. During the uprising, I kept thinking, if this were different, if it were my own children in my own home, I'd do the same thing. That's the power of love. And I found out just how deep it runs.

⊙

In 1999 Mark and Lola were still in Albania when Kosovar refugees — some half a million of them — flooded across the northern border, fleeing the crisis in the Balkans. Trying to manage the overwhelming numbers, the government began dispersing them throughout the country. Vlora got its share.

"It was winter, freezing cold and wet," Mark told me. "The refugees started pouring into the city by the thousands. Having traveled for days by foot to get across the border, they were put in the back of dump trucks and driven twelve to fourteen hours south. I have never seen so much misery. Some of them were literally carried off the trucks, sick and throwing up from not having eaten for days. They were filthy and stank, covered with mud and muck. They had nothing but the clothes on their backs. It was the saddest thing I have ever witnessed."

The refugees were moved into a temporary camp area. With the government unable to adequately care for them, many NGOs arrived to help. "We, too, had a large work with the refugees, bringing in five hundred tons of clothing and food. Most of the refugees were women, children, old men. The young men were back in Kosovo, either fighting or killed. We heard one horror story after another."

During the refugee crisis, Mark witnessed a side of the Albanian people he hadn't seen. "So many Albanians opened their homes, and I mean families who were already living with six or seven people in a two- or three-room house. They barely had the means to feed themselves, not to mention these strangers from Kosovo, and still they took in six, eight, ten refugees."

Six years after I first interviewed him, I tracked Mark down in Portland. He wasn't stateside raising money for the orphanage. He was home for good. One of the first things he said to me was how worn out he was, utterly exhausted.

Much had changed in his life, including a wrenching separation and divorce from Lola. "When we first went overseas, we were extremely close to our kids, they were our life, we'd been in New Guinea with them. Then all of a sudden, we wake up in Albania, our kids are grown, and it's just me and Lola sitting at home without electricity much of the time, looking at each other and thinking, *Now what? Now what do we do?* We had to restructure our whole life, which we did, through our work.

"I became dedicated to ministry at all costs, above and beyond all else. I was working six, seven days a week, sometimes twelve hours a day. There was no separation between our personal lives and our work." As a result, he says, he lost sight of his relationship. "I didn't slow down enough to look at the impact the work was having or the problems that weren't getting addressed. We let ourselves get busy and never solved the core issues, so they'd always crop up again. I took Lola for granted; I didn't nurture our relationship. I should have dealt with the issues instead of ignoring them. It was stupid, all my fault. There came a point when so much damage had been done to our relationship that there was no repairing it."

Apparently, Mark got little empathy from his brethren. "The churches, the Christians I knew, most of them cut me off completely because I got divorced. It's the unpardonable sin. Some of my closest friends wouldn't give me the time of day, wouldn't even hear me out, treated me like I was a child."

Now resigned from the ministry, Mark is in Portland facing a dreary job market. "I came here thinking I'd go to work in another social agency, a shelter for homeless families, a school for teenagers or troubled youth, but I couldn't have picked a worse time to come back. The economy is so bad that the social agencies are laying off people."

To make ends meet, he went back to work at the refrigeration company he had left so many years ago. "Talk about a major life change. Everything I ever had, everything I ever worked for, from the ministry to my family to my health, has changed. It's like riding high for a while, and then the next thing you know, you're on the bottom."

In his ministry, Mark has only one regret. "Looking back at the work, all the precarious positions we put ourselves in, I wouldn't have done anything differently. I made the right decisions, beginning to end — except one. I kept the former director on staff, hoping that I could change her thinking, and she became a millstone around my neck."

His deepest regrets center around Lola, the divorce, hard times with his grown children. "Not a day goes by that I don't mentally replay what happened. But I just can't keep beating up on myself. What's done is done. I made mistakes, I've owned up to them. I'm sorry, I've repented, I've asked for forgiveness, I've apologized, but I can't turn back the clock.

"There comes a point when I have to leave it behind and go forward."

Now remarried, Mark is rebuilding a life with his Albanian wife and young stepdaughter.

# TWO

## Leaving the Reasoned Path

Do not go where the path may lead, go instead where there is no path and leave a trail.

*—Ralph Waldo Emerson*

## Into the unexpected with the tough and the timid

When I began *Women of Courage*, my first courage book, I had misconceptions about the word, what it meant, where it could be found, *and* what it took to be courageous. My parameters were narrow. I saw it as victory over seemingly insurmountable physical odds, overcoming tragedy, confronting danger. I was looking only at the most visible, the most apparent acts and not seeing that even these may or may not be courageous.

I also thought that, to be courageous, I had to become fearless. And before even *thinking* about doing something daring, I had to become gregarious, hugely self-assured, confident. Finally, I thought there were courageous people, and then there was the rest of us. What I've learned is that courage is always accompanied by fear, and that the term *courageous people* is an oxymoron — sometimes we're courageous, and sometimes we're not. (I'll talk more about that in part 6 and, in part 5, we'll explore ways to work with fear.) And confidence? Confidence in a courageous moment is not always what it seems to be. While some people I interviewed, like Mark Nyberg, exuded a ballistic kind of confidence, and others, like Shannon Meehan, a calm confidence, *timid* and *shy* were words I heard frequently. *How could that be?*

A common misconception about people who dare is that confidence is encoded in their DNA — that they possess an uncommon strand that enables them to take risks that others wouldn't take. Their confidence is uncommon, yes, but in ways you might not expect, especially if your point of reference is the *Webster's* dictionary, where I found this definition of the word: "A state of mind or a manner marked by easy coolness and freedom from uncertainty, diffidence, or embarrassment." Not likely in a courageous moment.

On the surface, courage may look cool and easy and certain, but underneath, it's hot. People often said to me, "I thought I was nuts" or "People thought I was crazy" or "It made no sense." But. "But I did it anyway." Others told me they were shy or timid or cowardly. "But I did it anyway." When it comes to daring, confidence is not the absence of uncertainty, doubt, perspiration, fear, timidity, or shyness, but rather the willingness to act in spite of them.

Having been shy and insecure myself, I thought courage was beyond my skinny reach, but the more I listened to people's stories and tuned in to my own sense of true confidence, the more I saw that it's *what I do with* my shyness that makes the difference. When I let it get in my way, it does. When I'm consumed by it, I'm unable to be present in the moment, and I miss out on opportunities. When I criticize myself for it, I become even shyer.

We may feel silly for being shy or insecure, uncertain or afraid. We may be convinced that people are judging us, talking about us behind our backs. On the courage board that I hosted at iVillage.com for two years, we had a lively and touching, funny and moving conversation about being shy. People opened up and shared stories. Susan was one of them.

Thirty-two, a military wife with four children, Susan struggled with nerves in the most ordinary circumstances. "When my husband and I went looking for an apartment, the people were nice," she told me. "But I felt uncomfortable with the way they were looking at me. I was, of course, nervous — it happens every time I go somewhere — and my guess is that they noticed it and judged me. No matter what I do to feel good about myself, I end up feeling lousy. When I'm about to leave the house, I prepare myself so I can project a positive image and seem like a secure person. But I still doubt. I know I'm doing something wrong."

Had Susan not been motivated to stand up for herself, to speak her mind and be true to herself, she would have been stuck. To change something, we have to admit we have something to change. Much of the judgmental chatter in her mind was self-generated. It was a reflection of how she saw herself. Like my friend Julie says, "You can trip over the front doorstep and people will think nothing of it if you're confident." Bottom line, nothing Susan did on the exterior was going to help in a way that she could trust. The work had to be done from the inside out, starting with acceptance.

Every time Susan left the house, she geared up to appear positive and confident, but underneath she felt lousy. What if, every time she left the house, she acknowledged that she was nervous and shy? What if she let the truth rise up rather than pushing it down? What if she stopped being defensive about it? What if she were able to laugh about it, to see it as part of being real, being human? What if she accepted it? "Yesterday, I went out with my husband and didn't feel as nervous," she told me after doing just that. "When my anxiety appeared, I floated with it until it went away. It felt great. I had control of my feelings and thoughts for a change."

Being shy or insecure doesn't have to work against us. It doesn't mean we're incapable, unworthy, weak. It doesn't mean anything — good or bad — about us. Many great people have done great things while being shy and uncertain. So if you're holding back because you're shy, don't. You're not alone. If you're waiting to be gregarious and outgoing, don't. Be you. And go ahead. You're good enough.

Adonal Foyle

## The Maggot Dog Becomes a Golden State Warrior

*Leaving All That's Familiar*

One of the scariest things we can do is to let go of the familiar, to step into the unknown. Good Lord almighty, what's out there? Will we be safe? Will our old familiar ground still be here if we need to return to shelter? Do we really have to do this? Isn't there another way? Couldn't we just forget about it?

Years ago, when Lourdes Saab was the chief of protocol in the mayor's office in Los Angeles, she told me, "You have to risk stepping outside the circle that has been drawn around you." That pretty much says it all. Circles get drawn around us — consciously or unconsciously, and not necessarily maliciously — by family, friends, colleagues, or folks keen on the idea of keeping us tidy, under control, ever so predictable. We draw our own circles out of fear, doubt, and insecurity. We make up miles of excuses why we shouldn't step out. We can be utterly convincing.

At times, what drives us beyond the circumscribed safe space of a circle is the unwanted, the uncalled, something beyond our control. We feel we have no choice, no other option. We go because we have to, because something has happened that demands it of us, or because some compelling force inside us shoves us forward.

At other times, there's no need to go, no hand pressed at our backs. We don't have to take that step outside the circle. No one will be the wiser if we slide our foot back in again. No one will think less of us if we stay put. But we are haunted by the thought that we'll be forever looking back, wondering what might have been if we had just had the guts, if we had only dared. Something has gotten hold of us and won't let go. It lives inside us. Maybe that something is a call to adventure, a curiosity. Maybe our integrity is at stake, our values, our principles, our ability to feel right about something. Or maybe what's gotten hold of us is a sublime longing to make sure that our lives matter, that we live a full life, not dawdling on the sidelines.

In a way, these are the most daring of moments, because we don't have to take the risk — we really don't. And yet we choose to. We choose to expose ourselves to the vagaries of the unknown. Because.

And so we shove off into places we have never been.

I was sixteen when I left my home in the Caribbean. I came to the United States on a piece of luck, a dream, and an opportunity of a lifetime. A basketball would be my delivery. But how do you move away from the only life you've ever known? How do you leave the people you care about most?

I was born on Canouan, one of the Caribbean islands of St. Vincent and the Grenadines. We lived a simple but not a calm life. My father drank and was abusive. He left when I was six. With four children to feed, my mother decided to move to one of the bigger islands, Union Island, where she could stay at the family house of her brother and work in his restaurant or at the market.

As the oldest male in our family, I was left behind to care for my grandmother. In the Caribbean, boys do whatever needs to be done, and the first son is the unlucky one responsible for anything unpleasant. As a child, I didn't fully understand; when my mother left, I thought I'd done something terribly wrong, that she didn't like me. I felt betrayed, stuck with an old woman who was a total nut. Just me and my grandmother and my donkey on an island that was only three and a half miles long.

As time passed, my friends started leaving for other islands to continue their education. I was still in primary school, and watching them go was hard. It seemed like everyone was leaving except me. Determined to get off the island, I studied extra hard, long into the night, by kerosene light and candles. By some miracle, I was able to pass an examination to move on to high school. And that meant leaving Canouan — oldest male or not.

Leaving my grandmother to live with her sisters on Canouan, I say goodbye. I'm on my way to Union Island, a metropolis of two thousand people.

The reunion with my family is mixed. I've forgotten what my mother is like and have to relearn what sets her off so I can get out of her way when she's angry. Being with my little brother and sisters isn't easy either. We fight a lot, and I always get blamed.

My first day of school, I'm terrified and paranoid because even though

I've worked so hard to get here, underneath I don't think I belong. I want to blend in, but I'm six foot five. Walking up the steps of the school, I'm a scared, skinny kid heads taller than everyone else. Off to the side, I see a boy watching me. *What's going on? Does he want to fight me?* I'm big, but I'm also afraid.

"Hey! You gotta play basketball."

*He talking to me?* I'm rigidly shy. I don't talk much, and I sure don't want to talk to this kid. What's basketball, anyway?

"Hey! I gotta take you to the court."

For a week, the kid bugs me about playing; he won't let it go. Finally, I give in and go take a look at the court. It's outside and pocked full of holes. The backboard is made of wood; an old car engine holds it up. The rims have no nets. It's the middle of the day, a hundred degrees. And this is what the kid's so excited about?

"Okay, I'll play. Once."

In ten seconds, he explains the game and the rules, and that's it, we start playing. No, he and the other kids start playing, and I try to keep up. My big moment comes when I get a rebound. I'm so excited, I run the full length of the court with the ball tucked under my arm to go for a layup. When I look back, thinking I'm pretty hot stuff and expecting them to be right behind me, I see them falling on the ground, laughing hysterically. I forgot to dribble. I'm so embarrassed, I run off the court.

That's the end of that.

Or so I think. About a week later, as I'm walking home from school, members of one of the competitive island teams come up to me: "How you like to come at night and learn how to play the game?" All these guys are much older than I. In the islands, cricket and soccer come first. The old guys — in their mid-twenties, even into their thirties — play basketball. I agree to play with them because I want to get back at the little bastard who embarrassed me.

Even though I learn quickly, I can do only two things well: blocking shots and rebounding. I'm not good at dribbling without looking at the ball, and I can't shoot worth spit. I'm sure my teammates are thinking, "He's not that good, but at least he's long."

A few months later, we go to the Organization of Eastern Caribbean States Championship on Dominica. It's a big tournament by Caribbean standards, and every year an American professor comes in to help with the refereeing. Sometimes his son, Jonny, comes with him, and this time he sees me play. Even though I'm raw as can be, he thinks, "Wow, this guy looks like he could be a star."

"You gotta see this Adonal guy," he tells his dad, Jay Mandle.

"If he's playing basketball, he's probably thirty years old," says Jay.

After snooping around to find out how old I am, Jonny goes back to his dad. "He's sixteen."

"Impossible!"

When Jay and his wife, Joan, introduce themselves, they ask whether I've ever thought about playing basketball in the United States and using it as a way to get a good education.

"Yes! Wonderful! Of course!"

Mind you, they're not saying they'd like to take me to the States; they're only asking if I've ever thought about it. In the meantime, everybody on my team thinks I've just been discovered and that I'll soon be playing professional basketball in the United States.

"No, no, that's not what we meant," say Joan and Jay.

I'm so embarrassed. The possibility of being discovered is always there, sure — everybody wants to go to the United States — but it's a dream, not a reality. Which is why, some time later, after talking with me and seeing me play, when they actually do invite me to go with them, I think, *This can't be real.*

⊙

To this day, there is no logical explanation for why Joan and Jay decided to help Adonal. They were both working professionals with no spare time dangling from their schedules. "Truth is, I don't know why," Jay laughs now. "It was a fit of madness."

They'd been making a pilgrimage to the Caribbean for twenty years. An economics professor, Jay took his first teaching job at the University of the West Indies in Jamaica in 1966. Their son, Jonny, was born there. Jay loved basketball and had been refereeing games for as long as he could remember. When he and Joan, a sociologist, first encountered basketball in the Caribbean, they weren't looking to conduct a six-year participant observation study.

"Because everybody is nuts about sports, you can learn about other aspects of people's lives by studying it," Joan told me. "Particularly in the Caribbean, people who play basketball are very, very poor... it's called the grassroots. Really what we were doing was studying poverty. We had access to Rastafarians and people to whom nobody else had access; they loved us because we taught them how to play basketball. Over time, we grew close to many people and in that way gathered important information about Caribbean society from the bottom up. What started as a project to help folks by teaching them basketball became a window on a society in a deep and complex way. Once we recognized the kind of information we were getting and realized that other people didn't have access to it, we started writing what became our first book on the subject, *Grass Roots Commitment*."

Over the years, they'd had plenty of opportunities to take a player home with them. "Everybody wants to come home with you," says Joan. Adonal wasn't even the most remarkable basketball player they'd ever seen. So why? "He was the only player we'd met who was still in school. Most had dropped out at fourteen or fifteen and were now twenty-six and wanting to go to America to get a basketball scholarship. We thought, geez, this is ridiculous, here's a kid who's going nowhere who, if he were in the States, would go to college. How could we leave him there?"

They asked around about Adonal. "He seemed like a nice child," says Joan. For confirmation, they visited his school. Yes, they were told, he was a very nice child. "We went up and down the one dirt road on Union Island and asked everybody about the Foyle family, and everyone seemed to think they were good people." Joan talks fondly but realistically of Union Island. "We loved Union. It's a neat place, very much a backwater; they'd only recently gotten electricity. But it's also a hard-luck place with no jobs, a rock with a couple thousand people on it and no place for folks to go."

Joan and Jay wrestled with an idea that would significantly alter their lives. They had made the decision years before to have one child. Jonny was ten years older than Adonal and working on a PhD in philosophy. They were done with their parenting. They didn't need this kid, nice as he was, taking up space in their already busy lives. "We were absolutely distressed," says Jay, "because we didn't know what to do about Adonal. At one point, I turned to

Joan and asked her, 'If this were a person with a prodigious capacity to be a violinist, would we leave him here?' In Adonal we saw a wonderful kid with a talent as an athlete, not specifically as a basketball player but as an athlete. And it was impossible not to give him an opportunity. Yet it would be unlike anything we'd ever done."

They went to Adonal's mother to ask permission to take her son to America. Joan was upfront with her about the risks. "I told her that there are all kinds of awful things in the United States. It's not like this idyllic little Caribbean island. There are drugs and violence and other terrible things, and I wanted her to understand that we would do our best to shield Adonal, but it was a big decision with risks."

It was up to Adonal, said Patricia Foyle.

Two weeks after meeting him, Joan and Jay invited Adonal to come to America. "We're the least impulsive people in the world," Joan told me. "We have extremely stable lives. This was ridiculously fast."

Was it kismet? "All I can tell you is that it was weird," says Jay.

They had only recently moved to the small town of Hamilton, New York, to take teaching positions at Colgate University. With Jonny out of the house, they knew next to nothing about high schools in Hamilton and decided that Adonal would go to Philadelphia, where they'd lived and taught for years, where they knew the educational lay of the land and were sure that Adonal would get solid basketball coaching. They'd go down every other week to check on him. They'd call every day. That was the plan.

Soon after returning home, Jay ran into the chair of his department at Colgate. "I said to him, 'I just ruined my life.'" He laughed, but perhaps on some level he knew what lay ahead. Perhaps not. The full brunt of consequences is not always apparent to us when we dare. Sometimes that's a good thing, because it allows us to move forward and then grow into the bigness of the challenge.

⊙

"I gotta go, Mom. I need to do this." I haven't been with her for more than a year, and now I'm leaving. She's worried. "I have to go because it's an opportunity to get an education, and an education means a chance to be something other than a fisherman or farmer. An education means not working road construction for the government. It means not washing dishes in a restaurant all my life."

She looks at me and, inside, she knows it's right.

Not until I call my grandmother does the significance of what I'm about to do settle over me. She's in her eighties, and I might not see her again, ever. *What am I doing? My God, by the time I come back home...* The magnitude of the thing starts to hit me. This is bigger than just going to the States. For all my wanting to get away, saying good-bye to the woman who raised me is the saddest departure of all.

By the time I board the plane, all kinds of emotions are running through me. I don't know the people who will be meeting me on the other end. I don't know if I'll be able to keep up with the academic work. I don't know if I'll be a successful player. I don't know what it's like where I'm going. I've never been off the island, least of all to a place as big as the United States.

What is America to a Caribbean boy born on an island of eight hundred people? Mind-boggling. And very, very scary. The plane lifts off.

⊙

By the time Adonal left the West Indies, Joan and Jay were already back in the States. In detail, they had told him how to change planes at JFK in New York. They would meet him at the airport in Philadelphia.

⊙

My feet first touch American soil at John F. Kennedy airport in New York. I've never seen such a huge place. As the plane empties, I follow the people who were onboard. *What was it Joan told me about where to go?* I fumble in my pocket for the piece of paper with the instructions she gave me. *What did Jay say about catching the next plane?* I'm sure that I'm going to get killed, that someone is going to lead me astray. I'm so nervous that I start to slow down, and people rush past me.

"Adonal! Adonal!"

I spin around.

Unbelievably, it's the prime minister of my country, who has come up on the same plane. "Where are you trying to get to?"

I pull out the piece of paper and push it toward him, trying not to look scared. "Someplace in Philadelphia."

"You're going the wrong way."

He and his delegates, some twenty of them, lead me with my little bag through the airport to the right gate. What a sight we must be.

As the plane lands in Philadelphia, it's night, and I look out the window at a sea of lights, not candlelight but bright electric light. It's unreal to me, freaky. On the ground are islands of cars, cars, and more cars. On Canouan, there were two. We could walk around the whole island.

In Philadelphia, the plan is to visit a private school where I'll apply for a scholarship. But it doesn't quite work out. My grades are terrible, and I fail the entrance exam. We have to shift gears, and I end up enrolling at a different school. It seems like a quiet place. It's summer when I visit.

Before school starts, I go to the annual high school basketball camp. When I arrive at the hotel where the team is staying, I'm told that my room is on the third floor.

"How do I get up there?"

"The elevators are right over there," says the man behind the registration counter.

I go over, step into the box, and turn around. Nothing happens. I don't know what to do, so I stand there waiting for something to happen. A man walks in and presses one of the numbered buttons, and the door closes. With a jolt, I lurch. *What's happening?* I'm afraid to breathe, literally.

"Are you all right?" the man asks.

I nod, still holding my breath. The elevator jerks again, and I start shaking. I must be purple; I'm thinking, *I'm gonna die! I'm gonna die!*

At the camp, even though Joan and Jay come to make sure I'm all right, I'm a wreck. On the court, I don't know how to plant myself, how to play good defense. I'm a tall, skinny stick — back on the islands, they called me Maggot Dog because I was so emaciated — and when guys elbow me, I lose my balance. I get beaten up on the court and don't know how to defend myself and fight back. These kids have been playing for years and are skilled. Me, I'm raw as can be and trying to compete with guys who can put my head in the basket. It's a nightmare. Much about that first year is a nightmare. Everything is new.

Fall arrives, and with it my first day at an American school. To my surprise, two thousand kids suddenly jam the hallways! I tower over everybody and am terrified of stepping on someone or knocking someone over. I can feel people watching me. Everyone seems to know who I am, at least superficially, and they all expect me to know who they are. I've never experienced anything like it. Even though I've been playing basketball for maybe seven months, everybody thinks I'm the kid from the Caribbean who's going to save the team.

One of the first people I stay with is a friend of the coach who lives alone and has an extra room. I come home at the end of the day to find him drinking and no food in the house. The experience brings me desperately close to what it was like growing up with my father. I stay out of his way and try not to cross any lines, knowing where that led when I was a child. If I knew Joan and Jay well enough to talk to them about what's happening, I would tell them that this person is drinking like a fish, that there's nothing to eat, that I don't know how to drive, I can't go to the store, I don't have any money. But when they call and ask how I'm doing, I say, "Fine," because I'm afraid they'll send me back to the Caribbean, and I don't want to go home a failure.

I have nobody to talk to. I'm scared and lonely.

⊙

Joan and Jay had no way of knowing what was going through Adonal's head or how he was being treated. They'd gone to the school several times to talk with the teachers and principal before school started. They called regularly. "No matter how well you try to prepare someone, they're going to experience culture shock," says Joan. "Even though we explained things, even though we checked in with him, he felt alone and adrift. After all, we were all strangers to him; he had only just met us."

⊙

During this time, I miss my grandmother something awful. I miss my mother, our culture. Growing up in a more communal society, I knew just about everyone on Canouan. For better or worse, everyone looked out for one another, and I always had people around me whom I could trust. One of the hardest things for me is being in a culture in Philadelphia where I know so few people, and the people I do know want something from me and aren't necessarily looking out for my best interests. I'm sixteen and have to be mature enough to understand and make decisions that adults normally make. I have to grow up fast.

I work very hard to sustain, to make do. At school, even if I don't know what's going on, I pretend to, so that people won't think I'm an idiot. On the court, my progress is slow, and I'm a very big project for my coaches. Talking with my teammates is awkward because my Caribbean accent is hard for them to understand.

I start spending more and more time at the house of one of the kids on the team who does understand me. Every time he offers me something to eat, I wolf it down. "Hey, are they feeding you?" he keeps asking. Finally, I tell him the truth, hoping he won't squeal; I'm so afraid that the coach will get mad at me and send me home.

But eventually, I have to speak up. I go to the coach and tell him. When he gets upset, I don't know if he's upset with me or the guy I'm living with, and I don't know what he'll do. I keep thinking, *It's my fault, he's going to send me back to Union.* Instead, he moves me into the home of the assistant coach.

I begin to settle in, and I make some progress on the basketball court. After those first games, where the crowd is overwhelming — there are more people in the gym than on my entire island! — I find that I have a natural feeling for the game. My coach is great, and with organized structure, a better understanding of the fundamentals of the game, and practice, practice, practice, I begin to improve dramatically. Playing center, I have the height, the strength, and the agility to be good.

Where I don't do well is in the classroom. Even though I love to learn, even though my driving motivation to be in America is to get an education, I fall further and further behind.

That summer, I return home for a visit. Seeing my mom waiting for me when I come off the plane is wonderful. My whole island team comes out to greet me. I'm their baby sent out into the world, and they want to be sure I'm all right. It's fantastic but strange at the same time.

⊙

That was to be a summer of both basketball and academic training. Jay knew a coach in Trinidad with whom he wanted Adonal to work. The plan was to mix the court with the books and prepare Adonal for the S.A.T.s.

The plan quickly fell out when Joan gave Adonal a practice S.A.T. test, and his deficiencies were glaring. She was shocked. "He couldn't read any better than he had a year before. Finally, he broke open and told us the whole story. We went crazy about his living situation and were furious about the academics. We had impressed on the people at the school that Adonal was there for academic reasons, that school was the most important thing. Yes, yes, yes, they'd said, but instead they'd been grooming him intensely as a basketball player — by the end of the year, he was ranked number one in the country — and keeping him in the lowest academic track so his studies wouldn't interfere. So, here's a bright kid, and no one was helping him. We thought it was racist, and when we found out, we raised all hell."

But what to do right now with Adonal, fresh from his confession in Trinidad? "In that moment, we faced the full magnitude of the task in front of us," Jay remembers. How could they tell Adonal without overwhelming him? "We had to make him aware of the extent of the work ahead of him, and that was wrenching."

It was wrenching because Adonal wasn't quick to grasp what would be demanded of him. "How could he be?" says Jay. "It wasn't part of his life experience, his upbringing. He'd never done the kind of work we anticipated he'd have to do. Joan and I had to be as honest, clear, and explicit as possible in describing the situation, because we didn't want to mislead him."

They contemplated moving him into their own home so they could work with him on weekends and evenings. "But we had to be sure that if he came to live with us, he wasn't coming under false pretenses. It was going to be arduous."

Their conversation grew intense.

"We were all sitting around crying for days and days trying to decide what to do," recalls Joan. "We weren't going to force him to come live with us, and yet we saw so clearly what would happen if he didn't. Our close Trinidadian friends said, 'This isn't the way people in the Caribbean do things; just pick him up and take him, don't give him a choice.' But we couldn't do that. It was for Adonal to choose. And it was very, very hard because he had become a huge basketball success already. I don't know how he made that decision at seventeen."

⊙

I'm so conflicted about moving to New York, because I'll be leaving the good people who took me in, the assistant coach and his family, and other people I've come to care for. In my world, we live by a code of loyalty: You don't turn your back on the people who help you. But I can't end up as a basketball star without a high school degree. Joan and Jay are professors and are willing to tutor me every spare minute. I finally agree it's the right thing to do.

Understandably, some people in Philadelphia are upset. I get cussed at, called ungrateful, and I feel guilty. Some people call the newspaper and say that Joan and Jay are kidnapping me. It gets ugly. Some people are desperate to keep me on the team; some have other motives about which I don't care to speculate.

Instead of arguing, we try to go about our business and focus on what's ahead.

In New York, I'm faced with a new environment and the new rigors of study at Hamilton Central High School. Seven days a week I study, using shoeboxes of flash cards to learn enough vocabulary to take the S.A.T. exam. I have extra classes, extra writing, extra math. Ahead of me are two years of unbelievable tenacity trying to master this thing. I need a miracle to get into college.

◉

Even though Joan and Jay thought they were prepared, bringing Adonal to live with them was challenging.

"I couldn't have foreseen the dimension that it would take up in our lives," says Jay. "It was impossible to see ahead of time."

It's not that they weren't fully versed in the raising of a son, although, says Joan, "trying to raise a basketball prodigy is no joke." Rather, it was the compression of fitting in everything that needed to be done in a tight span of time. "Just getting Adonal oriented to what it took to accomplish something was daunting," says Jay. He wasn't just learning vocabulary and math and history; he was learning how to study: the elemental skill preceding the absorption of knowledge.

"We had plenty of moments of hollering at each other, because some major changes had to be made, and not all of it was easy, by any means," says Jay. "We even had to work with Adonal on his socialization skills so that he could do what he was capable of doing."

At any moment, either Joan or Jay could have given up and sent Adonal packing. Or Adonal could have bolted. "Without his absolute capacity to work, his strong motivation, his diligence, it couldn't have been done." Jay easily hands the credit to Adonal, because for Joan and him, the reward was huge. "It was so gratifying that there was no turning back — hard but also exciting and gratifying."

As the months passed, Adonal became voracious for knowledge. "We took him to theater, ballet, opera, museums, and he loved it all," Joan remembers. "He couldn't get enough. Yes, it turned us upside down and was disruptive to our lives... but it was wonderful."

Over the coming years, the kid they called the Maggot Dog back on the islands would lead the Hamilton Central High School basketball team to their first two state championship titles and receive McDonald's High School All-America as well as third team USA Today All-America and third team Parade All-America. Adonal graduated with honors and went on to college, but not to one of the traditional basketball schools. In part to be close to Joan and Jay, he stayed in upstate New York and enrolled in Colgate University, a small liberal arts school: The size was right, its academic reputation was strong, and the coach promised to give him individual attention and teach him skills in all aspects of the game. Adonal didn't want to get pegged as a defensive specialist. He wanted more. He wanted all of the game.

"I've come a great distance from Canouan. And yet a piece of my heart remains there. Life is complex now. But I know what I'm capable of, and I know who I can be and how my stepping into these bigger shoes gives hope to kids who, like me, want to be more."

At Colgate, Adonal was named the Patriot League Rookie of the Year and was the first freshman ever to earn First Team All-Patriot League honors. As a sophomore, he was named the Patriot League's Male Scholar-Athlete of the Year. He was named the 1996 Patriot League Player of the Year during his junior year. He was also a finalist for the John R. Wooden

Player of the Year Award and the All-American team, and was named Second All Team All-America by the U.S. Basketball Writer's Association, First Team All-Conference, USBWA District II Player of the Year, and First Team GTE/CoSIDA Academic All-America during his junior year.

By the end of his junior year, Adonal was ready to enter the NBA draft. He was selected in the first round of the 1997 draft by the Golden State Warriors in the San Francisco Bay Area. While playing in the NBA, he continued working on his degree, and in 1999 graduated magna cum laude from Colgate University with a degree in history. He's currently working on a master's degree in sports psychology at John F. Kennedy University in Moraga, California and, at the same time, writing a memoir.

A man of many passions, Adonal has taken the NBA Read-to-Achieve program to his Caribbean islands. Enlisting NBA players to go with him, he holds two camps a summer, taking books to encourage kids to read and bringing in balls and rims and hands-on coaching from the pros. "Everybody's going to be guards on my team," he laughs.

Describing Adonal in the *Mercury News,* Mark Emmons wrote that his "world is not flat. Its boundaries extend beyond the dimensions of an NBA basketball court." Calling him the "Player Most Often Referred to as a Renaissance Man," Emmons included in his profile of Adonal: "Reads and writes poetry. Played Stanley Kowalski in a college production of *A Streetcar Named Desire.* And might be the only NBA player to ever use the word 'idiosyncratic.' [He was describing one-of-a-kind teammate Gilbert Arenas.]" Emmons went on to call Adonal "one of the most politically active athletes in professional sports."

Ever aware of the gift of freedom, Adonal founded Democracy Matters, a nonpartisan organization that develops leadership skills in students and gives them a venue to voice their opinions through teach-ins, letter writing and petition campaigns, educational seminars, and voter-registration drives. Joan Mandle left Colgate University to become executive director of the Democracy Matters Institute.

Adonal's outreach and service in the Oakland schools and Bay Area community earned him the mayor of San Francisco's 1998 Sports Hero Award for his "commitment to the underprivileged children of the city of San Francisco." In 1997 the American Heart Association named him their "Athlete with a Heart."

It took Adonal a few years to find himself as a Golden State Warrior. In his sixth season, he played in all eighty-two games for the first time in his career, averaging 21.9 minutes per game. He was the first Warrior to reach the two-hundred-block mark in thirteen years and ranked among the league's top ten in blocked shots for the third consecutive season — becoming the first player in the Warriors' history to do so.

Janet Yang

# The First Wave
*Refusing to Be Boxed In*

She was sixteen the first time she went to China, one of the first to reunite with families on the mainland. She and her mother went alone. The rest of the family stayed behind, just in case. "China was considered a mysterious black hole," Janet Yang remembers. "If you went in, you might never come out. With a Communist regime in power, it was considered dangerous, unpredictable."

The year was 1972. Nixon and Kissinger had come back from a trip to meet with Chairman Mao Tse-tung. Permission was granted for Chinese Americans to travel to the motherland. Janet's parents hadn't seen their relatives since the 1940s, when they separately left Shanghai and Hunan Province for America and the University of Michigan, where they met and fell in love. Neither of them had intended to remain abroad, but by the time they graduated, the economic and political situation in China had caused relatives to urge them to wait: *It is not a good time for you to come home.* As the years wore on and the proletarian revolution surged, setting workers, peasants, and soldiers against the intelligentsia, the time for return was delayed again and again.

Yang Tienyi and his wife, Tsien Chungtzu, moved to Queens, started a family, and bought used furniture, certain that the stay was temporary. Janet came along in 1956. As news arrived in bits and pieces from relatives in China, her parents' plans to return faded. Her mother adopted an English name, Anna, and took a job at the United Nations, which raised suspicions back home. "In China, anybody who had experience abroad was suspect, and with the U.N. job, my mother was branded a spy."

In the meantime, the Red Scare gripped America, and Janet's parents were no longer seen simply as Chinese but as potential Communists. They were now caught between worlds, suspect both in China and in America. Her father couldn't get a job. Years later, Janet would cry as she read the letters he wrote to potential employers pleading for work. "He was desperate and said he would work for free just to get experience, and still no one would hire him. Finally, he got a job, for no pay." That would lead to a salaried job and, forty years later, he would retire from the same company, having reached the position of senior vice president.

In 1972 her parents were eager to be reunited with their families, but they were not without grave concerns. "We split up so that if something happened to us, the rest of the family was here in America to get us out."

Janet and her mother flew to Hong Kong and walked across the border, the only way to enter China at that time. "I'd never seen so many guards," Janet remembers. "They separated me from my mother and started interrogating me, trying to intimidate me. My Chinese was spotty, and I didn't fully understand what they were saying, but I got the gist: 'How are you treated as a Chinese in America? Do they discriminate against you?' They were harsh with me because they didn't believe I couldn't speak the language fluently."

As a teenager now living a middle-class life in suburban New York, Janet wasn't prepared for what she would see and hear and feel over the next three weeks. Meeting relatives for the first time and seeing her mother reunite with her family was emotional, a "time of many tears." Conversations often took place in whispers to foil bugging devices. "Stories were told about the suffering of the family as a result of my mother being branded a spy. Suspicions were raised about how my grandparents had really died, whether they'd committed suicide or were killed, as was common during the Cultural Revolution. It was all very mysterious and disturbing at times, but also full of celebration and the joy of reconnecting with family."

During the Cultural Revolution, any remnants of a nonproletarian life or a life outside China were destroyed. Photographs sent by Janet's parents from America had been confiscated. "Before we arrived, the photographs were suddenly returned." Because Janet and her mother were one of the very first families from America to return, the government did what it could to ensure they were treated well. "A government representative would go to the villages where my relatives lived and make sure there were fresh chickens to be caught and killed so we had something good to eat, which wasn't the norm." Other experiences were bizarre. "I helped my younger cousins with their homework because they were all studying a little bit of English. I'd open up the textbook and the lesson would read, 'Down with American imperialistic paper tigers.'"

The cumulative effect of those three weeks was life altering for Janet. "Being in this ancient country, a Communist country, a have-not country, my homeland, was overwhelming. All at once, I was experiencing for the first time the complete opposite of everything American. Everywhere we went, we saw military people, guards in uniform."

She didn't fully grasp it then, but she came home with a curiosity that would take hold in her and grow into an obsession with China. Years later, she would connect the dots between issues that had plagued her parents — living in limbo, being suspect — and her own return trip to China.

⊙

I return to China when I'm twenty-four. It's 1980, and China has been officially recognized by America. The first wave of journalists, business-people, and exchange students are going over to live, and I want to be part of it. I can't articulate why, only that I intensely want to go... maybe part of me is romanticizing the idea.

I'm working as the assistant to the editor-in-chief at *Book Digest* in New York City when I get a letter from the Chinese-language professor I studied with at Harvard. "They're looking for someone like you at a place called the Foreign Languages Press," she writes.

In the past, the Foreign Languages Press published only the collected works of Chairman Mao, translating them into many languages. But at the end of the Cultural Revolution, when Deng Xiaoping assumed control and started talking about industrialization and democratization, the idea of sell-ing to the marketplace began to gain acceptance. The Foreign Languages Press branched out to publish magazines and literature, history and art books.

Sooner than I imagined, I'm on my way to China. By myself. For a year.

I fly to Hong Kong and take a train into Canton, where I go through customs. The process is unbearably bureaucratic and primitive. I fill out endless sheets of tissue-thin paper and glue them to my bags, which then must be weighed and processed by a guy in an office that seems to close every time I approach. I miss my next train.

Arriving late in Beijing, I'm picked up by a reed-thin man with a hangdog look who appears to be worn down by his job. Lao Shen is a deputy head of my division at the Foreign Languages Press and undoubtedly a Communist Party member, because one of his main functions is to "handle" foreign affairs issues.

For years, a select group of foreigners with language expertise has come to China, starting in the 1950s with the Soviets. Others followed and were treated with utmost reverence, a tradition left over from China's colonial past, when virtually any Caucasian person coming into China was given the red-carpet treatment. Eventually, the government realized that they could find experts of Chinese descent who would feel like they were returning to the motherland, even if they weren't born there, so they would be willing to come for less pay and fewer amenities and to live like the natives. In every way, these new experts would be closer to the populace, and I'm in that experimental group. We're not called experts; we're called foreign workers, which means I'll be living in a dormitory.

As we arrive at the Foreign Languages Press compound on the outskirts of town, an uneasy feeling begins to settle over me. The cement building is badly in need of paint. A short woman with cropped hair and a rough edge approaches. She's one of two women assigned to take care of me and shows me around the compound. My uneasiness turns to shock as a stench from the plumbing follows us through the work building and, behind it on the other side of a courtyard, to the dormitories. She opens the door to my living quarters, and I stare into a stark room with a plain wood-frame bed with two woolen blankets laid on top as the mattress. In the morning, I discover that the building has no hot running water. Even though I'm in one of the better housing units for the Chinese, this is a great distance from New York.

*What did I get myself into?*

It's March and freezing cold. The next day, I'm taken on my first trip outside the compound, to the Friendship Store. The trick to staying warm is to wear heavy wool or cotton-padded leggings and cotton-padded jackets. Right off, I startle the woman with me by not opting for the standard issue for women, which is flared in all the wrong places. I purchase a men's jacket, which I'll end up wearing 24/7. Because the buildings aren't heated, everyone wears the same clothing indoors as outdoors.

*What am I doing here?*

The food in the commissary includes protein in the form of cubes of lard laced with pork, rice that almost always has pebbles in it, and the one and only winter vegetable, cabbage, which they bury underground to make it last until spring.

The first week, as I try to adjust to my surroundings and wrap my brain around the language, people at work are friendly, but I can feel a tense undercurrent. The English section is made up of about thirty people, and I hear stories like the one about a worker killing another worker's husband. These are people who worked together in the same office before, during, and after the Revolution. Nobody got transferred out or could leave. The dynamic of their still working in the same place is bizarre.

In spite of the initial shock and tense undercurrent, the wood bed and odd stench and commissary food, I'm determined to make friends and have a good time. I tell myself that everything will be fine.

My second weekend in Beijing, I have one of the most frightening experiences of my life.

It's Qing Ming Festival, one of the biggest holidays in China, a spring tradition of honoring and sweeping the graves of ancestors. In the new Communist regime, honoring ancestors is considered bad, so former leaders are honored instead. This year, rumors spread in the press that a leader named Liu Shaoqi is going to be politically rehabilitated and honored during Qing Ming. The number-two guy to Mao for many years before being deposed, he's popular among the people, and his resuscitation is especially symbolic. Like Democracy Wall, where people are allowed to write whatever they want on public bulletin walls, this is another concession to the people, to make them feel better about their history.

The festival is held in Tiananmen Square, which must be the largest public space anywhere in the world. Until you've stood in it, you cannot fathom the enormity of it. It's endlessly huge. Literally millions of people can stand in this square, it's that vast. Chairman Mao gave his speeches to the throngs here. And this is where big public celebrations are held, right in the heart of Beijing.

Just before Qing Ming, I get a call from a guy named Frank Hawke. He's a friend of a friend back home and in a student exchange program at Peking University. "Why don't you come with me Saturday morning, and we'll see what's going on at Qing Ming Festival?" Sounds good to me.

Frank is a tall Caucasian American from Stanford University. He picks me up on his bicycle, which is the only way to get around other than by bus, and off we ride toward Tiananmen Square. Several things inform what transpires next. First, I think it's going to be hard for me to blend in and be like all the other Chinese. In actuality, I have no idea how easily I'll pass as a native, and, in fact, it will be harder for me to prove that I'm American. Most of the places frequented by foreigners are very restricted, whether hotels or embassies or restaurants, and I'll regularly find myself in situations where I'm barred from them because I appear to be native Chinese.

Second, I don't realize how conspicuous I'll be with a foreigner. It's the most natural thing in the world for me to hang out with Americans who speak English, but a most unnatural thing for a Chinese woman to do. The third thing I haven't anticipated is how good Frank's Chinese is and how entertaining he can be. He's been living here for a year, has picked up a lot of Chinese slang, and has great fun using it; people laugh and think he's a riot.

And last, these celebrations look extremely organized from the outside. All the schools show up, with students from each class wearing bandannas of the same color or carrying the same colored flags. From the outside, it looks like everybody belongs to a group or is part of a work unit. But beneath the surface lies chaos in the form of *xiao liumang,* fringe elements of society who are unemployed, often young people who were denied a full education because of the Cultural Revolution and haven't been able to find work. They fit nowhere, and on celebration days they show up in gangs of their own.

As Frank and I ride into the square, we check out several celebrations, dances, and musical performances and notice a lot of activity around the memorial of Liu Shaoqi, the leader who is being resuscitated. We get off the bike and walk around. Frank starts fraternizing with some of the *xiao liumang.* They're fascinated by him because they haven't seen many foreigners, much less foreigners who speak Chinese, much less slang.

As Frank gets going, the *xiao liumang* think he's hilarious and start laughing. They're having a grand ole time, and pretty soon, people start to gather around us because it looks like we're having such fun. *But why are they looking at me so suspiciously?* I wonder. More and more people gather around, and the looks they give me are chilling.

Pretty soon, a mob surrounds us, and people are hurling themselves in, pushing and shoving. The square is already jam-packed, and now we've got more than a hundred people immediately around us, cramming us tighter and tighter together. As the crowd starts to sway back and forth, back and forth, I lose sight of Frank. I've never experienced anything like it, being in the middle of an uncontrolled crowd and literally being swept off my feet by the movement of the masses. Before I know it, I'm down on the ground. *My God! I'm going to get trampled to death!*

Out of the blue, a man shouts in English, "Get up now! Move away now!" He manages to move some people aside, and soon guards in uniform are parting the crowd. I lurch to my feet, frantic to find Frank. There he is. He sees me, and we start walking and then running away as fast as possible. At the other end of the square is the Peking Hotel, one of only two hotels for foreigners at the time. We get to the front door, hurrying to go in. Frank slips through, and, abruptly, I'm stopped. "Ninar?" demands the doorman brusquely. Who are you? Where are you from?

"I'm American. . . ."

"You can't go in!"

What? "I'm American," I repeat.

"I don't understand you!"

I pull out my passport. "I'm . . . "

"You can't go in!"

". . . American."

"Speak in Chinese!"

This exchange will take place every time I try to enter a hotel or restaurant for foreigners. No one believes I'm American. If I speak English, they demand that I speak Chinese. If I speak Chinese, that's proof I'm really from the mainland. The interrogation is intense.

Frank bails me out, and we hurry into the lobby. A guard approaches quickly. "Ninar? Neige? Danwei?" Who are you, what work unit are you from, what are you doing here, who are you here to see? *Oh my God, this can't be. . . .*

"I'm American. I have my passport." This will happen even at the café when I try to get orange juice.

"Ninar?"

"She's with me, she's American," Frank says. He's staying here, and we hurry to the elevators. When we come out on his floor, a *fuwu yuan*, a worker, stops me abruptly.

"Ninar?"

*Unbelievable.*

I learn later that a Chinese woman fraternizing with an American is either suspected of being a spy or disdained as a slut. I also learn that I've been followed from the moment we entered Tiananmen Square and that the man who shouted is a plainclothes policeman.

But I know none of this as, later that night, I head over to the other hotel for foreigners, the Friendship Hotel, where privileged Chinese also come. I've heard that the Chinese are just beginning to experiment with dances, and one is being held that night, sure to be an interesting experience. As the evening wears on, I end up talking with a nice, good-looking, young Chinese man who wants to learn English. He lives near my dormitory, so at the end of the evening, we share a ride home with the foreign affairs woman from my work unit. Once again, I'm naive about the ruckus I'm causing.

That entire weekend, I'm followed.

Two weeks in, and I've already become a highly suspicious person. Come Monday morning, officials arrive at my work unit to inquire about me. They've taken pictures and written copious notes about my activities.

As a biologically Chinese person who grew up abroad, I'm an enigma here. The presence of white or black or Asian people is understandable. But not of Chinese people who come from places like America. They don't know what to do with me. At first they think I'm a young, loose woman fraternizing freely with Americans, a big no-no. When they find out I'm a foreigner, they become highly suspicious because I drove home with the Chinese guy after the dance at the Friendship Hotel. What was I doing with him?

In one weekend, I set in motion a series of events that leave me with a constant gnawing fear about how I'm being perceived. Am I doing something that's bad or forbidden? Should I not be seen with this person? Is that person spying on me? I'm aware of eyes watching me everywhere I go. I become highly self-conscious, either trying to be more Chinese or to prove that I'm *not* Chinese. I'm caught in the strangest paradox, which is eerily reminiscent of what happened to my parents when China thought my mother was a spy and America thought they could be Communists.

Every time I go to a hotel, every time I go anyplace that's primarily for foreigners, I'm interrogated. The irony is that, when I was in China as a teenager, I was grilled about what it was like to be discriminated against in America. Growing up, I had felt discomfort at times, but I'd never experienced raw discrimination. Now, here in China, people are unbelievably rude to and suspicious of me.

Whichever way I turn, I'm afraid of getting caught for something — whether being with Chinese and going into a military compound or into a place closed to foreigners, or being with foreigners and going into places closed to Chinese. When I'm with Chinese, I'm uneasy because the culture is so different. When I'm with Caucasians, I can feel people's eyes on me, and I know they're thinking, "You slut, trying to get yourself out of China by sleeping with American men."

I feel like I'm in a no-man's-land, and I don't know which way to turn at times.

I belong nowhere.


Although I never feared for my life in China, I heard scary stories about people being arrested, journalists imprisoned for talking with someone they were forbidden to talk with or for entering an area that was closed to foreigners.

I regularly went into areas that were closed to foreigners and did things that could have gotten me into trouble. In a strange way, every day, I also feared for the lives of the people around me because I realized that simply by socializing with me, they could be put under suspicion. That fear and paranoia came back with me to the States. Walking past the Chinese consulate in

New York City and seeing the guard wearing the green People's Liberation Army uniform made my heart race. Because everywhere I had gone in China, I had felt eyes on me, I developed a real fear of that uniform and that look.

During my initiation into China, I wanted desperately to blend in, and I tried hard to be Chinese. Then, when I saw the repercussions of blending in, I wanted desperately not to blend in and I purposefully dressed as a Westerner. I lived a double life. On a Saturday afternoon, I might meet some Chinese friends to go to a park or a museum in town and I'd wear my baggy padded pants and jacket with my dusty, clunky shoes. That evening, I might be going to dinner at a foreign journalist's place or an event put on by the embassy, so I'd have a change of clothes with me and make a stop at Frank's to borrow the bathroom, take a hot bath — such a luxury! — and get myself dressed up for the evening. I always carried a change of clothing. If I was in a public place, I'd dress down. If I was hanging out with foreign friends, I'd dress up.

I wanted desperately to belong, and yet I couldn't stand being boxed in. It would have been easy for me to say, "Okay, I should just be Chinese" or "I should just be American" and go with it. But the real challenge was refusing to give up one for the other. I suffered for it, I really hurt, because every day I was being judged, and I hated that with a vengeance.

It took courage for me to get through the suspicions, the branding, the prejudice, and not back away from it. Over time, I recognized what a privileged position I was in, being able to go into Chinese homes. All the foreign reporters and newsmen wanted nothing more than to get a taste of the real China. But they were restricted, sequestered, and could only go from their foreign hotels to their foreign office buildings. If they tried to have too much contact with

Chinese, they got into trouble. And many Chinese were afraid to talk with foreigners, especially foreign journalists.

I had access that everybody was dying to have because the times were so rich. The Cultural Revolution, which had halted economic activity and purged China of a generation of intellectuals, had come to an end. The Gang of Four, Communist Party politicians who tried to continue Mao's legacy, had fallen. Student elections were being held at the university; for the first time the seeds of a democratic elective process were being planted, and I was able to be there, inside, observing history in the making. Because of my access to places and people, I ended up stringing for reporters, giving them story ideas that they couldn't get firsthand. I took great joy in bringing my foreign and Chinese friends together on those rare occasions when I could.

The year passed, and when I left China, I escorted out the young Chinese man I had met at the dance at the Friendship Hotel. Seeing great potential in him, I had helped him to get a scholarship at UCLA and assisted in the arrangements to get him out of China. I wanted to be with him as he left to make sure that he was okay. Once in America, I tutored him in English and taught him how to drive a car, open a bank account, and carry on with daily life, seeing him through the transition. He's still in the States, an extremely successful businessman. He barely spoke a word of English when he came over, and now he lives here with his wife and three daughters and is a trade delegate to the White House.

My experiences in China as it opened to the West were pivotal in shaping who I am today. When it came time for me to leave, I seriously considered staying. Because somehow, in that weird betwixt-and-between existence of mine, there was something thrilling; I was walking in history, participating in it, alive like never before.

⊙

When Janet returned to the States, she went to Columbia Business School to get her MBA, and then took a job in San Francisco running a film company, World Entertainment, where she negotiated rights to Chinese films for American distribution. She also organized Chinese film festivals, obtaining films through the consulate and embassy.

When Steven Spielberg shot the epic movie *Empire of the Sun,* he turned to Janet for help in getting all the permits to shoot in Shanghai. Gaining entry to the highest levels of government, she worked intensely for six months in preparation for a three-week shoot that started with five thousand extras in period costumes. It was her first hands-on experience in film production, and yet no one could have done the job better, because few knew China the way she did. For the opening shoot, the production shut down the entire city of Shanghai for three days.

Working on *Empire* with one of Hollywood's most prolific and successful producing teams, Kathleen Kennedy and Frank Marshall, was kismet, the beginning of a film career that would include being an executive at Universal Studios, producing *The Joy Luck Club,* and becoming head of production at Oliver Stone's film company, Ixtlan. She made *The People vs. Larry Flynt,* starring Woody Harrelson; *High Crimes,* starring Ashley Judd and Morgan Freeman; *Savior,* starring Dennis Quaid; *The Weight of Water,* starring Sean Penn and Elizabeth Hurley; and the HBO movie *The McMartin Trial,* for which she won a Golden Globe Award and an Emmy.

Janet continues to bridge the East and West. She is a member of the Committee of 100, a national nonpartisan organization composed of American citizens of Chinese descent who have achieved leadership positions in the

United States in a broad range of professions. Collectively, they pool their expertise and experience to address important issues concerning the Chinese American community, as well as issues affecting United States–China relations.

"Going to China today is such a pleasure for me, because it's changed dramatically," says Janet. "No one speaks in whispers anymore. To the contrary, people openly joke about their leaders. Beijing and Shanghai are two of the most international cities in the world, and no one blinks an eye at seeing a foreigner and a Chinese together; interracial couples are commonplace. The cities are filled with five-star hotels, restaurants with exquisite international cuisine, and clubs full of hip, hedonistic youth who care little about the Cultural Revolution. Among the urban, sophisticated crowd draped in designer labels, I feel like a country bumpkin in my typical, casual American garb."

Still close to friends in China, she travels there regularly. "Being in China when it opened was a unique experience, one I shared with a handful of people who stayed on and whom I run into periodically. Frank Hawke never left, has a family in China, and works for a fertilizer company. We were there when the seeds for what China was to become were planted — the Gang of Four was deposed; the first privately owned company was formed with great fanfare and has since become an extremely powerful international corporation; and that first wave of businessmen and journalists has grown into a tsunami."

None of her relatives are clamoring to leave the country anymore. "People in general have an incredible national pride and confidence in China's future. If anything, many foreign-educated students are going back to invest their time and make careers in China. And, thank God, the formerly ubiquitous P.L.A. [People's Liberation Army] is only a quaint sight. For me to be in China now feels like the most natural thing in the world. I can truly be myself and blend my Western ways with my Chinese ways without a hint of conflict."

## Jim Garrison

# Buddha and the Fly
*Following What You Know to Be True*

What does it mean to make our lives matter? The question lives in each of us, residing at the very core of our being. It gives us pause. It calls us to live with courage, authenticity, and dignity. It calls us to show up in our lives, to be more than a spectator. Like gravity, it pulls us toward the center of our existence. The answer cannot be anticipated. For each of us, it is uniquely our own.

All of us long to matter, to know that we have left our imprint and that, in however small or grand ways, we have made a difference. The world around us, from our circle of friends and family spreading out through our communities, breathes a little bit differently because of us.

Some people seem to be born with a sense of leaving a footprint. Some find their authenticity at a young age. Jim Garrison is one of these people. Harvard and Cambridge educated, he became deeply involved in citizen diplomacy during the 1980s, eventually bringing former Soviet leader Mikhail Gorbachev to the United States to establish the Gorbachev Foundation in San

Francisco. He is currently chairman and president of the State of the World Forum, which he co-founded as an international think tank for authors, scientists, Nobel laureates, religious figures, actors, and human-potential leaders to address issues ranging from arms control to business practices.

Jim learned early in life to color outside the lines.

The most seminal event of my life happened when I was five years old. We were living in Taiwan, in a little village in the center of an island called Chou Shan, which was very small and rural. My parents were conservative Baptist missionaries, and we were the only Western family there. I scampered around with the other kids, becoming fluent in Mandarin.

In the village were a number of Buddhist temples, and one summer day, I was wandering around as any five-year-old would, just looking for mischief and something to do, when I came across a temple. Even though it was morning, it was so hot outside that I went in for some shade. The temple was one large open room, at the far end of which was an altar, and on top of the altar was a large statue of Buddha sitting in a cross-legged lotus position facing the door. As I stepped in, I noticed a bald-headed monk in saffron robes sitting on the floor in the same lotus position in front of the Buddha. Visually, it was stunning — the monk on the floor facing a Buddha three times his size on a raised altar. I drifted in.

I remember this as clearly as if it happened yesterday.

The monk is completely still. As still as the Buddha. I'm captivated and creep closer. A fly buzzes around his shaved head and lands on his face, right beside his left nostril. It starts to walk around his cheek and up onto his forehead and down the bridge of his nose. And the monk never moves. To a five-year-old, this is impossible; I can't believe he doesn't slap at it. And then off it flies.

Watching the monk, I become absorbed. He's quiet, impenetrably quiet. After a short time, the fly comes back. It walks around his head and down toward his ear. And still he remains as utterly motionless as the statue of the Buddha. Not a flicker of an eye, not a twitch of a muscle. It's unnerving.

Suddenly, I realize that he's somewhere else. His body is here, but *he* is not.

Creeping to the back of the temple, just in front of the door to the left, I sit down cross-legged, watching him and trying to be quiet, to make myself as utterly still as he is. It's impossible. I'm so wiggly that I can't stay still for more than ten seconds, which intensifies my sense of awe.

After a bit, another monk comes in and, with a wooden mallet, hits a large Chinese gong. The sound reverberates through the temple, and still that monk sitting on the floor doesn't move, doesn't twitch, doesn't register a thing. I run out of the temple, unsettled by what I've just seen. The monk is clearly in a place I know nothing about, a place quite separate from ordinary reality.

That Sunday morning, dressed in my starched white shirt and little shorts, I sit with my mother and three sisters, as we always do, at the back of my father's church. When he gets up to give the sermon and starts to preach, the most amazing thing happens. I don't believe him anymore. It's rather staggering. Because I experienced something in the monk that was as deep as the word of God, I realize how wrong it is for Christians to come to this village and try to convert people. This single moment of recognition indelibly changes my life. From that point on, both Christ and Buddha become the great archetypes — actually, polarities, as it turns out — around which my life orients.

Conflict with my father and with the missionary school is inevitable.

When I'm six years old, I'm sent away to a boarding school with my sisters. We're gone for six weeks at a time and then come home for long weekends and holidays. With the exception of a furlough year when I'm nine, I live nearly the rest of my school days in a dormitory at Morrison Academy in the little city of Tai Chung.

The academy is your classic authoritarian, conservative Protestant school where strict discipline is practiced. As expected, my thoughts about the Buddhist tradition aren't well received. It's inconceivable to my teachers and the headmaster that somebody as young as I would challenge them so fundamentally. And challenge them I do, because I'm in deep conflict with an institution so completely predicated on the notion that if you don't believe in Jesus, you're a sinner and go to hell, that Christ died to save you and only if you believe in Him will you go to heaven. On the one hand, it's an awful thing for a little boy to know with absolute certainty that there's another way. But on the other, my numinous encounter with the monk gave me a kind of clarity that made me unafraid of risk. It taught me at a very early age that when I'm sure of something, it's the only thing that matters.

Instead of reasoning with me, the teachers and headmaster try to discipline my beliefs out of me. At one point, I'm put in a room for two weeks and made to write commentary on various books of the Bible. At other times, I'm beaten, brutalized in ways that leave scars on my body, and then returned to solitary confinement. And still I believe that Buddhism and

Taoism and Confucianism are to be honored and that the Chinese people are to be respected, not converted.

When children are severely disciplined or beaten, they often don't understand why and so they internalize what's happening and feel guilty. Because I interpret my punishment in a deeply archetypal way, I imagine it as David fighting Goliath, Robin Hood against the sheriff of Nottingham. I'm Alexander the Great taking on King Darius of the Persians, Lawrence of Arabia battling the Turks. All these courageous figures out of history become my heroes as I deal with the beatings and the confinement.

In retrospect, I see that my experience was invaluable because it gave me an early appreciation for polarity and the necessity of lateral thinking. While other kids were going through the socialization process and being taught the truth according to Christianity, I knew that what I was taught was true for some but not for all. I remember being intensely curious about all this and intensely energized by the fact that, in the monk, I'd been witness to something very deep. I absorbed it with the totality of my being until it became a fact of life, as opposed to an experience that I toyed with intellectually and discarded. I never forgot it. It set up a dialectic between me and the culture that inevitably led me step by step to where I am today.

By the time he was eighteen, Jim had moved back to the States with his family and was in his senior year at Abraham Lincoln High School in San Jose, where he was student body president and politically active. The year was 1969. The Tet offensive had taken place, and the military was ramping up. Jim got his draft notice telling him to register, which he did. Then he got the notice to take a physical examination. "I thought the government had a right to know who I was, but it didn't have a right to give me a medical examination to determine if I was healthy enough to go kill people. That was beyond the bounds of government propriety."

He didn't go.

Some time later, as he was walking home from school, he saw his mother waiting for him at the front door. She was crying. "Jimmy, you just got a letter from the Justice Department." She gave him the letter, and it said something to the effect of *Dear Mr. Garrison, you did not take your physical. You're potentially guilty of felonies, you can go to jail for up to five years, pay up to a ten-thousand-dollar fine, and you'll never receive a passport. We suggest you reconsider.*

He was given a new date to take a physical.

When his father came home and heard about the letter, he said to his son, "Listen, you have to do this, it's the American thing, it's patriotic, we're fighting the Communists in Vietnam."

People began to pressure him to take his physical. His minister told him that, as president of the Baptist Youth Group, he should comply. Folks at school said that, because he was a student leader, if he didn't go along with the program, people would think ill of him and he might not get recommendations for college.

Wrestling with the issue, Jim took refuge in his room one day after school. He closed the door. "I just happened to be reading Plato's *Dialogues* and the great story of Socrates drinking the hemlock. Sitting quietly on my bed, I started to reread sections on Socrates, and I had that same feeling of certainty like I'd had when I was five years old, that there was a rightness here independent of social convention and that this rightness was the thing to follow. It wasn't a matter of antagonism against the culture; it was a matter of what was morally correct."

That night at dinner, Jim told his parents, "I'm not going to take the physical, and I'm not going to run. Whatever the government wants to do to me, that's what they're going to do, but it doesn't make any difference because the matter has been settled in my mind. It's not negotiable."

"Not negotiable" is a place unequivocally seeded with courage. We get there through a startling clarity that comes from peeling away distractions and facing an unencumbered view of who we are and what really matters to us. A kind of bone-deep lucidity. It may catch us off-guard, as when we have an epiphany, or we may go looking for it, like Jim did. Either way, clarity liberates us. It's our uncertainty that's imprisoning, the scattering in our minds as we vacillate between what we know intuitively is right and our fears and confusion.

When clarity comes, we *know*, we feel it in our belly. Listening to it takes courage. Acting on it is another matter.

"My parents were kind of blown away. But because I was so matter-of-fact about my decision, my father said, 'Okay, I think you're doing the wrong thing, and God may punish you, and the government may get you, but if that's your decision, you're eighteen years old and you're accountable now.'"

As it turned out, the government lost him in its files.

The following year at Pepperdine University, Jim had a sober awakening to the fact that he was political in an existential but not a sectarian sense. One afternoon, returning to campus from his part-time job, he saw a crowd of people lined up in front of the administration building. Across from them were a cordon of police and the vice chancellor of the university, who was speaking on a bullhorn. The black student union had taken over the administration building. "I didn't know much about African Americans; I'd grown up in the Orient and didn't have a feeling for the black rage that was sweeping college campuses."

Jim parked his car, and as he walked toward the building, the vice chancellor boomed out, "In five minutes, if you don't leave this building, you're all going to be under arrest." Jim stopped dead.

"This was a defining moment: I had to choose whose side I was on, whether I was going to be a bystander or whether I was going to support the black student union. Did I believe, without a shadow of a doubt, that they had legitimate historical grievances that needed to be honored?"

His mind raced: *What if I get arrested? What about my career? What about my education? What about my parents?* The vice chancellor counted down — three minutes, two minutes, one minute. "To my great shame, I couldn't move. I stayed back as a bystander. And the internal pain of the shame and guilt I felt by not standing up when I was being asked by the universe to take a stand seared me, and for the first time in my life, I knew the depth of what it meant to be a coward."

Nobody was arrested that day. The police and the university backed down. And Jim was left with the haunting thought, *You fool, you let a threat make a coward out of you.* "Tears streamed down my cheeks. I vowed that this was never, ever, under any circumstances going to happen to me again. And it never has. To this day, I've never betrayed that inner moral compass that points straight and true to my integrity."

From Pepperdine, Jim went to the University of Tel Aviv and then to the University of Santa Clara and on to Harvard Divinity School for a double master's degree in the history of religion and Christology. His final degree, he thought, would come from Cambridge. His father had aimed him there when he was ten years old. Standing outside their house in Taiwan, he had talked to Jim about the importance of education. "You mustn't waste your life. Aim high and hitch your wagon to a star."

"What are the best schools in the world?" his son had asked.

"Go to Harvard and then to Cambridge or Oxford for your PhD."

That had sealed it.

A future vision is like a force of nature. Jim was rejected by Cambridge, by Oxford, and by the London School of Economics. The only school that accepted him was St. Andrews in Scotland. On the train ride there, Jim stopped in Cambridge, future vision in hand.

Renting a bicycle at the train station, I ride over to Trinity, one of the colleges that make up Cambridge University. I park my bike and walk in unannounced on the man whom I had wanted as my supervisor, Bishop John Robinson. As synchronicity would have it, he's sitting in his study.

After introducing myself, I remind him that I had applied to study under him and was rejected.

"Yes, I'm sorry we couldn't take you."

"If I can get into one of the other Cambridge colleges, will you be my supervisor?"

"Mr. Garrison, that's not the way we do things at this university. We have time-honored traditions, and competition to get in is intense. I'm truly sorry."

"Well, I'm going to find another college to take me, and I'll be back."

He doesn't have time to get out of his chair before I'm gone.

I ride straight over to Emmanuel College, walk into the porter's lodge, and ask for directions to the dean's office, not knowing it's in that very building. I knock on the dean's door and walk in, and, serendipitously, there he is. I introduce myself and tell him I feel that I belong at Emmanuel. "I've just graduated from Harvard, and I guarantee you I'll bring honor to this college."

For some reason that I still don't understand, he looks at me and says something to the effect of "You seem like a nice young man, and I think this is against every regulation, but I'm going to let you in."

I should be bowled over, but I'm not, because I'm so certain that this is the right thing. "I'm deeply grateful, Dean. You'll never regret your decision." I shake his hand, run out, grab my bicycle, and quickly ride back to John Robinson.

"Bishop, I just got in."

His mouth drops open. "You can't do that; this is Cambridge, you can't just walk in and be accepted."

"I just did, sir, and I want you to be my supervisor. I'm going to write my thesis on why it is that after several billion years of evolutionary life, our species and our generation have brought the entire life process to the brink of extinction through thermonuclear war. There's something wrong with what's going on in the world today, and I want to study under you at the best university in the world and find out why."

He leans over his desk. "Mr. Garrison, you're crazy."

"Bishop Robinson, I'm not crazy; this is the most important question that I, as a young man of twenty-three, can ask."

⊙

That's how Jim Garrison got to Cambridge and how it was that he spent seven years studying the question of humankind's survival. His work — interfacing Jungian death psychology and Jewish and Christian apocalyptic literature — was eventually published under the title *The Darkness of God: Theology after Hiroshima.* That's how he came to believe that absolute weapons psychologically require absolute enemies and that the Russian threat was a function of the U.S. nuclear arsenal. That's how he came to dedicate his life during the 1980s to citizen diplomacy, how he came to meet Mikhail Gorbachev in Moscow and eventually to co-found the Gorbachev Foundation in San Francisco. That's how he came to do the work he does today with the State of the World Forum.

"Once you realize with an inner sureness that a thing needs to be a certain way, the universe moves in unexpected ways. Thoreau said, 'If one advances confidently in the direction of his dreams and endeavors to live the life which he has imagined, he will meet with a success unexpected in common hours.' That's a beautiful way to live.

"From the time I was five years old, my life was governed by critical choices having to do with integrity and seemingly innocuous junctures." As a little boy running down the street barefoot on a hot summer morning, he could have passed that Buddhist temple, could have trivialized the experience, denied what he saw. As a young man threatened by his government and pressured by peers, parents, and authority figures, he could have toed the line, even though he felt it was wrong. With Cambridge, he could have said, "I didn't get in, I tried my best" and kept riding that train on up to

St. Andrews. With Gorbachev, he could have stopped short, convinced himself "Who am I to counsel a world leader?"

What made Jim Garrison different?

"With deep authenticity, one comes to a place of embedded certainty, knowing with utter surety the rightness of the place where one stands. And in that place, the world moves around you rather than you moving with the world. That's what I think it is to dare to be great."

In addition to the Gorbachev Foundation, Jim founded the International Foreign Policy Association in collaboration with then Georgian President Eduard Shevardnadze and former Secretary of State George Shultz, focusing on humanitarian relief for the former Soviet republics. His State of the World Forum has launched and directed a number of action-oriented strategic initiatives that have evolved into their own organizations: the Global Security Institute, the Coexistence Network, Global Equal Access, the Whole Child Initiative, and the Ethical Globalization Initiative. The State of the World Forum also convened the Commission on Globalization in 2000.

In the late 1980s, Jim served as executive director of the Esalen Institute Soviet American Exchange Program, which engaged in private-sector diplomacy with Soviet counterparts. He has written several books, including *The Plutonium Culture; The Russian Threat: Its Myths and Realities; The New Diplomats;* and *Civilization and the Transformation of Power.* His most recent book is *America as Empire: Global Leader or Rogue Power?*

John Perkins

# A CEO and a Shaman
## *Doing the Right Thing*

A crossroads is one sure place to meet up with courage. We feel the ground beneath us shift and are split open to look anew at what matters to us — really. At first, we're likely to encounter more questions than answers. A crossroads is ripe with the lure, as well as the fear, of the unknown, the unexpected, the unresolved. Our life is about to change, and before us is the chance to compose ourselves in a whole new manner. The opportunity is at once daunting and exciting.

From marriage to a job change, the birth of a child, a move, a divorce, or a complete career overhaul, crossroads vary in intensity. John Perkins has met up with some doozies, starting with his recruitment by the National Security Agency while he was in business school, living in the Amazon as a Peace Corps worker, and spending time with indigenous tribes hostile to U.S. oil companies. When he returned to the States, he went to work as an economic consultant and later started an energy company. On the surface, his story becomes one that any entrepreneur might relate to, consisting of hard work, passion, drive, success. But beneath the normal life of this businessman lay intrigue, turmoil, and redemption, beginning with shamanic journeys and rolling inevitably perhaps toward the day when John Perkins confessed to being what he calls an "economic hit man."

When John sold his alternative energy company, Independent Power Systems, he made a bunch of money for his investors. Now what? Most of his friends encouraged him to do it again with his own money. He wasn't contractually bound by noncompete clauses, and, if he succeeded, he'd be an extremely wealthy man.

Tempting — very.

So why didn't he?

"I sat down with my wife, Winifred, and my nine-year-old daughter, Jessica, and we talked long and hard about my next step. We kept coming back to our strong commitment to the environment. Winifred was a manager in the environmental department of Florida Power and Light, one of the nation's largest and cleanest electric utility companies. During our conversation, I realized that more important than starting another company and becoming wealthy was leaving something to our daughter and her generation — not money but something deeper. But what? What could I do? And how would I do it?"

The answer began to take shape around John's history in the corporate world as a consultant to the World Bank, the United Nations, and Fortune 500 corporations. Working with international companies and development agencies, he noticed that in places like Java and Egypt, Sulawesi and Mexico, the power to shape the future was in the hands of tribal chieftains, priests, firewalkers, and healers. "In our country, the influential wear business suits, read the *Wall Street Journal,* and invest billions of dollars each year in advertising." John was pretty sure that if he were to play a part in shaping the future, it would not be in a business suit. "More than to corporate America, I was drawn to the Amazon rainforest and to the Shuar, who had taught me so much and changed my life."

John had first encountered the Shuar while helping Andean farmers colonize the Amazon basin. The town he lived in was surrounded by jungle, and John had set out on an arduous two-day trek down the eastern slope of the Andes to the end of a dirt road and beyond to the land of the Shuar. He'd heard that they were fierce warriors with savage rituals, famous for shrinking the heads of their enemies. In contrast, he found them to be a compassionate people gravely concerned about the impact that colonists were having on the fragile rainforest ecology.

By the early 1990s, some of the Shuar had given up their traditional ways and had tried to adapt to Western customs, which led to impoverished lives in oil-company and cattle towns. Those who were determined to maintain their way of life moved deeper into the forest, to places east of the Cutucú Mountains, shrouded in mist. John was determined to find them, driven in part by a lingering guilt. "For years, as a Peace Corps volunteer and as a consultant to the World Bank, I had promoted the construction of roads and dams in the rainforests, coming to realize later the terrible impact of this colonizing, this attempt to bring indigenous people into what we call the First World. Now that I knew what was going on in the rainforest, the ecological nightmares that these projects had catalyzed, I wanted to go back with a very different agenda. I had time. I had resources. And I wanted to help save the breathtaking forests so crucial to our survival on the planet."

So now, rather than follow business logic, John followed his heart. With his family's encouragement, he returned to the Shuar.

⊙

To travel deep into the forest beyond the Cutucú, I need the help of an Ecuadoran friend, who arranges for a single-engine, missionary plane to take me. It's the first time I've flown low over the canopy into the heart of the jungle; as a Peace Corps worker, I traveled by foot. My pilot nods at the cleared land of the colonists below, much of it still smoldering from slash-and-burn development, and I feel a nauseated sense of urgency. We head east, where the rainforest lies thick and undisturbed below us.

What would have been a five-day trek for the Shuar and at least twice that for most outsiders is an easy flight and one that gives me a heart-stopping view of Shuar longhouses, oval in shape and some forty feet long, made of upright staves with thatched roofs. The pilot noses the plane down and banks toward a path cut through the jungle that surely cannot be our landing strip. Trees skirt our wingtips; we hit the ground, bounce and race through the jungle, coming at last to a stop.

And there they are. The Shuar. A cluster of men stands quietly watching as we climb out over the wing. Expressionless, they wait. As I approach, a young man named Tomás, who speaks perfect Spanish, steps forward. "Welcome." A student at the university in Quito, he's home on vacation. One by one, the others shake my hand. "You wait here," says Tomás. "We'll go downriver in canoes."

As they set about unpacking the plane, I wander over to the edge of the jungle, where a path leads into the forest. I'm drawn in, out of the glaring heat. It's cool and deeply quiet, except for the occasional call of a bird. The heady smell of the earth, of soil and plants and flowers, envelops me as I wander in and follow the path, enchanted. Suddenly, I'm standing before a long, white, sandy beach that slopes off toward a river. I drift over and run my hand along the worn but beautifully crafted wood of the dugout canoes.

I don't see him at first. I feel his presence and turn abruptly to find him standing there, watching me. We simply look at each other for a moment. His eyes are hypnotic. "I am Numi," he says, coming forward. "You must be the gringo we're expecting."

I had heard much about him in my preparation for this trip. Numi is a powerful and highly honored shaman who at one time taught at a Catholic mission school. Part Shuar, he's married to a full-blood, an herbal healer.

Standing by the river, we talk, wasting no time in getting to the destruction of the rainforest. He says something that will possess me for a long time: "The world is as you dream it." He walks to the edge of the river. "Your people dreamed of huge factories, tall buildings, as many cars as there are raindrops in this river. Now you begin to see that your dream is a nightmare." He reaches for a stone and tosses it far out into the river. "The problem is that everything you do ripples across the Mother."

As he speaks, I think about the epiphany I had one day while driving the Florida interstate. It struck me that what we do best in America is build. We bulldoze and construct. We pave under and roof over. Lay down sidewalks, roads, highways. Build cars, trucks, airplanes, houses, skyscrapers, shopping malls, factories. We divert rivers, turn mountains into valleys, irrigate deserts, drain swamps. And the material wealth generated by all this building and reshaping benefits a small percentage of only one of Earth's thirty million or so species. As for the rest, the consequences are vanishing forests, polluted air, poisoned water, and loss of biodiversity.

"What can I do? How can I help?"

Numi doesn't hesitate. "Change the dream."

"Change the dream?"

"It can be accomplished in a generation. You need only to plant a different seed, teach your children to dream new dreams." He places a hand on my shoulder. "I will introduce you to people who can help."

I had been in a deep, almost unconscious despair about the destruction of the forests, the depletion of the ozone, the smothering layers of carbon dioxide. What was I going to do about it? How could I ensure that my daughter had a good future? Standing at river's edge with Numi, I realize that the question I'd wrestled with — how to secure the future for my daughter — was one that no shaman would ask. In the world of the shaman, the question is not what to do for your own child, but what to do for your child's entire generation, because your child cannot stand alone.

Later, having arrived downriver in the village, I spend time with many of the Shuar elders, some of whom I'd met twenty years earlier. They too are concerned about the terrible destruction going on all around them. I tell them that I want to devote a great deal of my time and energy to saving the rainforest. I expect this to be an exciting piece of news to them.

They simply look at me.

It isn't until the last day of my visit, alone with Numi swaying in hammocks in the lodge, that I understand their response. "We welcome your help," he says, "but don't come back and try to better us. We don't need to learn any new languages, we've got enough of those. We don't need to learn any new religions, they've all been in here. We don't need anybody telling us not to cut trees or how to run our lives. It's your people who need to change. Go back and change your people."

I understand what he's saying.

"Your people in the north have had this dream of material things, and your dream has come true," he goes on, "because when you give energy to dreams, they always come true. Now that you're beginning to realize it was a nightmare, all you have to do is give energy to a new dream."

"How? What can I do?"

"Bring people. Bring people here."

Surely he doesn't mean tours.

"Not tourists, but people who want to learn, who will help to change your dream of huge factories and tall buildings and more automobiles."

"But how will I know who should come?"

"They are your people. Find those who want to be agents of change in your culture, bring them here to learn from us. We have powerful techniques of dream changing and shape-shifting, and we can teach them. Don't bring people to change us, don't bring any more missionaries or medical doctors or economists who want to tell us how to do things. Bring those who want to learn from us so that they can help to change your people."

That night, I can barely sleep. With the sounds of the jungle all around me, my mind races with the possibility of a new kind of change.

In spite of my enthusiasm, when I return home, I struggle with the idea of taking North Americans into the rainforest. What Numi has in mind is a form of vision quest, a spiritual journey in search of wisdom that has been practiced for as long as recorded history. I've studied shamanic journeys and vision quests and their modern applications at great length. I know what Numi wants us "moderns" to understand. And yet I'm in great conflict because I feel it's wrong to intrude, that indigenous peoples should be left alone.

In the end, to honor the promise I've made to Numi, I organize my first trip, reluctant and anxious about each person who signs on for the journey. It's an onerous responsibility. Over the twenty months that follow, I make repeated visits to the Shuar, the Lowland Quichua, and other Amazonian and Andean peoples. And I experience firsthand the way that dreams, direct communication with nature, and inner voices affect their daily lives.

Making this transition is not without its difficulties. For all her support, Winifred married a business executive who spent most of his life in a suit and tie in the world of corporate men, a consultant to the World Bank, CEO of an energy company. Suddenly, she finds herself married to a guy who wanders around the jungle, leading workshops and taking groups of people into the rainforest, many of whom are women. It's a radical change, and I know it's hard for her.

The transition is equally difficult for me. I was at the top of my game, making big money, a player. Now the money I make goes into the Dream Change Coalition, a nonprofit I've formed to help promote the teachings of the Shuar. To a business school graduate, measuring success in any terms but financial ones is anathema. If not income, then what?

I haven't completely reconciled myself with this new yardstick. Indigenous people tell us that life is to be lived in the moment, in the present, and to be lived ecstatically. By ecstatically, they mean feeling our oneness with everything around us. There is no separation, they say, that's just an illusion.

Our own medical scientists and quantum physicists tell us the same thing, that we're made up of subatomic particles that are not mass, but probabilities. Many aspects of modern science are very shamanic. The shamans believe deeply in unity, and their ecstasy comes from feeling it all the time. To grasp this is to redefine what it means to be successful and to understand that accumulating goods and services doesn't bring ecstasy.

Another thing that's difficult is facing my peers with my new identity. When I write the book *Psychonavigation,* I'm still doing consulting work for Fortune 500 corporations and, once in a while, a chief executive says to me, "My God, I saw your book the other day. What on earth are you doing?" The people whom I had always regarded as the rational, solid, upstanding citizens are now looking at me like I'm nuts, and suddenly the people whom I used to look upon as hippies, radicals, and New Age groupies are embracing me. It's disconcerting. I feel as if someone is hanging me by my ankles and I'm looking at the world upside down.

As time goes on, more and more executives are interested in what I'm doing, and I begin to realize that the corporate structure is a good one for changing dreams. Business is an immensely effective agent of change. We need only to change the dream that defines what it is to be a successful corporation, and I believe that's happening.

Over the years, I witness phenomenal changes and increasingly find that, deep down, people are extremely concerned about the direction our species is headed in; if they have children, they're especially worried. The CEOs of some major corporations, some of whom I know personally, are deeply concerned; for the most part, they don't know what to do because if they go too far, they can lose their jobs. I get calls from some of them after they've read one of my books, *Shapeshifting* or *The World Is as You Dream It.* They invite me to dinner, and after a couple glasses of wine, they loosen up and start talking, and I discover that, at heart, we're not that far apart in our thinking. Several executives confide in me that they're glad Rainforest Action Network or Greenpeace went after them because, down deep, they want to do something to help the environment, but it's difficult to convince a board of directors or stockholders until somebody pushes them up against the wall. So I know that the corporate world is filled with people who want to change, to leave a better legacy for our children.

But at the same time, what I'm doing in the rainforest is upsetting some people. I go head-on with a number of corporate and governmental entities in Ecuador, some of them U.S. companies whose business is damaging the rainforest. We begin to experience strange incidents, death threats and harassment. My Ecuadoran partner, who sets up our trips, is drugged and thrown off a three-hundred-foot cliff, miraculously surviving. We begin to have problems renting airplanes to get in and out of the jungle. Some of the pilots are scared. The military starts harassing us, and we receive strange letters and messages, telephone calls, veiled threats.

And somebody in Ecuador tries to turn the Shuar against us.

During one of my visits, a bunch of renegade Shuar threaten to attack us. It's night and we're meeting with the community when a warrior unknown to us stands up, throws his spear into the ground, and says, "We don't want these gringos coming here anymore. The only gringo we want here is our special friend." Turns out that this "special friend" has been coming around the community, giving lots of gifts and talking strongly against us, accusing us of doing black magic. He's known as a mercenary, and

I suspect he's been hired by an oil subcontractor to get the Shuar roused up against us.

As we leave the lodge, we see warriors with weapons in the shadows all around us. I can feel the tribe being divided, people taking sides because I have many Shuar friends, including blood brothers who are warriors. The tribe holds a council meeting and things eventually calm down, but the experience is extremely scary.

In spite of the danger, I never consider backing off my position or stopping my work. I made a commitment that my life would be dedicated to the next generation, and this work needs to be done. Also, I believe in the Shuar concept that there is no death. There's transition, shape-shifting, but we do not disappear, we do not cease to exist. This is not only a shamanic belief; it is also consistent with modern science: matter and energy do not disappear, they simply shape-shift.

Being aware of the dangers of my work, I do certain things to take precautions; I've been a martial arts black belt for many years, and I keep in good shape. But I don't worry. I try to put the danger in perspective: Driving on Interstate 95 at eleven o'clock on a Saturday night when some people are out there drunk can be a lot scarier than what I face in the jungle.

My work with the Shuar may be the unfolding of a future I saw when I was young. In seventh grade, I wrote a history report that grew into a seventy-five-page novella based on the true story of Abnaki Indians who captured white people in the colonies and took them up to their village in Canada. They inducted them into the tribe so that, by shape-shifting the colonists, they could protect themselves against the cultural genocide that was threatening them. The story was based, in part, on my own family's history, which goes back about three hundred years in New Hampshire and Vermont. Many of my ancestors fought the Abnaki Indians, but a few married into the tribe, so I have some Abnaki blood in me. At the same time, my fifth great-granduncle was Thomas Paine, a man of great principle and thought-provoking ideas who wrote *Common Sense,* saying, "The birthday of a new world is at hand." On the other side of my family was Ethan Allen, who won the first victory for the colonists in the Revolutionary War.

After reading my history report, my teacher asked me to stay after class. As I nervously approached her, she held out my novella. On the cover, I had drawn an oval Abnaki lodge, with a warrior holding his bow and arrow standing next to it.

It wasn't the A she had given me that captured my attention but the photograph in the geography book she pulled out, saying, "See this picture?" It was taken from an airplane looking down on a house that closely resembled the lodge on the cover of my report, except that it was made out of bamboo and thatching; to the side stood a warrior pointing his bow and arrow up at the plane. "Because you write about them with such love, I want you to know there are still people in the Amazon who live like that." I promised myself that, one day, I would go there, to that place with the oval lodge and the warrior.

Over the years, I've seen that scene many times, looking down from the airplane as I fly into the jungle, taking white people to the Shuar to be taught, to be shape-shifted, so that the tribe is protected against the cultural genocide threatening them from the Northerners.

Life is as you dream it. And my life has become an ecstatic odyssey.

⊙

Through his Dream Change Coalition, over the course of thirteen years, John took more than five hundred people — many of them business executives, attorneys, investment bankers, and medical doctors — to the Amazon rainforests, the Andes, the Mayan lands of Guatemala, and the Himalayas. He conducted workshops in Italy for corporate executives and in the United States for public defenders and police departments. He geared his "Shape-Shifting the Corporation" program to executives wanting to alter their company's goals and commitments while remaining competitive in the marketplace. He also created the Pollution Offset Lease for Earth (POLE) program, enabling corporations to offset the greenhouse gases they produce by leasing carbon dioxide–absorbing rainforests.

John's most recent book, *Spirit of the Shuar: Wisdom from the Last Unconquered People of the Amazon*, was nominated for a Pulitzer Prize. The Arts and Entertainment and History channels regularly air a documentary featuring him and his work. *Headhunters of the Amazon* is narrated by Leonard Nimoy.

My story about John Perkins originally ended here. But recently he set out with great purpose on yet another journey. And what he was about to do greatly informed the story as I knew it. He was about to expose what he had really been doing as an economic consultant to the World Bank, the United States, Fortune 500 companies, and development agencies. Working at various times for the Shah of Iran, General Torrijos in Panama, the United Nations, and the royal family of Saudi Arabia, at one point he'd had a staff of fifty stationed all over the world, he said.

Several times he'd started to write a book about his work but had stopped, either because he was frightened to go public or because he was convinced — "bribed," according to John — to keep quiet. He'd gotten as far as a book proposal that one agency told him was "too hot to handle."

The proposal for *Confessions of an Economic Hit Man* that he shared with me began:

> Economic hit men are highly paid professionals who cheat countries around the globe out of trillions of dollars. They funnel World Bank, U.S. government, and other foreign "aid" funds into the coffers of international businesses and the pockets of a few wealthy families who control the planet's natural resources. Their tools include fraudulent financial reports, rigged elections, payoffs, extortion, and murder. They play a game as old as Empire but one that has taken on new and terrifying dimensions during this time of globalization. I know. I was one.

Economic hit men, according to John, belong to a small, exclusive club.

> We dress like bankers and dine with U.N. Development Program experts and International Monetary Fund bankers at the finest restaurants in Paris, Singapore, and Rio. We cover the conference tables of congressional finance committees in Washington with our spreadsheets and financial projections, and lecture at prestigious business schools. We are "sunshine," in the open. Or so we portray ourselves and so we are accepted.

But, says John, the dark side of the economic hit man is to encourage world leaders to become part of a vast network that promotes U.S. commercial interests, ultimately entangling them in a web of debt that ensures their commitment to serving our political, economic, and military needs. "We offer these leaders perks — loans for industrial parks, power plants, and airports named after them — and, if all else fails, outright bribes and threats. For the most part, our actions are legitimate or at least perceived as such."

The more he told me, the more his previous story shifted dramatically within a new context. He had hinted at this world. But he'd been speaking through a veil. Now he was lifting that veil. It was risky business — at best.

"I decided that I had to come clean, and now was the time to do it," he told me. That decision began to take hold in November 2001 after a long afternoon wandering around Ground Zero. As he sat on the steps of 14 Wall Street looking across at the New York Stock Exchange, the incongruity of his life was inescapable.

Only two months earlier, he'd been in the Amazon with the Shuar and the seventeen Northerners he'd brought with him. "Eerily, the Shuar told us that they were planning to go to war with the American oil companies that were destroying their lands. They knew they would fail, but they could not let their native lands be taken, like so many to the north, the west, the east, as Ecuador sells off land to buy down its debt. They would make their stand even if the United States sent in military to stop them. They would die fighting."

Later that night, John and his group sat together around a fire. As they talked about what lay ahead for the Shuar, they wondered how many other people around the globe felt this way about the United States, how many others were losing their lands and culture to oil, how many feared us, hated us.

It was September 10.

The next morning, John got on his short-wave radio to talk to his pilots up in the Andes. He wanted to make sure they were on schedule to pick up his group three days later. The pilots were listening to an international broadcast of the attack on the World Trade Center.

When John returned to the States, he went to Ground Zero, haunted by his past. "I'm absolutely convinced that, if people in our country knew what was going on, what our foreign policy is all about, they wouldn't put up with it. They don't know the system behind the system. Very few people do. And we need to know. We're moving increasingly away from the American Republic and into a global empire. All over the world, this model is being implemented, and it's getting worse." He is quick to point out that this model is nonpartisan. "What I'm talking about happened on many people's watches."

*Confessions of an Economic Hit Man* comes out in the fall of 2004 from Berrett-Koehler of San Francisco. Calling it "one of the most important stories of our time," John Mack, M.D., professor of psychiatry at Harvard Medical School and Pulitzer Prize–winning author, says, "This is a work of great insight, moral courage, and transformational depth."

John understands the risk of what he's exposing with this book. But, he says, "It's also a very liberating move on my part. I feel a great sense of relief." He has led his last trip to the Amazon, although the Dream Change Coalition will continue them. He has had long talks with his daughter and his wife, not unlike those long talks a decade earlier as he wrestled with the decision to go back to the Amazon.

With Winifred supporting his decision, he walked the beach with his daughter, now in college, and told her what he was planning to do, told her that he will probably be vilified when the book is published. People will undoubtedly go after him, try to smear his reputation. He wasn't so much concerned about his physical safety, but he was deeply concerned about the emotional impact on his daughter; she had to know the truth even if others tried to shred it. How did she feel about him going public? Would she be all right? With pure Perkins courage, she told him that, should anything happen, she would step in to carry the cause.

# THREE

## Loving beyond All Measure

To love deeply in one direction makes us more loving in all others.

*—Anne-Sophie Swetchine*

THREE

## Through the veils of misconception

As my first courage book took me places I hadn't expected to go, I saw that I would have to let go of my original agenda to follow the stories. I would have to open up to being surprised, to being fluid in the moment, flexible with the unexpected. Every interview, every story of courage was teaching me, revealing something that I needed to pay attention to, carrying me a little further across my own internal landscape...and closer to my true self. The experience was changing the way I saw myself, my place in my family, my place in my community, and my place in the world. I was stepping up and speaking out, I was being more authentic. It felt good.

My study of courage, in fact, would take me more intimately into the meaning of the word than I had ever imagined. Not merely the telling of stories, this work would take hold of me, rattle me, challenge me, wrest me free of little ideas and demand that I be bigger. Not by climbing Mount Everest, but in the way I lived my life every day.

Emotional, mental, and spiritual courage can be as daunting as scaling a mountain. Sometimes the most courageous thing we do is to say, "I love you" when it scares the pants off us. Sometimes, it's saying, "I forgive you." Or "I'm sorry." Or "I want to be more real with you." To be emotionally vulnerable, to let someone into our inner sanctum can feel like we're splitting ourselves open.

Traveling the emotional landscape of the heart is a daring journey.

Facing the truth of who we are, of how we're doing with matters of love and personal dignity, integrity and service, soul and spirit, with the substance of our higher purpose can be an expedition of great magnitude. Turning inward to take stock of ourselves requires not only that we risk seeing our emptiness, but also that we dare to see our fullness. "Our deepest fear is not that we are inadequate," writes Marianne Williamson in *A Return to Love*. "Our deepest fear is that we are powerful beyond measure. It is our light, not our darkness, that most frightens us. We ask ourselves, 'Who am I to be brilliant, gorgeous, talented, and fabulous?' Actually, who are you not to be?"

Many people squirm at the suggestion that they're courageous, exceptional, inspiring. Who could be deserving of such big praise? I've often heard, "To say I'm courageous feels arrogant" and "To talk about my courage feels narcissistic." Women especially can be too modest. The word *courage* connotes much and commands images of such a grand scale that we feel unworthy. And yet, there is power in owning our courage, admitting it, sharing it with others. And contrary to arrogance or narcissism, the people I've interviewed have three distinct qualities: a beautiful humility, a tremendous presence, and a deep authenticity.

Perhaps being modest about our courage is a way to ensure that we still belong as we step out, as we stand up, as we cross the boundaries of our familiar. "Oh, no, I'm just a housewife, small-town person, regular kind of guy," said many. "I'm only doing what anyone else would do."

Perhaps the responsibility of our bigness seems overwhelming. To be big is to have a big impact. What will be expected of us? Will we become too visible, too vulnerable to criticism? Will others envy us? Will we be able to sustain? Sometimes we are attended by an amorphous fear that, if we admit to our bigness, then something terrible will happen.

We may also be embedded with beliefs that make us hesitate at the threshold of our bigness. "It's lonely at the top." "The higher you fly, the harder you fall." To do what we say we want to do, to be who we say we want to be, requires dismantling cultural myths and our own personal myths, and redesigning our beliefs.

Why do we fear our bigness? What are we afraid will happen if we live a life that matters, if we have significant impact? What beliefs hold us back from it?

As we claim our courage, we set down our Little Story — the ways in which we keep ourselves small — and pick up our Big Story: why we're here, what we can learn, what we can contribute with this life, how we can be of service. As Marianne Williamson says, the world gains nothing by our playing small.

What will we do with our courage? How will we make our lives matter? How will our personal world and the world at large be different because of us?

⊙

A far cry from *bravado,* the word *courage* derives from the Latin *cor* or the French *coeur,* meaning "heart." Even with the boldest and most daring acts, courage is a matter of the heart.

Listen . . . we can hear courage all around us:

*In dreaming and daring to live our dreams*
*In daring to be different*
*In questioning*
*In challenging*
*In defying limitations*
*In changing the impossible*

*In doing the right thing*

*In taking a stand for ourselves or someone else*

*In bridging worlds apart*

*In standing by our principles*

*In stepping up to responsibility*

*In changing*

*In being honest*

*In answering the call to adventure*

*In listening to our inner voice*

*In being content but not complacent*

*In healing*

*In being vulnerable*

*In being passionate*

*In giving*

*In caring*

*In forgiving*

*In loving*

*In loving*

*In loving*

In claiming ourselves as the magnificent beings that we are, in honoring ourselves at the deepest level, lies courage. *I will not be kept inside a box. My voice will not be muffled. My spirit will not be denied. I will be heard. I will use my life well.*

## Karen Murray

# The Mother Love
*Persevering When No One Believes You*

Courage can take us down a path with unforeseen consequences. The far-
ther down that path we go, the less we want to be on it. But we're compelled to follow it, led by instinct, intuition, a gut feeling. We know we
need to be on this path to do the right thing, even though chaos swirls
around us, even though no one believes in us, even though we're alone in
our conviction. The risk may be great, but we know that we risk even
more by turning back.

How are we to understand what it takes to stay the course? What makes
one person keep to the path regardless of how messy and uncomfortable
things get, while another steps back and retreats into safety? Is it that courage
is like a muscle and the more we use it, the stronger it gets? Every time we
do something daring, is it then easier the next time? Would Karen Murray
have been able to stay the course with the greatest challenge of her life had
she not had all that practice in her twenties? Or is it just in her nature?

I first met Karen at the Fortieth and Broadway New York offices of Liz

Claiborne, where she is the group president of menswear. Her assistant brought us lunch from a restaurant around the block, and we sat in her office on that winter day and ate our salads on either side of her desk. This was one smart woman, likeable to the bone. Two things in that office meant the most to her: the photo of her son and husband and an essay by Emily Perl Kingsley, which brought her to tears as she read it to me.

Karen started knocking down the doors of convention right out of college. She graduated with a degree in criminal justice and planned to go to law school. In between, to shore herself up financially, she took a temporary job at Gant, a men's shirt company in New York — an odd turn of events for her, because Gant was a traditional, conservative company in an industry occupied almost exclusively by men.

Hired as a receptionist, she threw "temporary" out the window when she was promoted to office manager. Her new position included going into showrooms and cleaning up after the guys, putting away swatches and samples shown to buyers. That grew old quickly. She was pretty sure she could do as good a job as the men selling in those showrooms, and she began to question why she wasn't allowed to work with the buyers. Well, it just wasn't done. Without much to lose, she decided to tell her boss that she'd leave if she didn't get moved into sales.

Her break didn't have as much to do with that demand, she figured, as it did with the tough times that Gant was going through and the numbers of men with families to support leaving to join more stable companies. "In the end, I think management thought, Hey, the company's falling apart, let's take a chance and give her some accounts." She took over Bloomingdale's, Lord & Taylor, and Saks Fifth Avenue.

The men in the traditional department stores were accustomed to being wined and dined at the big restaurants, taken to baseball games, football games, bars. Karen didn't do any of that, and, inevitably, one of the buyers went to her president and complained, "We want her off our account. We can't work with her."

When Karen heard this, she went straight to her president. This time, however, she had something to lose. "I remember it clearly; it was my first courageous moment. I was so nervous I was shaking. I told him I had a job in my back pocket. In truth, I was interviewing at Calvin Klein, but I didn't want to take it because I loved Gant. But if my president had said, 'Karen, we're taking you off the account,' I would have resigned." Instead, he said, "Let me think about it overnight."

Overnight, Karen tried to chase away images of going to work the next day and having no job. The next morning, her president stepped into her office. "We want to keep you on the account." Bloomingdale's, Lord & Taylor, and Saks Fifth Avenue became Gant's biggest accounts, and Karen soon became salesperson of the year. She got the plaque. She got the Rolex. And at age twenty-five, she was promoted to vice president.

She never went to law school.

It was inevitable, of course, that others in the industry would pay attention. And sure enough, a few years later, she got a call from the president of Bugle Boy asking her to come work for him. She hadn't been fishing and wasn't interested. "I'm happy in my career," she told him. "I want to stay where I am."

"What would it take?" he asked.

That night, she told her new husband, Jim, about the call. "Tell them it would take tripling your salary," he said off-handedly. They laughed, not thinking in a million years that Bugle Boy would agree.

When she called back the next day with her answer, the president said, "Okay, when can you start?"

She stayed at Bugle Boy for some three years before making a fortuitous move to Liz Claiborne. By then, she was thirty-four and pregnant. "Life was good. I had successfully broken into the predominantly male industry of menswear and was pulling in a substantial salary. I was happily married, wanted to be pregnant by thirty-four, and conceived right on target. What could be more wonderful?"

She was about to step onto the most daunting path of her life.

◉

Following a beautiful, healthy, full-term pregnancy, Michael is born in August of 1991. My labor is short and the delivery uncomplicated. The doctors give my new son a perfect score after checking his vitals.

All is well.

Later that day, I shuffle down the hall, drawn like a moth to light, to soak up the sight of my baby again. Through the window of the nursery, I see that Michael isn't alone. The doctors and nurses are looking at his fingers. *Why are they doing that?* No one says anything to me, so I assume everything is fine.

The following day, I notice the doctors in the nursery again, looking at the roof of Michael's mouth and at his fingers. Rather than forming the tight fists of a newborn, his hands are open, his fingers bent backward. "Your son has a dislocated hip," one of them says, coming out into the hall.

*A dislocated hip? What does that have to do with his fingers and his mouth?*

They put Michael in a little harness and say it's fine, don't worry, this sometimes happens during birth, it's no big deal, the harness will come off in eight weeks. But I feel uneasy. I know something isn't right. When I bring Michael home, I want to hold and caress and nurture him, but I'm afraid I'll hurt him or disturb the harness.

"Big deal, our son has a brace," says my husband as he passes out cigars. "It doesn't mean anything."

While people around me celebrate, I grow more and more upset and depressed, thinking something is wrong with my baby. As much as I love my stepchildren, who are with us for the summer, I want to be alone and withdraw to my bedroom. Flowers come from my business partners and from my office. I can't look at them.

By the time I take Michael back to the hospital for a checkup, Jim and I are barely talking. He refuses to believe that anything is wrong. His other children are perfectly fine, and this child is going to be perfectly fine as well. End of discussion. This time, I go to the hospital with my mother.

Being new to motherhood, I think the checkup is routine. In retrospect, I think the doctors were concerned about Michael's fingers and hip, even though they didn't tell me. They measure the size of his head, his fingers and arms, and, once again, say everything is fine. They check his hip and tell me it's progressing, to keep the harness on and bring him back in a couple of weeks.

The months go by in a blur. I remember Michael getting a cold during a trip to Cape Cod with Jim, who has a sales meeting. I remember feeling scared and paranoid the entire time. I'm anything but a normal, calm mother. When we return to New York, I set about finding the right woman to care for Michael while I'm at work, knowing my leave of absence is ending. I'm not thrilled to be leaving Michael during the day and am careful about the choice of his caretaker.

Not long after returning to work, I get the call that I'm hoping not to get. "Michael is sick, he's very congested." I speed home and run into the house. Michael is almost blue. I rush him to the hospital. He has a respiratory virus called RSV, which is dangerous in a baby under six months because his lungs aren't developed and he's susceptible to asthma. Doctors put him in an oxygen tent, and I stay in the hospital with him for ten days.

The ugly part of this story is that Jim and I are going through increasingly more difficult times and aren't communicating. While I'm trying to find out what's wrong with Michael, he's on the golf course or on business trips. We argue often, and our marriage deteriorates. I feel as if I'm losing my son and my marriage at the same time.

Michael continues to grow disproportionately fast. His fingers are long. His toes are long. I pick him up at the nursery school, and he's a full head taller than everybody else. But what concerns me more deeply is his loose joints. When he starts to walk, his ankles won't hold him up. When he sits in the high chair, he leans over. He's flopped over in the stroller. It's as if he doesn't have enough glue in his body. And he's getting an indentation in his chest bone.

Something is wrong, very wrong.

During the next several years, I take Michael to joint-disease doctors, orthopedic surgeons, physical therapists, occupational therapists, regular pediatricians, every doctor you can imagine in New York City. Every special-ist. Everyone but a heart specialist. I don't have a clue that anything might be wrong with his heart.

Without exception, every doctor tells me that he's fine, not to worry. Yes, he's tall, but you're tall, they say. I'm five foot eight, and my husband is six foot two. "But I have no indentation in my chest bone," I press. "My hus-band doesn't have one. Why does Michael? Why are his joints so loose? Why are his fingers so long? Something's not right here."

You're fine. He's fine. Get over it.

Even his pediatrician writes in the records that I'm a hypochondriac, that I'm a neurotic mother, and that nothing is wrong with Michael. "If the doctors say he's fine, then he's fine," says my husband. "Why are you look-ing for something to be wrong? What's the matter with you?"

Even though Jim thinks I'm crazy, I continue to search. I continue even when we separate and sell the house. I don't care. I'm on a mission more crit-ical than anything in my life. For five years, the only one who believes me is my mother.

For Michael's fifth birthday, I buy him a computer. It comes with a free CD called *The Family Doctor*. Late one night while Michael is sleeping, I put in the CD and enter all his features under "rare disorders." I list the height and the loose joints and the indentation and the long fingers and toes, all of it. The word *Marfan* pops up. I remember one of the doctors in the nursery saying that word . . . *Marfan*.

I hold my breath.

And double-click.

The window loads.

And I read....

Children with Marfan syndrome grow taller than their peers, their arms and legs are disproportionately long, their joints are loose, they have an indentation or protrusion in their chest bone, and their fingers can be contracted at birth. Every single symptom that Michael has ever had.

My heart pounds in my ears.

As I continue to read, I slow and then stop. Marfan can be fatal. All the connective tissue in the body is weak, and the aorta, which is our primary blood vessel, is thin and weak and can tear and dissect, causing sudden death.

Through the night, I sit in front of the computer, reading, searching, digging deeper. The next morning, first thing, I dress Michael, hail a cab, and take him to the same hospital where he was born, the best hospital in the city. I head straight to the geneticist and the doctors who had said Michael was fine. "I think he has Marfan syndrome."

"Just because he's tall doesn't mean he has Marfan," one of them says.

How many times had I heard *Just because...?* "I want you to check his heart."

"If you really want us to, we'll check him again." I can hear the undertone of condescension as one of the doctors tries to show me the door. "Come back in a month, and we'll do an echocardiogram."

"No, I want it done now!" I start to cry hysterically. "I want you to check his heart, and I want it done right now!"

Maybe they think it's the only way they can get rid of me, but they take measurements, like they had done so many times before. Yes, he has a long arm span, and that's one of the signs. Yes, he's got the indentation. They take Michael to the scanning room for an echocardiogram.

I sit in the waiting room with a million feelings running through me.

When the doctors come back out, they're white as ghosts. "His aorta is twice the size of a normal aorta in a child of his age." Yes, Michael has Marfan syndrome. Immediately, they put him on beta-blockers to lower his blood pressure and to reduce the strain on his aorta. I had called my parents and asked them to meet me at the hospital. Now they take Michael home, and I break down, right there in the hospital. I can't even call Jim. I ask the cardiologist to make the call. Jim is devastated.

In the months that follow, I slide deeper and deeper into depression. I finally know what was wrong with Michael from the start, but the diagnosis is devastating. I take a few weeks off from work. I contact the National Marfam Foundation, which supports Marfan families, and I go to support-group meetings, but they're so focused on the pain and suffering of the disease that they depress me even further. It's as though I'm living every day with the real possibility that my child will die that very day. How does a parent do that?

When I return to work, people are wonderfully supportive and understanding of what I'm going through, and my staff steps in to take on a bigger workload to help me out. One day, I'm working with NBC on wardrobing for newscasters and morning talk show hosts. Jack Ford, one of the morning hosts, is in my office when I get a call from a doctor. Overhearing my conversation, when I hang up, he says, "I know what Marfan syndrome is, and I couldn't help but hear how you diagnosed your son. You should come on *The Today Show* and talk about the signs and symptoms and help people who are trying to figure out what's wrong with their child." I tell him I'll consider it, not thinking he'll actually follow through, but he does.

In a seven-minute segment that airs on a Saturday morning, Michael and I are on *The Today Show* with a doctor from Johns Hopkins Hospital.

We list signs and symptoms, and I tell our story. More than ten thousand calls come into the foundation from people frantic to talk about their child's symptoms. The doctor at Johns Hopkins will be booked for a year as a result.

Over the following months, I talk to parents around the country who are panicked about their children, and I connect them to doctors at Johns Hopkins or the foundation. Several dozen children are diagnosed, their lives saved by surgery or by being monitored. Cards and letters pour in from people saying, "Thank you for helping to save my child's life."

With the airing of *The Today Show,* my life begins to shift significantly. Where I had felt depressed about Michael's illness, about losing the child-hood I thought we would share, losing my husband, losing my home, I now feel that I'm saving lives. It is the most gratifying feeling I have ever had.

I start getting involved with the foundation, which is based in Port Washington, New York. I can't let what happened to me — the struggle I went through for five years — happen to other parents. That commitment becomes my breakthrough. It gives me a huge amount of strength and courage. I work tirelessly to raise awareness and money for research, because if you're diagnosed with Marfan syndrome, you live. If you're not diagnosed, you die. It's that simple.

Since Michael was diagnosed, Jim and I have worked hard at mending our marriage, and we're committed in a way we never were before, dedicated to being the best parents we can be for Michael, who is now thirteen years old and doing well.

What has kept me going has been the determination to give my son a life and not to succumb to the disease. Although he can't be involved in physically demanding activities, he plays golf and attends a camp where the focus is on nature and hiking, boating and fishing, instead of soccer and baseball, basketball and tug-of-war. He understands his condition and takes beta-blockers every day to preserve his heart, which we monitor with an echocardiogram every six months. When need be, he'll have surgery. Although his life is different, and he can't do the physical things that most children do, we focus on what he *can* do, not on what he *can't* do.

In the midst of my depression, someone sent me an essay written by Emily Perl Kingsley, "Welcome to Holland":

> I am often asked to describe the experience of raising a child with a disability — to try to help people who have not shared that unique experience to understand it, to imagine how it would feel. It's like this...
>
> When you're going to have a baby, it's like planning a fabulous vacation trip — to Italy. You buy a bunch of guidebooks and make your wonderful plans. The Coliseum. The Michelangelo David. The gondolas in Venice. You may learn some handy phrases in Italian. It's all very exciting.
>
> After months of eager anticipation, the day finally arrives. You pack your bags and off you go. Several hours later, the plane lands. The stewardess comes in and says, "Welcome to Holland."
>
> "*Holland?!*" you say. "What do you mean Holland? I signed up for Italy! I'm supposed to be in Italy. All my life I've dreamed of going to Italy."

But there's been a change in the flight plan. They've landed in Holland and there you must stay.

The important thing is they haven't taken you to a horrible, disgusting, filthy place full of pestilence, famine and disease. It's just a different place.

So you must go out and buy new guidebooks. And you must learn a whole new language. And you will meet a whole new group of people you would never have met.

It's just a *different* place. It's slower paced than Italy, less flashy than Italy. But after you've been there for a while and you catch your breath, you look around...and you begin to notice that Holland has windmills...Holland has tulips. Holland even has Rembrandts.

But everyone you know is busy coming and going from Italy...and they're all bragging about what a wonderful time they had there. And for the rest of your life, you will say, "Yes, that's where I was supposed to go. That's what I had planned."

And the pain of that will never, ever, ever, ever go away... because the loss of that dream is a very significant loss.

But...if you spend your life mourning the fact that you didn't get to Italy, you will never be free to enjoy the very special, the very lovely things ...about Holland.

When I read that, I cried for two days straight, literally, and I am still brought to tears every time I read it. I thought, my God, Karen, you're not going to Italy, you're going to Holland. The pain will never go away, but you can't spend the rest of your life mourning. That's what changed me. I had to find beauty in what was happening, I had to look for the best I could find in Michael's condition, because if I didn't look, I'd never find it. And if I didn't find it, I'd never be able to show Michael that his life could be beautiful.

It is said that moms have an inner strength and courage. When Michael was diagnosed with Marfan syndrome, when I saw the power of listening to my intuition, when I stepped up to educate and help people save the lives of their children, I found strength and courage like I had never known before.

Every day now is a gift.

⊙

Karen received a Mother of the Year Award from the National Mother's Day, Father's Day Council. Michael and Jim were with her at the award ceremony in New York City. "As I walked across the stage to accept the award, I looked out at them and saw them beaming up at me. It is an image I carry with me always." Karen is often recognized for her impact on families, and it is not uncommon for someone to call out across a room, as a woman did at a Chicago Marfan conference, "Karen, Karen Murray, I saw you on *The Today Show,* you saved my son's life!"

While also sitting on the board of the American Heart Association, Karen continues to be extremely involved in fund-raising for Marfan research. Because so few doctors are knowledgeable about the syndrome, fewer than half of those afflicted with it are diagnosed, leaving the others vulnerable to sudden death from aortic failure that could have been prevented.

An estimated two hundred thousand people in the United States have Marfan syndrome or a related connective tissue disorder, making it nearly seven times more common than cystic fibrosis. Karen remains hopeful that the medical community is getting closer to new ways of strengthening connective tissue.

Robert Lewis

# For a Kid Named Domestic
## *Cooling Revenge and Healing the Pain*

Is a man's courage different from a woman's?

When I first started interviewing men for this book, I had a real attitude about that question. I thought a woman's courage was much more interesting. More real. Deeper. I had spent a good many years interviewing women for the first two courage books. Easily, graciously, they had gone into vulnerable, intimate places with me, telling their stories with great emotional honesty. At times I was startled by it. But women are like that. We can turn ourselves inside out and share our sadness, our love, our fear, our shyness, our tenacity, our strength, our determination, our will. Just for starters.

So as I readied myself for the first of my interviews with men, I thought, *How on earth am I going to get these guys to open up and be emotionally honest and vulnerable with me? Say the word* courage, *and most of them are going to go straight to the macho testosterone thing.* I was irritated out of the gate.

Every one of them proved me wrong.

Every one of them was right there with me, intimate, honest, showing their weaknesses, their fears and uncertainties, and all the ripe emotions that inhabit a courageous moment. Here's what I've come to think: Each of us has feminine and masculine aspects within us, and we need both when we do something daring. Whether man or woman, we need both heart and action to bring about something truly courageous. Heart without action is inertia. Action without heart is hollow.

One red-hot night on the back end of a summer, Robert Lewis Jr. struggled with both. His heart was on fire; he was angry enough to do something dangerous. Instead, he needed desperately to defuse a whole crowd of kids on boil and to keep them safe.

Robert was a gang intervention worker in Boston. He was good at it. Mayor Ray Flynn dubbed him the "gang czar" for his ability to work the streets. When he got the call that there'd been another shooting, he'd already been to fifty funerals of kids killed in gang-related incidents. But this one was different. This one was personal.

Today the president and executive director of the National Conference for Community and Justice in the greater Boston region, and a man not known for showing his private emotions, Robert cries as he tells the story of that summer night in 1992.

⊙

His name was George Ramos; on the street he was known as Domestic. His death nearly made me strike out in a way that I had come to expect from the kids who killed him. I wanted revenge. Immediate. Without mercy.

The night of the shooting was one of the longest in my life. Working the streets, my job was to catch violence before it happened or cool it down when it erupted. When I heard that Domestic had been shot, when I saw the blood on the playground, I didn't know how I'd do that.

When the shooting happens, I'm already emotionally beat, drained from my work on the streets. Operating out of community centers, I've been running the street workers' program, Boston's answer to gang intervention. It's the first in the city that actually puts workers out into neighborhoods to work with a population that a lot of people fear. Ninety percent of youth workers' were doing their business in buildings, but 70 percent of the young people are on the streets. That didn't make sense. Which is why the street workers' program was started, to provide support, advocacy, mentorship, guidance, and resources.

We're the voice of a big brother, a big sister, and we work hand in hand with the police and the courts. Our mandate is to prevent gang violence and, short of that, to create a safety zone for people affected by it and to prevent retaliation. We also work proactively by getting kids into programs to help them get their Graduate Equivalency Degree, doing job counseling, setting up sports leagues. Our best weapons are our knowledge, experience, and commitment. A licensed clinical psychologist meets with us weekly and teaches us to mediate conflict, to deal with grieving, to handle domestic violence and abuse. We have to have sharp instincts. And even sharper wits. We deal with a lot of shit.

I've spent too much time in the emergency room at Boston City Hospital. I've gone to too many funerals. I'm fried, just holding on. I've got the car, the beeper, the cell phone. I'm always on call. It's time to make a change. This is what I'm thinking as I sit down at home on Sunday night with my wife and kids. I've scheduled a meeting the next day with City Year, an organization that puts a corps of young people to work in the community as volunteers — a kind of urban Peace Corps. Is it the right move for me?

Not unlike other nights, I get beeped. 9-1-1. Before I get to the phone, I get beeped again. 9-1-1. By the time I pick up the receiver, my pager goes off again. I pick up the phone and make the call.

The panicked voice on the other end screams, "Junior! Junior! Shots fired! Shots fired! O'Day playground!"

The O'Day playground is near West Newton Street in the community of Villa Victoria. I started the first youth service program there and worked with kids in the community for seven years. When I left, I still coached some of them in sports. They called me Junior. I grew up in Villa Victoria.

I race to my car with my beeper and my cell phone, trying to get more information as I peel out. At O'Day, as I fly out of my car, a young man grabs me: "Rayton's been shot, Domestic's been shot, José's been shot, a young woman's been shot." People are frantic. Blood is on the playground.

"Hold tight!" I start grabbing people, trying to chase Domestic's name from that list. "Just hold tight! C'mon!" The place is going crazy. "Keep it cool! Let's chill!"

People are crying. People are angry, a hundred people on boil on the playground. "What happened?" I ask a brother I've known forever. No information. People start pressing in on me, thinking I must know something. "Wait a minute, damn, okay, hold on, hold on, let me make a call." I call the police station. Nothing. I call the hospital. Nothing. I'm getting nowhere. I need information. Badly.

I call City Hall's twenty-four-hour hotline. "Robert, we can't talk to you right now," says the operator. "Is there a number where we can call you back?" I give her my beeper and cell phone numbers.

I call one of my street workers: I need you over here! Now! I call my supervisor, Charley Rose, but he's dealing with a death in the family. All hell is breaking loose, and I'm the only adult who can keep things together. I finally get through to someone at the hospital's emergency unit who knows what's going on. I ask about Domestic.

"Hold on."

I wait. It seems like forever.

"I'm sorry..."

No!

"...George Ramos died."

I almost lose it. I want to explode. *Who did this? Goddamn sonsabitches, who did this?* I spin around. *Someone knows who did this! I want to know! Who did this?*

Domestic. Dead. This kid I've known since he was little, who worked hard to get out of the gang life, to go straight, and then to help other kids go straight. I love this kid like my own. I want someone to pay. It takes everything in me to put a grip on revenge. I cannot go there. I cannot. I look around at all the young people, angry, hurting, and I know I cannot fuel their anger with my own. I have to help them through this.

A young person calls me on my cell phone and says frantically, "I heard Domestic was shot!" I have to break the news now, and I know it's going to be bad. Quietly, I tell a few people. Within minutes, the word is out, and the place goes off, with people crying, breaking bottles, pulling up fences, swearing and cussing and talking about retaliation.

No one knows what happened or why. I call the hospital again and find out that Rayton is still on the operating table and might not walk again, and that José was shot in the foot. Everything in me and around me is going nuts. I've watched fifty kids go in the ground. Fifty. But this is not just fifty-one, this is Domestic. My insides are all fucked up.

I don't know what to do. I call my wife and tell her Domestic's been killed. "I gotta stay out here, I gotta be with the kids."

My mind rivets sharply on the safety of the young people on the playground. *Keep things cool, don't let it explode.* My street workers have answered the call, Charley has broken free, and the cops have arrived, some of whom I know. If we can keep the crowd within the confines of the playground, we'll have some kind of control.

Through the night, I hang with the kids. Folks are drinking, folks are getting high, and I don't try to keep them from it. I know what they're doing, they're sedating themselves, they're numbing the pain.

I wish I could tell you everything that happens that night. We cry, we hug, we kiss, we hang onto each other to keep from exploding. The cops cordon off the playground. I work with Captain Cellucci to be the go-between so the cops and the kids don't get pitted against each other, to let the kids vent their emotions without erupting into violence. And all the while, I'm thinking, *Domestic was in my house a couple of weeks ago. I talked to him just a couple of nights back when he was out front. He lived next door. I know his sister. I know his mother. Who's going to tell his mother? I cannot make that call.*

I'm at O'Day playground all night.

The next morning, I call City Year. "I can't come in today, I gotta stay out here with these kids." That Monday turns into two weeks of being with young people from Villa Victoria, being a part of their anger and pain, and trying to figure out how to galvanize the community in a positive way. I talk to Teen Empowerment, a program for young people making changes in the community. I talk to Boston against Drugs to get youth workers and counselors to come out to Villa Victoria for basketball games and barbecues. I talk to the social-service agency for Villa Victoria. And I help make preparations for the wake and the funeral, which are going to be deep.

The night of the wake, people start out from Villa Victoria to walk the two-plus miles to the Puerto Rican church at Egleston Square in the neighborhood of Jamaica Plain. Hundreds of kids are on the walk, and it cuts through rival gang territory. An incident almost erupts on the way there. By the time I get to the wake, a line stretches out of the building and around the corner. Sixty cops are positioned around the area, some in riot gear. The tension with the police here is high because a kid from the neighborhood was killed by a cop a year earlier.

Before I get into the building, some kids from a rival gang show up, and all hell breaks loose, right there at the wake. A kid coming out of the church cracks with emotion and slams his fist on the hood of a car. I go over to comfort him, but just as I get to him, a cop throws me up against the wall and pins me with his nightstick. It's a cop I had asked Cellucci to rein in at O'Day and again just before the walk to the wake; I was concerned he'd incite the young people. He catches me at the throat and pins me on the wall, choking me. Now, I'm a big guy, at the time probably 205 pounds, but this guy gets me off the ground with that nightstick under my chin. I won't be able to talk for three days.

Later that night, I go over to O'Day to make sure the young people who got their butts kicked are okay. This kid, Angel, got his head split when he jumped in to defend me. He walks up and asks me if I'm okay. I'm looking at this nineteen-year-old who got his head whacked protecting me — and he's asking me if I'm okay. These are my kids.

Over the weeks that follow, Villa Victoria reclaims its community and its young people who are in pain. And I realize, more than ever, the vulnerability of these kids. What happened at O'Day playground happens many a night in our city. This time, it touched home because I grew up in Villa Victoria, I worked there, and I knew people. The shooting violated a space that was personal. It crossed the boundary of home. And it made me understand how folks feel all over the city, all over the country, when their people are killed in drive-bys, when their people are violated. It made me think hard about what families and communities go through. Even though I ran the gang program, even though I'd been to fifty funerals, it hadn't become personal in such a painful way. This brought it close. Brought it close because it was Domestic. Brought it close because it could have been me, it could have been my son. I've spent many a night at O'Day playground shooting ball, on nights not unlike the night Domestic was killed.

That night in August was one time I wished it hadn't been me with the cell phone and the beeper. I was angry. I was hurt. I was struggling.

Death is permanent.

Domestic was a lovable, fun-loving kid. He'd crack you up. He'll never make me laugh again. I won't see him again, won't have the chance to say,

"Hey, man, I hear you were out until three last night — you make sure your mother knows if you're going to stay out that late, she shouldn't have to worry." She shouldn't have to worry. And now her son is gone. Forever Years later, I still see the pain in her. It's heart-wrenching.

At O'Day playground is a small memorial ground for people from the community who have been killed. Some young people created it and laid a peace rock there to honor Domestic, to be a focal point for remembering him and other young people. Someone painted a mural of him.

Eventually, we put together some of the pieces of that night: Domestic and Rayton and José were out on the basketball court at O'Day playground, hanging out, playing ball like they did all the time, nothing different. Some young people were on the other side of the fence just chilling. Folks didn't know them but didn't mess with them. And then all of a sudden, this thing just opened up, guns going off in the park, and those kids no one knew took off. Who knows, maybe it was retaliation. Maybe somebody said something to someone's mother, father, girlfriend. Or maybe it was an initiation, some kid earning his way into a gang by shooting up the playground.

I didn't want to find out who killed Domestic. I had the power to, from working with the mayor and the police, but I knew that if I got a name, I'd nail the son of a bitch. And I didn't want that, because it would keep the violence going. Someone would have to do the payback for the kid I nailed. And, if any of the young people of Villa Victoria knew who did the payback, they'd retaliate and there'd be more killing. It had to stop. Nobody stepped forward, and, to this day, no one has been arrested.

Several years after Domestic's death, a youth worker named Melvin was shot and killed. It shook me like Domestic's death had. A line is crossed when someone who is out there giving his heart and soul to help young people is killed. Stepping over that line declares open war on youth workers and street workers and people who make a difference in the lives of others. That's not right. These are folks who don't make a lot of money, who work all hours of the night, who are always available to help young people. And then some punk takes his life? No, no, no, you don't cross that line.

When Melvin was killed, I began to think about all the young people I'd talked with during hostile situations. I'd hear someone going off about retaliation, and I'd punch him in the chest and say, "You ain't doin' nothing." I'd be working the street, hanging out with young people, rapping with them, and if someone gave me shit, I'd walk up and grab 'em and say, "Look, man, you keep goin' and I'm gonna kick your ass." I had conversations that got hot, when I had to grab a young person and push him against the wall and say, "Yo, I ain't gonna play." So when I heard about Melvin, it threw me, threw me hard. Because who's to say that any one of those young people I'd punched in the chest or pushed against the wall or stood down wouldn't decide to bring out a gun? It knocked the wind out of me for a while. It made me reassess myself, my own vulnerability.

Eventually, I kept that appointment at City Year and saw that I could leverage a job there to provide critical opportunities for young people. I could be a catalyst to ensure that kids out on the streets who want to cross that thin line from gangs or the criminal life would be able to get the skills and resources they need while also becoming productive citizens.

As executive director of City Year, I wasn't on the streets 24/7 like I had been. I wore suits and raised money and administered a program that was turning around the lives of hundreds of young people by getting them out into the community to volunteer and be of service, to learn leadership skills, to bridge racial divides. I leveraged my position to get in the doors of corporate America to raise money that enabled us to put 230 young people to work in the community each day. They renovated housing for the homeless, turned vacant lots into community gardens, led programs for senior citizens, ran after-school programs, served as teachers' aides in public schools. It was a process of changing individuals and changing the world through the power of civic action. These young people would go on to do great things.

At the mid-year basic training retreat at Grotonwood, I address my City Year corps. I've had a couple of stressful days at work. We've had to kick two kids out of the corps, and I hate doing that. Plus, I'm dealing with a budget crunch. So whereas I'm normally energetic, hugging people and upbeat, I've been distracted and anxious. As I walk up to deliver the keynote, a few kids stop me and give me cards that say things like, we love you, we're with you, keep your head up. Then a few corps members give me posters with kids writing: "Robert, we love you," "Where's your smile?" "You're our mentor," "You're our leader," "You're our inspiration." Someone writes, "We want to know about you, Robert, we're with you."

I usually don't go into personal things at work. I talk about why I do what I do and why the work is important, but not about the details of my own life. It's the first time that they ask me to tell them more about who I am, and I share the Domestic story. In front of more than two hundred young people, I break down and cry. I tell them about my younger sister, who died a year and a half earlier, thirty-one and trying to recover from drugs, making changes, working to do all the right things when she got sick. I tell them about the emotional times when I've spoken at funerals and said to the families and friends, "Stop crying to the stiff, turn around and cry to the congregation, show the kids your pain. It's not going to make any difference to the stiff, 'cuz he's dead. Show it to the kids, show them that when you die it affects your family, your friends, your neighbors, your community." I tell them about the times I took young people on field trips to hospital emergency rooms and to the morgue so they could see a cold body, see what it looks like up close. I wanted those young people to see death, let it stare them in the face, and ask themselves, *Is this what life is all about?*

What young people have to offer is a magnificent thing. I've seen it in the hundreds of people who work with City Year. I know what's possible. But I also know the pain and hopelessness, the hurt and anger that drive our young people to violence. I felt it course through me with Domestic's death. It would have been so easy, so righteous, to strike back, to numb the pain with revenge. I know how that feels. But it wouldn't breathe life back into Domestic. The only way to rightly honor Domestic was by healing the pain, keeping on with the kind of work he was doing in the end, and by lifting out . . . lifting out of the cycle of violence.

Promoted to senior vice president of the national organization of City Year, Robert traveled the country overseeing regional offices and witnessed the first international expansion. As part of that expansion, he went to South Africa and met President Mandela. Yet he told me, "Something was missing. I had a void in my heart. And the void was local. What keeps me going is working on local issues that impact and affect the quality of life in the place that I call home."

That longing led him to the National Conference for Community and Justice office in Boston. "When I came across this organization, I was blown away by its mandate to fight bias, bigotry, and hate and to promote understanding and respect among all races, religions, and cultures. Finding NCCJ, a small organization taking a big stand for equal access and equality for people . . . oh my goodness, I said to myself, I've come home. I get to work with individuals, organizations, and communities, empowering them so that all of our people — not just some, but all — are able to participate in American democracy."

Robert still travels and lectures at places like Harvard University, the President's Summit in Philadelphia, the State of Texas International Youth Conference, and the NAACP Martin Luther King Day Celebration. He has testified before the U.S. Senate during the Crime Bill Hearings. An overseer of the Boston Plan for Excellence in the Boston Public Schools, he is also co-chair of the Massachusetts State Summit and a founding member of the South End Athletics and Activities Association.

"I wake up every day," Says Robert, "and look at my wife and kids, and when they say, 'Good morning, I love you,' I know the world is great."

Paul Cox

# Koki, the Chiefs, and a Rainforest
*Looking for a Cure and Finding the Power of Love*

For Dr. Paul Cox, courage rode in on the cancer that claimed his mother's life. She was not only his mother, but also his scientific hero. His childhood memories are etched not with cookies baking in the kitchen but with microscopes in the laboratory and cell dissections his mother did as a fisheries biologist. She opened doors to a whole new world for her shy young son, a world of wonder that would capture his imagination for a lifetime.

When she got sick, he tried everything to help her fight the cancer. He found the best oncologist in the country to treat her, lavished her with comfort and care and love. He fasted and prayed for God to intervene. He did everything he could and yet was unable to save her. "I had never felt so helpless," he told me.

Shattered, Paul was plagued by the thought that he must do something to help find a cure for cancer. "Because I'm an ethnobiologist and my work is the study of how indigenous peoples use medicinal plants, the only thing

I knew to do was to go to the rainforest, to the healers, to the plants, to try to find a cure." Twenty years earlier, at age nineteen, he had followed his call as a Mormon missionary to Samoa. Later, he had done field research there for his doctoral studies at Harvard. Now he would go back to try to find a treatment for breast cancer. "It was a long shot, but I had to do it." He would have quit his job as professor of biology at Brigham Young University in Utah, but they gave him a leave of absence. And the Presidential Young Investigator Award he had just received from the National Science Foundation financed the project.

With his wife, Barbara, and their four young children, Paul left the twenty-first century for Savaii, the least-developed island in the Samoan archipelago, which he describes in his book *Nafanua: Saving the Samoan Rain Forest* as having "perhaps the largest and most species-rich rainforest remaining on any South Pacific island." Sitting on a fifty-five-gallon drum on the stern of the Samoan ferry taking them the three hours to Savaii, he looked out over the ocean toward the island, its interior mountains and small volcano cutting the horizon. How could he take his family to such a remote and foreign place? What had he been thinking?

The village of Falealupo is on the westernmost tip of the island. It was late afternoon when Paul and his family, tucked in their van, descended the steep grade toward the tip of the peninsula and the vast canopy of rainforest came into view. The stifling heat dropped perceptibly as they entered the forest, and the air filled with the sounds of birds, nothing like the "exotic cacophony" portrayed by Hollywood but rather, as Paul describes it, "the gentle purring of fruit pigeons calling to their mates and the rustle of honeycreeper wings."

And then there was Falealupo, a mile of white-sand beach licked by the bluest South Pacific seas you've ever seen and dotted with brown thatched huts. Women were beating their wash with sticks, and fishermen were returning home, pulling dugout canoes out of the water and hanging fishing nets out to dry. Paul and his family would spend a year in this village, living in a thatched hut without running water or electricity. The Falealupo people took them in warmly and, over time, made them honorary members of their village.

In Falealupo, Paul hoped to find a lead in treating the deadly cancer that had claimed his mother's life. "I gambled that, if there were any herbalists left on the islands, the best might be found there, far from civilization." Apprenticing himself to the healers, he made detailed records of plants and their medicinal uses and sent samples to the National Cancer Institute in Washington, D.C., to be tested. One of these plants was *Homalanthus nutans,* which the healers used to treat hepatitis.

When Paul and I first spoke, he made no claim to courage. "In many ways," he said, "I'm a coward." This was before we talked about his dangling from the canopy of a rainforest, gathering medicinals at dizzying heights. "I'm a tropical botanist, and I'm terrified of snakes, which is the rough equivalent of being an airline pilot petrified of heights. I'm even afraid of spiders. But I was desperate, and I took a leap that forever changed me."

What we do in the name of love is staggering. For Paul Cox, it was just the beginning. "I came to love Falealupo as one can love only a home, a place to which one is deeply connected through the soul. Here the chiefs governed in harmony with an ancestral wisdom passed through the centuries. It was a true refuge, and even when our year was over and we returned to Utah, I knew I would be back."

⊙

With the National Cancer Institute doing lengthy studies on the plants I had sent, I return to Falealupo, this time to research an incomparable species of flying fox. So rare were these creatures that my petition for a grant to study them was nearly rejected out of hand because there was no record of them; ergo, they "simply don't exist." Except, of course, I had seen them. They were huge, breathtaking, and obviously endangered. They've drawn me back to Samoa, and the return is like coming home.

As the ferry churns toward Savaii, I look out over the sea toward the silhouette of the island with great anticipation. Barbara and the children aren't with me this time, but academic colleagues with a deep passion for the preservation of the Samoan flying fox will be joining me soon.

Once I'm on land and traveling across the island to Falealupo, an uneasy feeling settles over me. The island has changed dramatically. Eighty percent of its lowland rainforest has been logged, converted into wooden pallets for the tuna industry. Huge logging trucks roar down narrow roads, smelling of diesel and creosote, the odor of rainforest death. Villages around the sawmill glow at night with electric lights powered by a generator. The traditional thatch roofing on houses has been replaced with corrugated iron.

I've heard that the Falealupo forest is threatened because the village needs money for a new school, but I'm convinced they'll find a way to protect it. For ten years, the chiefs have refused to sell. The forest is simply too integral to their life. Snaking along toward the sea and that lush canopy of forest, I realize that it's become integral to me as well. I'm deeply, emotionally connected to it. I can't imagine life without the forest.

Shortly after I arrive in the village, my friend Lamositele tells me that loggers have arrived in Falealupo. "They're cutting the rainforest."

His words suck the air out of me. I'm literally struck dumb

The Samoan government has given the village an ultimatum: Build a new school within nine months or the existing school, which they've deemed inadequate, will be shut down and the Falealupo children will be denied entrance into the Western Samoan educational system. As often happens with mysterious coincidence in the Third World, the demand for a new school was followed shortly by an offer from a logging company to harvest the thirty-thousand-acre Falealupo forest. Not surprisingly, this particular offer was exactly the amount of money that it would take to build the new school, sixty-five thousand U.S. dollars.

Wanting their children to be prepared for life in a modern South Pacific world requiring more than reef-foraging skills or the tending of taro patches, the chiefs borrowed money from the logging company to start construction of the school in exchange for logging rights. Rather than sacrifice their children's future, they made the unthinkable decision to sacrifice the forest.

I hurry to my van, tailed by villagers, and, with some of them packed inside, speed off toward the lowland rainforest. Soon we hear the sound of heavy equipment. From rainforest to clear-cut is like passing through the gates of hell. These aren't guys who come in and cut down trees like Paul Bunyan; they come with bulldozers and push the whole forest over, leaving a huge gaping wound that looks like someone set off an atomic bomb. Stately banyan trees with lianas and vines trailing from them crash behind us. Precious plants found nowhere else, plants that hold the promise of cures for some of our most devastating modern-day diseases, are torn out of the earth and strewn in horrible, rutted piles.

The chainsaws, the diesel loaders, the roaring engines of the logging trucks, the smell of creosote...the shock is so great that, initially, I feel a stunned detachment; forests are cut every day, nothing unusual is happening here. Then my eyes catch on Samoan children standing off to the side, watching a truck loaded with massive trees barrel past them. What must they be thinking? These trees are their heritage, a part of their sacred connection to spirit. I am witnessing the rape of the very soul of the Falealupo people.

I look over at the other villagers who are there, watching this death. Many of them are weeping. Not since my mother's death have I felt so devastated, helpless, small, inconsequential. The despair is paralyzing.

Another logging truck screams by, and I turn to walk back to the van. *I cannot let this happen.* My mind rages against the despair, shaking loose, clarifying: The medicine coming out of this forest can help millions of people. There isn't another one like it anywhere, and there isn't another village like Falealupo. *I have to do something.* But this is no academic issue I can bring up for debate in a weekly seminar. No subject for a symposium with economists and resource specialists. There is no time to enlist overseas environmentalists in a fight to save a forest few have ever heard of.

In the walking distance between the clear-cut and the van, I know that I have to take my own stand. I cannot let this happen. I have to stop this travesty that will raze a hundred acres of precious forest a day. Whatever the cost, I have to stop it.

On the way back to the village, I say quietly to Lamositele, "I must meet with the village chiefs." The chiefs will not gather in their entirety until the following morning, and speaking before them will be tricky. The Falealupo are a proud people. Even though I've lived with them and have become like family, I'm still a foreigner. Asking them to reverse a decision made by the chiefs, especially regarding their land, will be a delicate matter.

Before the first light of morning, I awake to the sweet smell of taro and fish cooking on beds of hot stones covered with banana leaves. Anxious about my audience with the chiefs, I pray before leaving my hut, asking for powerful words to move their hearts so that the forests can be protected. That I, an untitled man, am given a chance to address them is extraordinary.

Out into the haze of sunrise, past the smoky fires toward the beach and the dugout canoes, I walk into the sea and stand quietly for what seems like a long time. As the waves wash over my feet, I rehearse the chiefly language I learned so many years ago as a young Mormon missionary. I will need to speak eloquently in the native rhetoric, which I have not used with the chiefs before. An articulate and well-spoken use of their tongue will hold great sway.

The gentle motion of the water is calming.

When I feel ready, I go to Lamositele. "Do you have any suggestions for me today as I approach the chiefs? Do you think I have a chance to sway them?"

My friend is unusually solemn. "It will be very hard. We know and trust you, but land issues are difficult, the hardest. Any proposal involving land is bound to arouse suspicion."

"But you will be there to help me if I have trouble, won't you?"

"Koki," he says, using my familiar name in Samoan, "I'm sorry, but I can't go. The village might suspect that my family put you up to this and that we are somehow trying to seize village land. It's important for us to stay completely out of the matter."

I will have no backup in the first chiefs' council I have ever attended.

When the time comes, a young girl runs up to me with the news that the chiefs are waiting. Carefully, I adjust the formal lei that Lamositele has lent me for the occasion. I pick up my long, slender kava root, used in ceremony, and walk along the beach to the north side of the village, where the chiefs meet in a rustic hut on stilts decorated with red hibiscus and pink torch ginger. I climb the notches in the coconut-trunk ladder, feeling ever more the foreigner, a man from a different culture, a different time.

Inside the hut are twenty large men stripped to the waist, their bodies glistening with scented coconut oil. A few wear leis. All the most important chiefs of the village are present. I step in, still more nervous than I want to be, and sit down on a mat. From the back, I hear someone murmur, "What's Koki doing here? Doesn't he know this is the chiefs' meeting?"

The most highly regarded chief, a formidable Polynesian man who looks like a statue from Easter Island, begins the formal welcome. In turn, I respond with high greetings to those gathered and give honor to the sacred chiefs of Falealupo village, all in their native tongue. The men smile, surprised that I can speak their esoteric language. And then they carry on with their business. My request will be worked into the back end of an intricate and lengthy investiture ceremony for two new chiefs that day.

By late afternoon, the investiture ritual is over, and I'm finally invited to speak my mind before the chiefs and the villagers. I slide forward on my mat, as is customary when speaking formally, and briefly close my eyes, knowing the importance of beginning with composure. Here, in this place, form will matter more than substance. Regardless of the merits of an argument, the most eloquent and persuasive orator rules the day in Falealupo. I need to speak without fear, without hesitation.

I begin slowly and loudly, in the precise intonation and cadence I learned so many years before, giving much time to the proper honoring of sacred entities and chiefs, living and dead, thanking the council for accepting and hearing me. Well into my speech, I finally come to the point: "Yesterday, I saw the terrible destruction caused by the loggers. I know that you are not happy with this situation because the forest is precious to you. Therefore, I gently approach your sanctity and sacredness with my humble opinion. I scratch the roots of the *fau* tree and beg your indulgence. Could I pay for your school so that you can save your rainforest? I have no other objective than the preservation of the forest. I do not wish to control your land or to make decisions concerning it. I am merely proposing a covenant: I will raise money to pay for your school if you will protect your rainforest. I believe the forest is sacred because it was created by God's holy hand. We must find a way to save it.

"Thank you for the opportunity to visit you in clear skies and in health. I pray that God will cause the orbit of the moon to be high above the heads of the high chiefs. May God also bless the orators that their whisks may never fall or their staffs ever break. May my voice continue to live. May our morning be blessed."

Silence fills the space between us. I wait.

Suddenly, the chiefs burst into applause. Like I said, a good speech is highly respected. I have done well. As to the substance of the matter, saving the rainforest, the chiefs will have to consider my offer with great deliberation.

A day passes. A hundred acres are razed as I await word from the chiefs. Two more days pass. Two hundred more acres.

No decision in the village is made without the full consensus of the chiefs. Without that, an issue simply remains unresolved. I seek out one of the healers, hoping for some sign of how this precipitous judgment is going but instead am told yet another story about the chiefs' suspicions when it comes to foreigners and land: Long ago, Germans came to the South Pacific, passing out cigarettes to the chiefs and in return securing from them a mark on a piece of paper that, unbeknownst to them, deeded away vast tracts of land. Those memories are still painful to the Falealupo people, making them cautious to a fault of foreigners.

The next day, I hear that the chiefs have accepted my proposal.

To preserve the forest, they've decided to take a perilous step, trusting that I, a white man from a foreign land, have no hidden agenda. In council with them again, I explain the details of my offer, starting with an immediate trip to the Development Bank in Apia to have the mortgage on the school signed over to me. In the end, I will formally renounce any rights to village lands or forests. "I know that this has required a tremendous leap of faith on your part," I say to the chiefs, "and I thank you from my heart. I will not let you down."

When word of the chiefs' decision reaches the loggers, they apparently think it's a hoax, because they show up the next morning anyway and continue bulldozing. When Fuiono, one of the high chiefs, hears this, he literally runs the three miles to the logging site with his machete in hand. "Don't cut another tree!" He brandishes his machete at the loggers. "This forest is now taboo!" To violate a taboo, especially in contradiction to a chief, is unthinkable to a Samoan, and all the logging company employees are Samoan. Quietly, they pack up and leave.

That Monday, I fly over to the capital island to meet with a director of the Development Bank of Western Samoa and sign a personal mortgage for sixty-five thousand dollars for the school. And then I catch a plane home.

Now I have to find a way to tell Barbara that we're selling our house and close to everything we own to save a rainforest.

Barbara and the children are waiting for me at the Salt Lake City airport. The abandoned flying fox that I've brought home to nurse back to health is a good distraction until the children are in bed and I can get Barbara alone. Then I tell her what I've done. To this day, I cannot talk about it without getting emotional. Barbara takes my hand, looks in my eyes, and says, "Paul, what a great opportunity. How often in a lifetime do we get a chance to do something like this?"

My emotions are close to the surface for days. Watching the movie *Bambi* with the children, I burst into tears. At night, my dreams are ransacked by monstrous bulldozers grinding through the forest, majestic trees crashing to the ground. Falealupo lives in me, breathes in me, catches in my throat.

Friends and family soon begin to find out what Barbara and I are doing, and people come together in an extraordinary effort to help. Two startling donations are made spontaneously on a conversation and a handshake: one from Ken Murdock, owner of Nature's Way, a large herbal medicine company, and the other from Rex Maughan, who owns Forever Living Products, the largest manufacturer of aloe vera products in the country. It's almost all the money we need to cover the cost of the school.

Around this time, I learn from the National Cancer Institute that the *Homalanthus nutans* plant I had sent to be tested, the one used by Samoan healers to treat hepatitis, has shown remarkable activity against the AIDS virus, stronger than AZT, with nearly complete protection of human cells long before signs of toxicity. *Don't say anything about this,* cautions the institute's director of natural products, who ran the tests. *We don't want the patent trail to become clouded. This may be an important discovery.* He doesn't know that I found the plant in the area of the Falealupo forest where the loggers have already decimated the land. Has a cure for AIDS slipped through my fingers? The urgency of my return presses in on me.

With the money for the school in my backpack, I return to Samoa. Wasting no time, the Falealupo village chiefs and I head straight to the logging firm and, taking them by surprise, pay off the money already advanced for logging rights.

It's done.

I turn as the villagers cheer, filled with a deep, abiding satisfaction. It is one of the greatest moments of my life.

"Purity of heart is to will one thing," writes Kierkegaard, one of my favorite philosophers. Since that first fortuitous trip to Falealupo, I have come to believe that if you decide you're going to do something, whatever the cost, and if it's a good thing, then God somehow makes way for it to happen. A whole village depended on my promise to raise that money to save the rainforest. I had no idea where it was going to come from, only that it would come. And a way was provided.

My experience has taught me that we're not limited by our resources; we're limited only by our dreams. If you can dream it, you can make it happen, if it's right. In Samoa, I laid everything on the line. Spencer Kimball writes that faith is like moving down the tracks on a train at night. Beyond the reach of the headlamp, the tracks appear to stop, but if you keep going to the edge of that light, you find that the darkness retreats. I had to confront the abyss, to stare into chaos, to not know how it was going to work but to take the leap anyway. And once I had, the light moved forward and I could see the way again.

Now I take those kinds of leaps all the time, because I know that if I'm engaged in a good cause, if it is the right thing, if I'm not in it for my ego, if my motive to help other people is pure, then miracles will happen. I simply have to step up, become a piece of a much bigger picture, and let God move me around.

I did not go to Samoa to save a rainforest. I went out of despair at the death of my mother. I did not go to be made an honorary chief of the Falealupo tribe. I did not go to lose my heart to a people and place uncommon in all ways. I did not go expecting to be so irrevocably altered. But in a place where the sun sets in the sea, I found myself. I became human again.

Through Paul's efforts, not only in Samoa but in Haiti and Tonga, sixty-five thousand acres of forest have been preserved, and water facilities, schools, and clinics have been built. The plant he found in Samoa, *Homalanthus nutans,* was developed as the new drug Prostratin, part of a combination therapy to treat AIDS that will soon enter human clinical trials. In a landmark arrangement between the Samoan government and the AIDS ReSearch Alliance of America, the people of Samoa will receive 20 percent of all commercial revenues from Prostratin. The monies will benefit not only the Samoan government, but also the village of Falealupo and each of the families of the healers who helped Paul discover it. As part of the agreement, the HIV drug must also be made available to poor countries at little or no cost. Paul told the *Financial Times,* "The drug industry has had a strained relationship with poor countries. I hope this will serve as a working model."

The Goldman Environmental Foundation in San Francisco honored Paul with a Goldman Environmental Prize, considered the Nobel Prize of the environment and awarded annually to a grassroots environmentalist from each of the six inhabited continents. He has written more than 130 scientific papers and three books. Today Paul serves as King Carl XVI Gustaf Professor of Environmental Science at the Swedish Biodiversity Centre in Uppsala, Sweden, and as distinguished professor at BYU-Hawaii. He is chairman of Seacology, a foundation that preserves island cultures and habitats throughout the world, and director of the National Tropical Botanical Garden in Hawaii.

PART

# FOUR

## Living Replete

Life loves to be taken by the lapel and told, "I am with you kid. Let's go!"

*— Maya Angelou*

## Mistakes, defeats, and believing in yourself

Courage requires a willingness not only to act on faith, to trust ourselves, but also to make mistakes, to be embarrassed, to change course, and to be wrong in the pursuit of what's right. I didn't come easily to this idea. I spent the better part of my life not doing things unless I could do them perfectly, or at least well enough to make an impression or not be embarrassed. As a result, there was much I didn't do and much I missed.

On a winter night as I watched CNN's *Rise to the Top* success stories, I was struck by a segment on Taryn Rose. Doing rounds as a resident in orthopedic surgery, she recognized the price that women pay to wear fashionable shoes. She was so struck by the pain women endure that she decided to do something about it. So she started a shoe company. In her garage. It was a risky, unexpected turn of events in her medical career. Five years later, Taryn Rose International is a multimillion-dollar company.

"I reached a point," she said, "when I was more afraid of regret than of failure."

To live replete is to encounter failure. As we take risks, show up more audaciously in our lives, as we find our true voice and use it, we will goof up. It's bound to happen. And it's okay. In case I forget, I taped this Albert Einstein quote to my computer: "I haven't failed, I just found 100,000 ways that don't work." Reading that helps me to keep a healthy perspective and reminds me that the greatest risk is risking nothing at all.

Coming up short helps us to see more clearly where we're going and how we are going to get there. Missing the mark can spawn new strategies and innovative ideas, tempering our will and conviction with new energy. Talking about the defeats in her life, Maya Angelou said, "If you never had to stand up to something, to get up, to be knocked down, to get up again, life can walk over you wearing football cleats. But each time you do get up, you're bigger, taller, finer, more beautiful, more kind, more understanding, more loving. Each time you get up, you're more inclusive. More people can stand under your umbrella."

By being patient with our failures, listening closely and intently to what they teach us, ultimately we will succeed. Forgiving ourselves for what needs to be forgiven and laughing at the foibles that make us human, we emerge wiser and more confident in who we are.

Garrison Keillor advised the 2002 graduating class of Macalester College to "have interesting failures." My mind still twists around that comment. *Interesting failures.* The idea lifts the burden of failing and invites us to play, to give our all, to go for it — not cautiously but exuberantly. The notion urges us not to let the fear of error hold us back and confine us to a life less lived.

Consider where you stop yourself. Why do you do that? Are you afraid of defeat? Are you afraid of making the wrong decision? Maybe you're more afraid of success, afraid of the responsibility of it. Maybe you're afraid of standing out, being visible. Afraid of other people being jealous of you. What are the fears, small beliefs, and constricting thoughts that stop you? When we flesh out the things that keep us safely tucked in the background of our dreams, when we expose and defuse the things that put the skids on our being all that we can be, we are freer and freer to live the life we've always imagined — to live replete.

One way we keep ourselves small is by thinking we're not good enough. We're not smart enough, not gregarious enough, not witty enough, not savvy enough, not pretty enough, not educated enough, not clever enough, not romantic enough . . . endlessly not enough. When rooted in childhood, these feelings of not being enough can come from parents, teachers, authority figures, cliques we never belonged to, kids we wanted to be like, or friends who dumped us.

Somewhere inside us are dreams and desires we haven't made good on because that little gnat keeps buzzing around our heads: "You're not smart enough to do that" or "You're not clever enough; are you kidding?" or "You're not experienced enough for that!" What does your gnat have to say? What about you isn't good enough? Who told you that? What does it keep you from doing? How would you feel if you knew it was just a belief? What would you do if you knew you were enough? Who would object to that? What do you need to say or do to reassure that person or to dispel their influence over you?

Imagine what you could do if you knew, without a doubt, that you were enough. What would you do? Who would you be?

Belief in oneself makes all things possible, including an agility with our fears, insecurities, and doubts. The very things we fear or shrink from may be the things that, once done, we love.

It happened for me that way with public speaking. After writing my first courage book, it would have been easy for me to stay home — holed up with my computer, where I am eminently content — and not tour, not lecture, certainly not create a courage theater performance and put myself *in* it. *What on earth was I thinking? Hadn't I nearly fainted the last time I'd been in front of a group of people?* Before my book tour, I had nightmares for six months, at least. I was up in the middle of the night, panicked about sitting in front of a television camera, with my mouth full of cotton and eyes glazed over with fear. Mercy me.

It took two television interviews with sweaty palms for me to discover that I loved doing television. I went on to love radio. And being on stage was electrifying. If I hadn't let myself feel nervous and out of my element, I would have stayed comfortably glued to my computer. I would have missed out on the goose bumps, on the fun, on the thrill of what my work was becoming.

Imagine what you could do if you were willing to be out of your element, if you believed in yourself enough to sweat bullets. Imagine that you are enough even if you're shy and insecure. Imagine making mistakes and being fueled by what you learn. Imagine not being afraid of being afraid. Imagine yourself standing strong with a new brand of confidence. Imagine who you can be. Imagine. . . .

# Nelly Rodriguez

## *Cita con Nelly*
### *An Unexpected Voice for Her Latino Community*

Nelly Rodriguez was a woman with much on her mind in the fall of 2003: her daughter, Daniela; the grandbaby who would be born in March; her two-year-old television show; the article that had called her the "Latina Oprah"; her work as a loan officer; the stores she owns; and her corporation. She was the queen of multitasking.

As she walked me through El Grande Grocery Store and La Placita Latino, I was struck by how the stores reflect the quintessential Nelly, with her many interests and eclectic ideas. Pushing through the front door, we came first to the CD counter, with phone cards on the right and the imported groceries, like dried chili peppers, on the left. Passing the fresh meat counter at the back, we swung left through an opening made to join two commercial spaces in a minimall, and there were the cowboy boots and men's Western clothing. But wait, there was more. To the left were the women's cocktail gowns, bridal gowns, lacey wedding pillows, tops for wedding cakes, and bridesmaid and flower-girl dresses, as well as white gowns for girls coming of age at fifteen.

215

In the midst of this chaos was Nelly's desk, where she works as a loan officer for United Mortgage and handles the wiring of money as part of her NORCA Corporation. At the desk next to her was a woman she's known almost thirty years, Margarita Paredes, who manages the store. Peel through the dresses, and you may find Daniela, a realtor and notary, at yet another desk. I've missed endless details of curios and imports packed tightly in a store wanting only for space. Think of the old-fashioned five-and-dime, compressed and catering to the Latino community.

If Nelly has a mission, it's to help the Spanish-speaking people in her city learn the ropes of life in America and not simply survive there, but thrive. She herself came as a young woman from the Dominican Republic.

Like her brothers, Nelita, as she was fondly called by her family, was sent to the United States to improve her English, which she had learned at the knees of American nuns at Colegio Santo Domingo. The youngest, she was the last to leave the island. "In my country was a big revolution. Trujillo, the dictator, was assassinated, and it seemed every day, we wake up to a new person ruling the country. The United States sent in troops, afraid some radicals and Communists would take over because we're so close to Cuba."

Nelly was fresh out of high school and working in the media department of an advertising agency. "Everything closed down for a few months, and I had nothing to do. My father said, 'You're not working, you're not doing anything, just talking all day on the phone. I will send you to the States.'" For a young woman who was allowed to go nowhere without a chaperone, coming to the States from the islands was intoxicating. "It was the sixties, time of the rock and roll. I'd seen the movies, dancing in the streets, convertible cars, having fun, no chaperone. Yes, yes! I'm ready to go!"

Her brothers, all six of them, had been sent to New York, and that's where Nelly might have ended up had it not been for one of her brothers, Forrest, who busted out of the Big Apple and went West. "He wasn't learning much English because he was always with a group of Dominican Hispanic people in New York. So he looked on the map and said, Let me see the farthest place I can go." Portland, Oregon, was about as far as he could go. A friend knew someone there, and Forrest found his way to a different life and a city that Nelly would soon be calling home.

She flew to Portland on images of living the rock-and-roll life with her brother, freedom, unfurling herself... oh, yes, and taking an English class now and then. Forrest picked her up at the airport and showed her around the City of Roses. Then, still speaking in Spanish and as naturally as can be, he said, "I'm gonna drop you off."

"What do you mean, drop me off? I'm living with you."

"No, you're going to a Christian school."

"What?"

"The same one I go to, only you'll be living in a dorm."

Nelly burst into tears.

At Cascade College, one person spoke her language, the Spanish teacher. "Her Spanish wasn't that good, but she was really nice." Homesick for her native tongue, Nelly took to talking to herself in the mirror. Her brother didn't call.

A week after landing in this foreign place, she was walking down the stairs of the student union and coming up was Forrest. "*¡Hola, Forrest! ¡Que bueno que por fin te veo, estaba loca por verte y también por hablar español!*" How wonderful to finally run into you; I was dying to see you and to speak some Spanish! She was ecstatic to see him, to be with *la familia.*

He barely stopped. "What did you say? I don't understand."

*"Forrest, por favor háblame en español, solamente la profesora de español me habla en español y no lo hace muy bien."* Please Forrest, speak Spanish, no one speaks to me in Spanish but the Spanish teacher, and I can't even understand her at times.

"I have to go to my class; see you later."

Not a word in *español.* Not a word of warmth, no *la familia.*

"I cry so much."

Forrest wasn't being malicious but thought his little sister needed to be cut off, on her own, if she was ever going to make it. Tough love, you might say.

People were good to Nelly, and as time passed, she warmed to her new home. One day, she noticed a young man working in a yard. "I recognized him because he drove a little sports car and was so handsome. I couldn't believe what he was doing, because in my country only the poor people do yard work." Both surprised and impressed, when she saw the sign go up at a nearby café advertising for a waitress, she decided to go in. "On my first day, I take the order from a table, and they ask for eggs over easy. I don't say anything, but I'm thinking, eggs over *what?*"

Proud of herself for acclimating to American culture, she asked one of the other waitresses to take a picture of her in her uniform so she could send it to her family. "Ah, my father cried," she gasps. "My mother couldn't believe that I was working as a waitress. They call me right away, they'll do anything, they'll send me whatever I need; they don't want me working as a waitress."

But Nelly was getting a taste of financial independence. "I was so embarrassed the first time I got a tip, I didn't want anybody to see. I hid it in my apron." She pantomimes furtively bagging the tip and laughs. "But I caught on pretty quick and figured out who was giving the biggest tips, maybe twenty-five cents. Making my own money that I could spend however I wanted felt good."

The heart of an entrepreneur was beginning to beat.

Nelly met and married a native Oregonian, Daniel Kaptur. When stability returned to the Dominican Republic, they began to think about moving there. "It was a brand-new country with so much opportunity." They ended up in Santo Domingo and built a million-dollar business from party supplies, catering, and the motto "Be a guest at your own party."

We're in the home of her daughter, Daniela, who is pregnant with her first child and glowing. Sitting on a couch in the living room, we're like two old friends catching up on time apart, except that Nelly's breast cancer gets only brief mention, stacked between stories. "Did I tell you about that?" She waves it off and launches into yet another story. I could stop her but don't, curious about what will unspool naturally. "You'll like this one," she laughs, knowing that as a mother I'll understand the lengths to which she went to get her only daughter away from a playboy, which ironically opened yet another bold new chapter in both their lives.

The same year I graduate with my master's degree in clinical psychology in the Dominican Republic, my daughter graduates from law school. We decide to take a trip, relax a little, maybe enroll in some workshops to enrich ourselves. Because we live on an island and my sister is a travel agent, we often go to Europe and Latin America. But this time, we decide to come back to Portland. Maybe I can get Daniela to stop thinking about her boyfriend. Every other trip I've sent her on was useless. She knows he's no good for her and forgets him while she's gone, but when she comes back, same story. I'm hoping it will be different this time with her mother and her brother to distract her.

Our first weeks away, she's talking to her boyfriend the whole day, thinking about him all the time. But slowly, things start to cool down. She meets the man who will become her husband, and that's that. She's finished with the playboy.

We're in no big hurry to return to the Dominican Republic; maybe we'll stay a few months. Over the years, Portland has changed dramatically, and we have plenty of people to speak Spanish with, *afortunadamente.* We even have an Oregon Council for Hispanic Advancement. I attend one of their conferences and am especially impressed with a documentary on HIV made by Richard Schwartz.

Daniela gets a job at a credit company, and I decide to help my friend Bertha, a loan officer who is so busy that she asks me to do the loans for the Latino community. I remember that this Schwartz guy is producing a local one-hour television show called *Connexion Hispanic* at Mt. Hood Community College. I call him up. "Richard, I have an idea. Why don't you do a show to tell the Latino community that they can buy a house, show them how it can be done?"

"Good idea."

I invite the only two realtors I know who speak Spanish to come with Bertha and me, and we go over to the television studio. The show is pretty good, but the girl asking the questions is a little bit nervous and keeps repeating herself. Poor girl, she doesn't know much about the subject. Maybe because of my background in clinical psychology, I start to talk and ask questions.

At the end of the show, Richard says, "Wow, you did really good. Why don't you give me another idea?"

I start to think about what else we could do. I'm a volunteer at the Women's Crisis Line and know about domestic violence in our community, which doesn't get aired because people are *muy* scared of talking about it. Maybe I could get people talking. Richard likes the idea, and I start putting together the show, finding the right psychologists and social workers. Hoping to avoid a repeat of the nervous girl forgetting what she'd already asked, I tell Richard about a very popular show in the Dominican Republic hosted by two women; while one of them is thinking about what to ask, the other is talking to the guest. Maybe he could get a second person to host.

"Why don't you do it?"

"No, not me, I'm suggesting you could..."

"Yes."

"...find someone else..."

"You."

"...to co-host."

"Nelly."

"You're kidding."

"No."

I have a whole month to get ready, it's a subject I've studied, and I'm a volunteer at the crisis line. "Well, okay."

The day of the show, I arrive at the studio extremely well prepared with questions and information. The people I invited are all there, everybody's getting ready — except the girl who hosts the show.

"Where is she?" I ask.

"She should be here soon."

More time passes, and I ask again.

I can see that the television crew is starting to get nervous. So am I.

The clock is ticking down to showtime. "Excuse me, but where is the host?"

"Nelly, you have to go on!"

"What? Me? No!"

"You're on the air!"

⊙

Telling this story, Nelly is making such a ruckus, laughing and exclaiming, that her son-in-law's mother comes in, wondering what on earth is going on.

⊙

My legs are shaking.

We're on air, live. Unlike the other show, which was taped, we can't edit out mistakes. I'm dying over here. Even though I'm shaking, *asustada,* people don't know because I'm so well prepared. When the show finishes, everybody starts to clap. The producer comes over, the camera people, the director, all saying, "You did so good, the show was so good."

The next week, the producer calls. "I want you to take over as host of the show."

What is he thinking? "No, I did okay because I have a lot of experience on that subject and I got prepared. But..."

"You were good, period."

"...I was so nervous. I'm not a talk show host."

"You have to do it."

I'm about to make a decision that will change the course of my life. I host the show for a year, and by the time Patty Leahy, producer and director of a news show called *Noticias de la Comunidad Latina,* asks me to come onboard, I think, what the hell. In the year that follows, we win two awards as the best targeted talk show of the Northwest.

Eventually, with both Richard and Patty moving away, I feel it's time to try something on my own, and *Cita con Nelly* (An Appointment with Nelly) is born. With the help of my son-in-law, Todd Gang, we set up a local show, first at Telemundo, which at the time has limited access, and later through Univision, the most-watched Spanish channel around the state. With Todd as executive producer, our first show on Univision airs on November 23, 2002.

⊙

*Cita con Nelly* had a strong first year. "This is a big deal," says Roy Larson, president of Larson Northwest Hispanic Research and Consulting. "It's the first time there's been a local Hispanic television show on a major Spanish-language network."

Nelly likes those "firsts," especially happy whenever she instills a Hispanic presence into Portland culture. She announced the halftime entertainment at a Northwest Timberwolves football game. "For the first time, the words coming over the microphone were Spanish when I introduced the Mexican singer and the salsa dancers." Another first? "Spanish words running across city buses." *Cita con Nelly* ads splay across TriMet buses, her picture as large as life in the bus shelters as well. The state's largest public transit agency is a major sponsor of the show and ran its first Spanish television ad campaign: Watch and *disfrútelo,* enjoy!

"The show is a terrific opportunity for Portland's Spanish-language Latino community to get a look at local current events in Spanish, local Latin cultural events, public affairs, issue-oriented topics," says Michael Hanna, general sales manager for KPOU-TV Univision Portland. "It's just a wonderful program, the first of its kind in the Portland area, and that makes it truly special."

What Nelly hasn't counted on is being treated like a celebrity. "Living in the city in the Dominican Republic, it was no big deal to know someone who was on television, go to dinner with them, be friends. But it seems like a big deal here. People stop me on the street, ask for autographs, want to take pictures with me, shake my hand."

At just that moment, a little boy comes bouncing through the living room, talking to himself. He's the son of one of Nelly's employees who makes extra money by cleaning the house and doing yard work. Rather than shush him away, Nelly admires him: "He's so intelligent." She wouldn't think of not having him underfoot, whether at the house or in the store.

"We're working hard to make our next year better," she goes on. "Even though the show did well, the first year was financially difficult. I don't think people trusted us yet. Some advertisers said, Come back when you've been on the air for a year." But Nelly is tenacious, and her audience is the fastest-growing consumer group in the Pacific Northwest, which augers well for those ad dollars. In the Portland area, Latinos spend about a billion dollars a year.

Hanna calls her a "true pioneer," saying, "She's one of a kind, the first person to make a strong effort to build a Spanish-language television program with broad appeal on a major network with a good loyal audience. People respond to what she's all about, and her success reflects that."

Unflappable, Nelly has snagged interviews with actor Edward James Olmos, members of the musical group La Onda, Mexico's consul general in Oregon, Martha Ortiz de Rosas. There she is at the governor's office, a credit union, grilling the police chief. In addition to educating her viewers, she takes them to places they're unlikely or unable to go themselves. *"¡Hola, amigos!"* she welcomes them. "Welcome to *Cita con Nelly. Oye,* I am so happy!" It's pure Nelly *chispa,* charisma. Partly filmed at her daughter's home, *Cita* mixes news, health, and self-help with *Cocinando con sabor* (Cooking with flavor) and a regular segment called *Conoce tus derechos* (Know your rights) to educate viewers about their legal options.

"The majority of Hispanic people in this town don't have much education; they're from the farm, away in the mountains. They're hard workers, but they only went to school maybe five, six years at the most. We want to teach them everything about this country, the traditions, the culture, the law, the services, without letting them lose their roots. And we're trying to be role models. On local and national news, what you see are the Hispanic people who have done something wrong. What you don't see are the hundreds who are hardworking, holding down three jobs a day, serious people trying to make a decent life. These are the people I feature on my show. Some originally came here picking fruit from the farm, and now they're lawyers or have a business. . . . I want people to know that they can make it here."

I wonder aloud what has been the most challenging part of this ride. "Being a woman, being from another country, having the skin of a Latina is not easy here, and also proving to people that we can do a good show. It's not the best, I know we can do a lot better. But it's good. The struggle has been paying for some of it from our own pockets."

Nelly has had plenty of experience in standing up for herself and for what she believes in, and the more challenging a situation, the more alive she becomes. "I get energized when I have to figure out how to keep a situation from knocking me down. I like to work hard, strategize, think about how I'm going to respond. The more difficult a problem, the stronger I get."

Maybe Nelly got that drive from her mother, who taught her to fight for the rights of others so they have a chance to better their lives. Maybe she got it from her father, Angel Rodriguez, who ran a farm outside Santo Domingo and was also an entrepreneur. "He's such a humble man; he would come from the farm with his driver and give him a seat at the main table in our house, not in the kitchen. He treated everyone the same, whether they were poor, rich, black, white, and he was very loved." Nelly remembers the early years at the farm, before the family moved into the city so the children could attend better schools. In the early days, they used candles for light, horses for getting around, and a bitter herb to keep the children from getting sick. She goes there easily in her mind. "Ah," she says, "we could talk forever. Did I tell you about riding down to the river...?"

The memory unspools. I listen, images playing across my imagination. Yes, Nelly Rodriguez is a woman with much on her mind, *chispa* in her heart, and many stories to tell.

George McLaird

# From Foursquare Gospel to Mysticism
*Looking Truth Square in the Eye*

Meeting a crossroads well takes courage because we turn into the wind, set our eyes on the truth, and do not look away. What we see may be discomforting if our outer and inner lives are not aligned, if our essential principles and values, our dreams and visions are compromised. On the other hand, we may be gratified if we've been true to who we really are, if we are leading our lives with crackling authenticity.

*Authenticity* is a word much bandied about these days. I myself use it regularly in my work. At a talk I gave to corporate women, one of them asked, "What is authenticity? How do you define it?" The answer seemed obvious to me: Authenticity is being true to who you really are. "Yes, but how do you apply it in your life? I'm a mother and wife. Every day, I'm making compromises. How do I remain authentic, then?"

Her question lingers with me because clearly we bump up against compromise all the time, which bumps us up against choices. And it's deep inside those choices that we claim our authenticity, that we author our lives, that we are genuine.

229

Whether we're aware of them or not, we are constantly making choices. Some of those choices take us where we want to go. Others send us on wild-goose chases. A seemingly small choice can have huge ramifications. A seemingly huge choice may barely ripple across our lives. Some choices we try to hand over to others: *Please decide for me; I don't know what to do.* Or *I know what to do, I know what is right, but I don't like it.* Avoiding responsibility for a difficult choice, letting someone else make it for us, gives us an "out" if it turns out badly: "I would have done it differently." But using blame and hiding behind another's choice keep us small.

To live a life of deep authenticity demands that we make conscious and powerful choices, and how we go about making those choices is important. The Reverend George McLaird faced the most potent choices of his life when he realized that his fundamental beliefs were flawed. It was as though the ground beneath him shook and fell away and he was at the mercy of knowledge he had not sought or welcomed. And yet there he was, stripped bare of what he had known to be true — but really wasn't.

What now?

Sometimes our courageous choice is in the staying. Sometimes it is in the leaving.

◉

When I graduated from the San Francisco Theological Seminary in San Anselmo, California, I set out to do what I'd always known I was meant to do. Married, with a new baby, I took my first job in the ministry — as assistant pastor at a conservative church in Southern California, perfect for a Barry Goldwater/Ronald Reagan Republican.

I was right with the world.

Part of my work was to counsel congregants, and one day a young man randomly walked in to talk with me. The church was large and prominently located, so he must have ventured that someone inside could help him. Out of the blue, he showed up in my office, wanting to talk about Vietnam. We sat down together, and, eventually, he came to the part that left me cold — his orders to kill women and children. His story was so repulsive that I have no memory of what I said to him. That night at home, I told my wife, "A young man came in today with a preposterous story, and I don't know why he would make up such a thing." With that, I dismissed it.

Several months later, a church member came in for counseling and told me the same story. This time, my awareness began to crack open, and I thought, *Something's going on here that I don't know about.* And yet even though the antiwar movement was picking up, I didn't join; I still agreed with our government and supported the U.S. involvement in Vietnam.

Then one night, I attended a meeting sponsored by St. Andrew Presbyterian Church in Redondo Beach, California, where I served as youth director for the junior and senior high school kids. The speaker was an Air Force pilot who supposedly was coming to the church to drum up support for the war. As I drove to the meeting, I listened to the news on the radio. I don't remember whether it was Nixon or Kissinger, but one of them was on the air admitting that we'd been secretly bombing Cambodia. Thank goodness the pilot was coming that night; I'd find out what was really going on and what was behind these stories.

Well into his speech, the pilot said something that I'll never forget: For several years, he said, he had been a pilot in Vietnam, and he guaranteed us that no bombs were ever dropped on Cambodia. Obviously, he hadn't heard the concession. I was shocked. Yet being brand new to the ministry and not knowing the people in the church well, I didn't say anything.

As I was driving home, I made a commitment to myself: *No matter what it costs me, I'm going to find out the truth.* Up to that point, I believed that the United States was ordained by God to be the savior of the world, to bring righteousness and correction to countries with political flaws around the globe. I'd elevated the Constitution as a God-inspired document. And now I found out that my beloved country not only lied, but also was perpetrating horrible atrocities in the name of freedom.

It was the beginning of an avalanche of things that caused me to reassess and that radically changed me, not only politically. My determination to discover the truth about the Vietnam War led me to question whether there were other places in my life where I wasn't facing the truth. To do so was huge, a massive, life-changing inquiry. I looked honestly at my ministry. I looked honestly at my marriage. Both were full of lies.

I fervently, ardently, do not want to admit that my marriage isn't working.

My wife and I were both brought up in conservative Christian homes. I was raised as a fundamentalist and, as a result, saw the whole world as black or white. Now we're in areas that aren't entirely black or entirely white, and we don't know how to deal with it. We've gotten along as well as any married couple gets along for the first two, three, maybe even four years, but then real life starts happening. We have a young son. We're away from home. We're practically broke and living in Los Angeles. I'm a new pastor. And my entire worldview has been overturned in a matter of months.

In some ways it's the most exciting time of our lives. But what we aren't acknowledging is that it's also the most disturbing. On and off for seven years, we go to counseling. We try everything that's suggested to us, and nothing works. The arguments and hassles prevail. I make myself believe that these are typical marital problems and that surely they can be fixed. The idea of getting a divorce doesn't even cross my mind; it's not an option. Period.

Facing the lies in my marriage, it is inevitable that I look to my theology for the refuge of truth. But behind closed doors, I learn that many clergy have two theologies: a private theology and a public theology. What is spoken from the pulpit isn't always consistent with what a pastor believes at heart. How can that be? Doesn't that make his public theology a lie? The church, I discover, has a party line, and, up to this point, I've bought it: what to say, how to say it, and when to say it.

Struggling with my marriage and my theology at the same time is deeply difficult. In the end, I know I must leave both. Filing for divorce is the single most courageous thing I have ever had to do. Theologically and religiously, divorce is off the charts for me. I'm a pastor; I should be a good example of matrimony, and instead I'm a failure.

But I'm not just divorcing my wife; I'm divorcing the church, which has been my bedrock my entire life. Both my parents were fundamentalist Christian pastors, and I was young when that first thought of entering the ministry had touched my mind: Sitting in a little Foursquare Gospel Church in St. Peter, Minnesota, and listening to the sermon, I had decided, *When I get up there, I'm not going to talk like that.* I had heard this particular preacher often and thought, *I'm not going to bore people with the same sermon every Sunday.* Little did I know how prophetic that would prove to be.

Since childhood, I had been headed in one direction: being a pastor. All my education was geared toward that end. My entire life was based on truths from the church, and now I'm about to abandon them, 100 percent. It's overwhelming. It frightens me. I don't know where I'm going. I have no plan B. All I have is a plan A that's disintegrated.

I approach my colleague at the San Leandro Presbyterian Church to talk about my crisis. Over the months that follow, we continue to talk about things I've begun to question in the church, where I disagree with the theology, places where I find paradox rather than firm answers. Finally, I tell him I have to leave.

The church has a process for those who want to leave, and my next step is to meet with the presbytery, a committee of three or four people, to tell them that I'm going to resign — not only resign but leave the ministry. Before the meeting, I'm terribly nervous and feeling vulnerable, certain that I'll be grilled. But instead, the members of the presbytery are empathetic and gentle. No one says, "You've lost your faith, you're a backslider, you've wasted your life." I suspect they've seen many pastors who either feel inadequate for the job or are unwilling to narrowly confine their spiritual beliefs, and I'm grateful for the way they handle me.

Part of the support for clergy who are leaving is to send them to a vocational counseling center that specializes in this kind of transition. I sign up for a three-day, intense vocational investigative workshop and set about doing the assigned homework, which takes about a month. In the end, my highest vocational marks are in the ministry.

The irony is too much.

I decide to start looking for a job. Maybe I'll be a salesman. Around this time, I get a flyer in the mail from another Presbyterian pastor, who is sponsoring a day on creativity at his church in San Francisco. I sign up, thinking that to become a salesman, I'll need all the creativity I can get.

That day, for the first day in my life, I meditate.

I have a phenomenal, mystical experience. A dozen of us are lying stretched out on the floor in the chapel, it being the only quiet, undisturbed place in the church. The leader of the workshop guides us through an hour-long meditation to get us in touch with our creativity. First, we relax every bone in our bodies, working up from our feet and saying internally, "I am not my toe. I am not my foot. I am not my leg," moving up to the top of our heads. Then we say to ourselves internally, "I am not my body." Then, "I am not my breath." Then, "I am not my thoughts." *What? If I'm not my thoughts, then who am I?* I have never, ever heard of such a way of thinking. Finally, we get to "I am." Period. "I am." And through my closed eyes, I see a being who is sixty or eighty feet tall. Instantly, I am that being, looking down at my body. I bolt upright, shocked. Everyone else is still lying on their backs, calm and quiet.

For the next five years, I will try to reproduce that experience but will never be able to. I see it now as a gift, a window that opened just for a moment so I could see that the essence of life is not theology or philosophy or being especially well educated about either. It's being in touch with the "I am," or the authentic self, and living from that place more and more every day.

Meanwhile, back at my home church, the pastor gets sick, and it's up to me to give the sermons. The congregation hasn't been told that I'm leaving, and I figure I have nothing to lose by being honest. My first Sunday, I step up to the pulpit and begin, "The church has taught us A, B, C. The Bible says A, B, and C. But I have some thoughts about it all, and I'm not sure that we've struck the truth yet." For the briefest moment, in the space of an exhale, I pause, waiting for the groans. Looking out over the congregation, watching for the scowls and disapproval, I continue, certain that people will get up and leave, certain that I'll be booted out by the time I finish.

Remarkably, my telling the truth gets an astounding reception. People are hungry for a pastor to tell the truth, and that truth may be, "I'm not sure about certain things, I have questions that may not have answers, but let's explore."

It's the opening up of my theology, and I decide not to leave the ministry. I'm going to stay and tell the truth. Having already resigned from the San Leandro church, I need a home church that won't fire me when I break with tradition. Most Presbyterian churches won't tolerate someone like me getting up Sunday after Sunday and talking about the truth as I see it today. They want people who will parrot the party line and reassure folks that not much has changed over the past two thousand years. Nevertheless, I start bringing up the idea, talking with other pastors at ministerial lunches. Everyone tells me it can't be done. I'd have to start my own church. And even then, what I'm suggesting just isn't done. It's better if I simply leave the ministry.

As I begin to scour the area for a church, I become more deeply involved in meditation, which is a revolution in my theology and, at times, life altering. One of my greatest desires is to see Jesus in meditation. I try and try and try. But nothing happens. Finally, I give up. Soon afterward, He appears. He's holding a big, empty silver platter, a serving dish, and He hands it to me. Behind him is a group of folks, and I ask, "What am I to do with this?"

"I want you to feed the congregation."

"But I don't have anything to feed them."

The people behind Jesus laugh. And with that, the meditation ends. I don't understand it, so I speak with several people who might interpret it for me. Nobody gives me an answer that makes sense. I'm so frustrated trying to understand that, one day, going into meditation, I demand, *All right, I've been trying to figure out that meditation for months now, and I want the answer.* I hear in my mind's ear — which is how we hear our internal thoughts — "All you have to do is pass onto the congregation what nourishes you."

*What nourishes me?*

That week, rather than trying to figure out what I'm going to talk about on Sunday, I watch for what is nourishing. I feel no pressure about preparing a scholarly sermon and am more present than I have ever been. That Sunday, the sermon I give is more real, more immediate, and, yes, more nourishing for everyone.

I have always found it distasteful that sermons can literally be bought; a couple of outfits sell them to pastors for their weekly posits from the pulpit. You can sign up like a book club and receive them. That's the worst. It's like getting up and reading the *Reader's Digest* to your congregation. It's not even your own stuff, your own experience. A parishioner once came to me and said that she had gone to an out-of-town church for

Sunday service and, about eight months later, went to a different church and heard an identical sermon. "How is that possible?" she asked.

It's junk-food theology.

Congregations are like spiritual restaurants, and just as restaurants run the gamut from greasy spoons to elegant, the spiritual food served in a church varies greatly. Are people being fed spiritually, are they growing, and is their theology being turned into ethical living and service to others? If not, people are getting fat on junk theology. They're unhappy on the inside and haughty on the outside, feeling that God likes them best, which is a horrible conclusion to draw.

Over the next months, I receive maybe forty rejections from churches, form letters that always start with something like "You're a wonderful person with exceptional talents... blah blah blah" and then end with "You just don't fit our needs. We're sure you'll find the perfect place."

Yes. I will. I continue to have a clear vision of what I want: to be in the ministry and tell the truth so that the truth itself nourishes people. The one prayer I pray throughout my search is "Lead me. Guide me." It's from an old gospel song, "Lead Me, Guide Me along the Way." I want to end up in the right place. And I do. My vision becomes a self-fulfilling prophecy.

All those years ago, I thought my two greatest failures were getting a divorce and breaking from the church. I had lived in such a way that I'd never admitted failing at anything. And now I had to admit publicly that I had failed at two very significant things.

"George," a friend said to me, "you just joined the human race."

I had seen myself as being above divorce and above failure. Now I had to admit that I had wiped out my marriage. I had done that, not my wife. I had destroyed our marriage by not mending the cracks in our relationship and by using work as my excuse. Workaholics abandon the people we're closest to, our families. I abandoned my wife and child and never thought anything of it, because my cover-up was that I was working hard for them. But I wasn't. I was working hard as a result of my addiction.

Unexpectedly, after the divorce, I developed a closer relationship with my son, Sean, and with my mother. I had turned over a good part of the parenting to my wife, and when Sean came to live with me, there was nobody to pick up the slack. I had to do all the parenting alone, which turned out to be a blessing. The same thing happened with my mother. I had also turned over my relationship with her to my wife. We'd get together, and they'd do all the talking and I'd listen for a while and then go watch a ball game or read a book. When I got divorced, there was no one to run interference. I had to do it myself.

What has happened as a result of that determination to find out the truth about the Vietnam War is that I have very little resistance now to the truth. If something isn't working, it's easy for me to say, "Okay, we're going to fix this, or we're going to get rid of it," as opposed to thinking I have to put up with it, because the truth is that we don't have to put up. We don't have to live in a protective cocoon, hanging on desperately to faulty beliefs. We can change. We can clean up the messes in our lives and choose the truth instead. Jesus and Buddha and Gandhi, Rumi and Yogananda are magnificent professors, geniuses in my life, and they remind me that I have to live by what is true for me today. Authentic truth is always evolving, never stagnant. Unlike contrived truth, it is not harmful.

That turn in my life also put me on the path of meditation, and my mystical experience in that first meditation is what carried me through the fear and grounded me as I was going through a theological earthquake, thinking that God — as I was taught and envisioned Him to be — didn't even exist. With everything falling apart, I would remember that experience and know that it was the smallest part of me, the most insignificant, that was afraid. The greater part of me *knew* that I'd taken the right path.

To this day, meditation is part of my grounding. It nourishes and irrigates my life and is my most important and powerful spiritual discipline. Revealing in many ways, meditation opens up doors so we can discover incredibly lovely things about ourselves and develop a sense of courage to continually face the truth rather than just live in our comfortable ruts.

The way I see it, courage is a holistic moment when we do the unthinkable and act on the truth, literally not playing it safe. It's the action we take when we are the most frightened. We do exactly what our instincts tell us *not* to do. Our instincts tell us to run and hide. And courage says, "You cannot do that. You cannot live authentically if you run and hide from this moment."

I did not run. And I did not hide. And in that authenticity, I found freedom.

⊙

George was the pastor of the Sausalito Presbyterian Church in Northern California for twenty-six and a half years, and under his leadership, the

church grew and prospered. He created a seminar on marriage enrichment and wrote a book, *The Marriage Maze,* to give couples tools to use
in building healthy relationships and in negotiating those times when
they hit the skids. He retired early following a heart attack and, once
again, is in the full embrace of change. His wife, Linda, who was a flight
attendant for United Airlines longer than George was the pastor at Sausalito Presbyterian, took early retirement following United's filing of bank-
ruptcy. Together, they're negotiating their own transition to places yet
unknown and undefined but sure to be hotly authentic.

Karen Gaffney

# A Team, a Dream, and a Swim across the English Channel
*Believing in the Impossible*

What makes it possible for us to be courageous when we face something that seems insurmountable? For us to walk straight into it. For us to not give up, not back down. Even when we have good cause to turn away. Even when everyone would understand.

Ask Karen Gaffney, and she would say that, hands down, what makes it possible is family. We first met at the family home, and it was eminently clear that she had been able to meet the challenges in her life because people believed in her and refused to see her as small even though others would expect less of her. Was it significant that both her parents came from large families and, as a result of all that love and support, she had big wind in her sails?

Her mother, Barbara, grew up at the knee of a woman who juggled eleven children and made every one of them feel important while also teaching them to make the most of whatever they were handed. "In a family of that size, organization and priorities were essential," she told me. "Whatever

243

you wanted to get done had to fit into a system. If something didn't go your way, you found another way. Things happened on the way to life, and you just made a way through, you never let them stop you." This unflappable will is part of Barb's legacy to her daughter.

Another legacy passed from mother to daughter is a surety of spirit. In the spring of her sophomore year of college in Santa Clara, California, Barb decided to take the following year off and go to Alaska to work with the Jesuit Volunteer Corps. "The only problem was, they rejected me." It was not in Barb's nature to take no for an answer. Over spring break, she hitched a ride with a friend going home to Portland, Oregon, headquarters of the Jesuit Volunteer Corps. At a meeting with Father Morris, SJ, she explained that people don't always fit into a neat pattern — four years of high school, four years of college, and straight into the workplace or marriage. Life didn't always work that way. Sometimes, people needed to take a year to give back or to gain a new perspective. "I didn't need him to be a hundred percent sold, just enough to get into the program. He was reluctant, but he accepted me."

In Fairbanks, she worked at a Catholic school where Inuit, Aleut, and other indigenous children were educated. They came into town from surrounding areas and lived with parish families during the school week. Many came from challenging backgrounds. "Their point of reference was different, their existence controlled by the elements, things like whether the fish were running. They naturally learned in a different way. Some of them had what we call learning disabilities." She couldn't have known how important this experience would be. "I learned about acceptance and how kids rise to our expectations of them."

A few years later, Barb gave birth to her first child, a daughter. She had Down syndrome.

And so it was that Karen Gaffney found her way into a large extended family with big love and tenacious, unbending support. "I couldn't think of a better family to have been born into, because I'm accepted and loved and encouraged," she told me. "They know how it feels for me to be excluded, and they always try to find ways to make me feel a part of rather than separate from, like asking a teacher to explain what Down syndrome is to the other students and to talk about why it takes me longer to learn things, how I have to work a lot harder, and why I made the decision to go to a regular school."

It was in this big lagoon of love that Karen first learned that she had Down syndrome. She was in Spokane with her folks, at her grandparents' house. "I'll never forget when my parents told me. I didn't know what it meant at the time. But growing up, I sure learned. It's meant a hearing loss, joint problems, heart problems, dislocated hips and a crippled left leg that makes me limp, and other things. Now I know the effects of Down syndrome because I live with them. And I've decided not to give in to them. I got my high school diploma, my associate's science degree and teacher's aide certificate. I've done a lot in my life. I've accomplished a lot and overcome a lot. And I'll keep going."

Some of the hardest times for Karen were in high school, when she desperately wanted to be like other kids. "I really wanted to belong, but I didn't know how. People would be talking about me behind my back, thinking I didn't know what was going on, that I didn't get it. But I did, oh, yeah, I understood. That was the worst."

Why not simply choose an alternative school, a program for disabled children, someplace where Karen wouldn't feel different? Why keep banging her head against the irrefutable fact that she was at a handicap around "normal" kids? Didn't she want to give up the struggle? To lay her head down just once without thinking that she had to take on the world and prove herself worthy?

"One time, over dinner, Mom asked me how it was for me in school, did I want to give up. I was in my junior year of high school, and I said no, I really wanted to go for it. I wanted to get my diploma. I had to continue. It's the same now. I have to continue my public speaking. I have to continue working with my foundation, I have to continue being a teacher's aide. I have to continue."

This is what I'm most profoundly left with as I drive away from the brick house overlooking the thick woods around the Gaffney home. Karen Gaffney will continue. Always.

"I've worked hard to get where I am, but I wouldn't be here if my parents and teachers hadn't believed in me and given me opportunities. I'm so grateful for that. More than anything, I want other people with Down syndrome or other disabilities to have the same kinds of opportunities." And that is like a religious calling.

Karen created a foundation to support full inclusion of people with Down syndrome and other disabilities. Not only does she do the one thing that scares the pants off most of us — public speaking — but she also makes educational and inspirational videotapes, talking to people who can help break down the stigma of disability: educators, parents, physicians, and others who, with the right knowledge about how to work with someone with Down syndrome, can make all the difference in that person's life.

In one of her videos for educators, she stands poised, hands clasped lightly in front of her, as she speaks unflinchingly and yet gently to the camera: "Yes, we are different. Yes, we have special needs. But we also are filled with potential and abilities and dreams that were never thought possible, even a few years ago."

Just a few years ago, Karen Gaffney was a child trying to find her place in the world. "Looking back, I wish I hadn't been so afraid to reach out to other kids. I kept waiting for them to reach out to me. That never happened. I wanted to say, 'Get to know me. Get to know me as a person and not just a person with Down syndrome.'"

⊙

All of us want to belong. For me, the first time I experienced that feeling at school was on the swim team. The girls treated me like I was one of them, not someone who had a disease they might catch. I was part of something. When I was twenty-three, I captured that feeling again and lived a dream that was impossible — swimming the English Channel.

My dad was the one who first put me in a pool when I was a baby. He knew water would be the great equalizer for me and would strengthen my muscles: one of the effects of Down syndrome is poor muscle tone. In our pool, he would hold onto me and blow in my face. I'd squinch up my face and hold my breath, and he'd dip me in just enough for me to get used to being underwater. Once I had that down, he started letting go of me, and I'd sink all the way until my feet touched the bottom, and then I'd push off and pop back up to the top. It was a great game.

Of course, he eventually got me swimming . . . with a lot of bribes, like candy. I created my own style, like a dolphin. Swimming helped me to focus and taught me about goals early in my life. I entered my first Special Olympics when I was six.

Because my hips were dislocated, I went through five surgeries. Yeah, five. Big ones. I can tell you, that wasn't easy. The pool is where I went to recover. The water was my best friend, where I was comfortable and could move with ease and without pain.

As I was growing up, my parents always pushed the envelope for me so that I could have a full life. People would say things to my parents like "You'll be lucky if you're able to teach her how to tie her own shoes," but they didn't listen. By the way, I was the one who taught my little brother how to tie *his* shoes. I learned about perseverance and confidence and not settling for less than I could be.

In high school, I started talking with my dad about swimming the English Channel. I know what you're thinking: oh, yeah, sure. That was real doable. But we talked about it anyway. If you don't talk about a dream, how are you ever going to make it happen? Well, it didn't happen right away. It kind of came through the back door a few years later.

By the time I was twenty-three, I'd done things that people didn't expect from someone with Down syndrome. Like getting my high school diploma from a regular school, St. Mary's Academy. Like getting my associate's degree from Portland Community College and a certificate to be a teacher's aide. Those of us with Down syndrome learn differently, and sometimes it was so hard that I'd have to study and do homework seven days a week.

Because I wanted to share with people what I'd learned about having Down syndrome, I started to give public talks. I wanted to change people's perspective about what's possible for us. In one of my speeches, I talked about the importance of dreams and said that I had a dream to swim the English Channel. Our local newspaper, the *Oregonian,* wrote about that talk, and a woman named Kathryn Haslach read it.

Kathryn Haslach had attempted to swim the English Channel in 1992.


When I finish my daily swim at the Multnomah Athletic Club pool, Kathryn Haslach is standing there.

"What do you think about a relay across the English Channel?"

*What? Is she talking to me?*

That night, I tell my parents about Kathryn showing up at the pool and her idea of doing a Channel relay with people who support my dream, a Team Gaffney of sorts. My folks are kind of shocked. I think they're scared for me.

Did I mention that Kathryn didn't make it across the Channel?

She offers to show us a videotape of her solo attempt, and we schedule an evening for her to come to the house. I've never seen the Channel before, and watching that video is pretty scary, all right. Kathryn started out in calm water, but two-thirds of the way across — that's eight hours and forty-three minutes — a storm came in. Watching her struggle through eight-foot swells with waves crashing over her head wasn't encouraging. Because of the rules of a Channel swim, she wasn't wearing a wet suit and had to have people from a pilot boat give her heated liquids to maintain her body temperature. When the water got so rough that they couldn't pass liquids to her, she started to become hypothermic. They pulled her out.

*And this is what I want to do?*

Even though my parents have always encouraged me, and I've always challenged myself, this is a big envelope to push: a twenty-one-mile envelope, to be exact, from Dover, England, to Calais, France. We talk with other swimmers who have tried to make the crossing. A few things concern us: the sixty-degree water, the currents that require a lot of strength to outswim, the stamina needed, and the jellyfish that can paralyze you with one sting. Oh, and the weather can change on a dime. I guess that's why the Channel waters are called "notoriously rough."

I'm four feet ten inches tall and weigh ninety-five pounds. Can I swim even one leg of a relay in those conditions? Honestly, in the beginning, my parents think it's unwise to try.

Me, I think it's pretty big. And I'd better get busy training.

No one with Down syndrome has swum the Channel. More than a dream come true, it's a way to show people what's possible. For me, that's the most important thing, to change people's ideas about what those of us with disabilities can do if we're not excluded and to show people with disabilities what's possible if we take away the limitations around what we *think* we can and can't do. It's all about having the confidence and the drive to actually do something and then gathering around you the people who will support you. Don't let your expectations limit what you can do, that's what I always say.

Kathryn begins contacting people who might be interested in joining the team. She starts at home with her husband, Tim, who was an Oregon State High School swim champ in 1979 and swam for the U.S. Naval Academy. Yeah, that's a good place to start. Like he would say no?

Gail McCormick, who also attempted a solo when she was twenty-three, joins. The rest of the team follows — maybe their names aren't important to you, but they are to me, so here goes: Gail's brother, Marc Bowen, who was a lifeguard on the Oregon coast when he was in college; his daughter, Kelsey, who at sixteen lifeguards at a local high school pool; Sara Quan, who at twenty-eight is one of the top open-water swimmers in her age group; Tom Landis, who returned to competitive swimming at age fifty-five and placed fourth in the world in the fifteen-hundred-meter freestyle for his age group; Mike Tennant, who swam for Portland State University and is training with a masters group; Joe Tennant, who competed for Georgetown University; Laura Schob, who coached when she was younger and now trains with master swimmers; and triathlete Lindy Mount. Splitting up into two relay teams, we're a pretty interesting mix, the youngest being sixteen and the oldest being fifty-nine.

Because I've already overcome a whole lot of challenges, I've learned not to let much get in my way. The only time I really doubt myself is at Coffenbury Lake, our first outing as a team to start training. No one has seen me swim until now. Remember what I said about creating my own style of swimming, like a dolphin? Well, when I'm nervous, I have a hard time getting my head down. I'm more like in a dog-paddle position, with my head up and paddling with my hands. I can't kick with my left leg because it's crippled. My strength comes from my arms.

When the team first lays eyes on me in the water at Coffenbury, they start thinking we might not make it on account of my legs. That's the hardest moment of the entire Channel experience. It's kind of embarrassing, and I come away feeling unsure.

But like I said, I've learned to overcome. I practice. And practice. And practice. Three times a week, I do workouts in the Multnomah Athletic Club weight room. Along with my daily hour's swim at the club, I do hour-and-a-half and two-mile open-water swims in the Columbia River, no easy feat, believe me. We train in Hagg Lake, in the San Francisco Bay, and in Nehalem Bay on the Oregon coast. My teammates are carrying my dream with me, and my confidence is growing. Together, we'll make this happen.

When we finally feel ready, we contact Duncan Taylor, the secretary of the Channel Swimming Association in England, and start the administrative process — filling out forms, setting our schedule, and sticking to very strict rules for Channel swims. We'll have four days within which to attempt our crossing. The captain of a pilot boat will go with us, and his take on the weather and the tides will be the final word. When he says go, we'll go.

With my family, I go to England early to adapt to the time change and the water over there. My brother, Brian, is with us. He's two years younger than I and an alternate on the team. He and I have been swimming together all our lives, and together we make this final training push.

We start swimming in the Dover Harbor, where all the Channel swimmers train, and then, with the help of Mr. Taylor, we go out into the Channel and swim along Shakespeare's Cliff to experience rougher water. I can tell you, it's a lot easier than going in the opposite direction, toward the Channel, where the tides are so strong you're swept in an S-shaped path from England to France and you have to swim fast enough to stay with the tides or it's all over. I remember how Gail McCormick had gotten within a mile and a half of the shore of France when the tides changed. For two more hours, she swam without getting any closer to shore. She would have had to swim four more hours in place before the tide changed again and allowed her to make headway. That close, and they had to pull her out.

The days leading up to our swim are anything but encouraging. The wind blows a gale, rain pours down, waves crash against the shore, there are whitecaps everywhere. Several swimmers who are scheduled to cross are turned away.

On July 23, the day breaks on calm waters and sunny skies. A more perfect day for a Channel swim you won't see, says Mr. Taylor. At 10:06 in the morning, the first swimmer of the first team enters the water at Shakespeare's Cliff, between Folkestone and Dover, England. The second team enters at 10:12. Each of us will swim one-hour legs.

*Will we make it across? Will I have the strength?*

I'm number five in our rotation. Kathryn swims the fourth leg, just ahead of me. As my time gets closer, I start to get nervous. It's going to be hard to get into the water because of my legs. In fact, I'm more nervous about getting down the ladder on the side of the boat and into the water than about the actual swim.

At 2:00, my dad and the captain help me step out on the ladder. I'm not entirely steady. But when I get to a lower rung, just above the water, I turn a bit and jump in. Oh, yeah, that's a moment. I don't know what to expect, being in the Channel waters, and it kind of takes my breath away.

At first, I start treading with my head up and take in a huge mouthful of seawater. I struggle, coughing it up and dog-paddling. Little by little, I start to feel my rhythm and get my bearing. Kelp beds are all over the place, and I have to keep pushing them away, which is kind of creepy because I know jellyfish cling to kelp and it's the time of day when the sun's heat draws them to the surface. I try not to think about that, and, fortunately, I don't see any. I'll find out later that they're there; people on the boat see them.

My dad is hanging over the side of the boat, giving me hand signals when I need to swim faster. I know that a couple of our team members have gotten seasick, one of them from being in the water and losing sight of the horizon. I make myself focus on my rhythm. It's not just me. We're a team. And my two and a half miles are going to help us get across.

When I finish, I'm exhausted and freezing, and climbing up that ladder is harder than going down. On board, we have oatmeal, tea and coffee, blankets and jackets to keep us warm. In five hours, I'll go back in the water. My second leg is at 8:00 that night. The wind will have picked up; the water will be rougher and the air colder. The challenge will intensify.

Fourteen hours and twelve minutes after leaving England, our team touches shore at Cap Blanc Nez in France. Tim does a victory dance on the beach, and a raft is lowered from the boat to go in and pick him up. Twenty minutes later, the second team comes in, with Kelsey Bowen making the final strokes to shore. We have a scare when we lose sight of her for five minutes as she swims back toward the boat. But there she is!

We made it. Exhausted. Freezing. But wow.

We turn around and start back toward England.

The greatest thing about the Channel swim was being with people who clung to my dream with me, who had confidence in me — even if not at the beginning. As we talked about all the challenges we faced and set out to accomplish a goal together, I was not only part of the team, I was a friend. With them, I'd done something important and courageous.

⊙

The Channel swim became a fundraiser for Karen's third motivational video, *Opening the Doors of Tomorrow Today*. With help from a long list of Oregon companies; former Olympic athletes such as Don Schollander, Matt Biondi, and Donna de Varona; ex–Trail Blazer Maurice Lucas; and others, the team raised enough money to make yet another video, *Imagine the Possibilities*.

Two days a week, Karen works at her foundation, and the other three she works at Early Head Start as a teacher's aide, with kids following after her as if she were the Pied Piper. She continues to swim every day, travels nationally to lecture, and loves hanging out with her brother, Brian. Already, she's got her sights set on another Channel swim — this one with an entire team of people with Down syndrome.

Kathy Eldon

## Out of Iowa and into the Untamed World
*Journeying to the True Self and Carrying Hope*

I first picked up the phone to call Kathy Eldon at the urging of a friend who knew her well and was unequivocal about her story being in this book. I hadn't heard of Kathy, but during the course of two years she would spill over into my life, most startlingly as I watched the documentary that she and her daughter, Amy, made. *Dying to Tell the Story* is about journalists in harm's way and, most significantly, about her son, Dan, who at the age of twenty-two was stoned to death in Somalia.

Dan Eldon was the youngest Reuters photojournalist, one of the first to bring the stark images of famine in Somalia to the rest of the world. The experience inexorably changed him. Some of the worst sights, he wrote, he could not bring himself to photograph. He returned regularly to Somalia even as he found himself in increasingly dangerous situations. He was there when the United Nations bombed the suspected headquarters of General Mohamed Farrah Aidid. Dan raced to the scene. Carnage was everywhere; the streets were bloodied by the bodies of more than two hundred killed or mutilated people, including religious leaders and respected elders of the community. As he and three colleagues began shooting photographs, an enraged crowd turned on them. The horrible irony of what followed was that they were killed by the very people they were trying to help by making sure the world saw what had happened.

As I watched *Dying to Tell the Story,* I wondered how Kathy could even draw a breath after hearing about Dan's death, such a public death, brutal, thrown across the covers of magazines and front pages of newspapers worldwide. Of this Kathy Eldon was certain: Her son had lived a full life, and she would find ways to continue to give his life — as well as his death — meaning. She would saturate her work with messages from Dan's life, almost as though he were still here, almost as though his voice were coming through her. She made the documentary, traveling to Somalia, to the place where Dan had come to know the local people and been nicknamed "the Mayor of Mogadishu." She and Amy and the camera crew walked the road where Dan had been stoned. She gathered up his seventeen journals, a vibrant collage of images and writings, into a book she titled *The Journey Is the Destination: The Journals of Dan Eldon.* With Amy, she created a television series, *Global Tribe,* to unearth and bring forward stories of unsung heroes who offer hope and ways to a better future. She launched a global movement of young people who believe in the possibility of change, a change that begins with the individual. She pressed forward to produce a feature film about Dan's life.

Anyone who lives replete inspires it in others. We cannot be in the orbit of such a person without feeling drawn toward color, lots of it. Life surges through our veins: This is who I am, this is me, truly. We are aroused to show up more fully in our lives, to unfetter our passions, to be of service. Like her son, Kathy had been on a journey of self-discovery, living intensely, taking a path at times pocked with painful consequences. In a way, doing so prepared her for the moment on a summer day when she heard the unthinkable.

⊙

I was born in Iowa, where horizons are big and cornfields stretch out until tomorrow. And yet I couldn't stop dreaming of a life far beyond.

Luckily for me, my parents were firm believers in the value of travel. When I was fourteen, they took my brother and sister and me on the grand tour abroad. We galloped through fourteen countries, and when we arrived in Russia, the Gary Powers spy trial was under way. We were continually followed, and the experience was exciting and intense and unsettling all at once. In Berlin, we visited the refugee camps for East Berliners who had gotten across the wall. For the first time, I was made aware of people's inhumanity, and it was beyond anything I had experienced in Cedar Rapids, where people weren't even rude to one another. By the time I returned home, something in me had shifted. I wanted to know more about the world.

When I was sixteen, I applied to be an America Field Service exchange student. I chose the Southern Hemisphere, because that meant I would leave in January and get out of chemistry class. I imagined I would go to South America. I hadn't paid any attention to South Africa, couldn't have even found it on a map. But that's where I ended up for seven months, beginning a lifelong fascination with what I saw as an unexplored continent that tests all who travel there.

Graduating from high school back in the States, I went to Wellesley College. For a Midwestern kid to pitch up on the train with a trunk of Iowa clothes and end up with the likes of Hillary Clinton and Diane Sawyer and so many hugely intelligent people was breathtaking. I was sure that I'd gotten in on a quota. *How on earth did I end up here?* I was overwhelmed.

That summer, I returned to Iowa to work in a summer camp for girls. That very same summer, a young man named Mike Eldon left his home in London and came to the States to do an internship at Quaker Oats. Thinking that Cedar Rapids was a suburb of Chicago, he arrived quite depressed after a four-hour ride that ended at the YMCA. Fortunately, the family of a local doctor took him in.

We met on a blind date arranged by the doctor. Mike was dashing, debonair, and funny, nothing like the engineers at Collins Radio, who wore white socks and were the only available bachelors in town. He swept me away. When I returned to Wellesley, he came out to see me, and we fell more deeply in love as we walked around the lake. Over the course of the next two years, we would write yearning letters across the ocean to each other.

Graduating from Wellesley with an art history major and a teaching credential, I ended up back at home. I had gotten the best education money could buy, and I was sitting on the shelf in Iowa. I thought my life was over. Having never taken a studio art class, I somehow managed to get a job teaching art classes to grade-school kids and spent many a late night trying to figure out what I was going to do the next day. And then came my first television experience, presenting an arts-and-crafts segment on a women's lunchtime program. I loved it.

In the autumn of 1969, Mike returned to Iowa — and proposed. I was so in love with him and so desperate to get out of Iowa that, having been with him for a total of nineteen days over two years, I jumped on the SS *France* and sailed away with him to start a whole new life.

Those early days in England were idyllic. We had wonderful friends and an exciting life in downtown London at a time when everything was stimulating and vibrant. The only missing piece was my work. Unable to get a job in broadcasting, I ended up sweeping floors and working behind a counter in a dreary gift shop to help out with our desperate finances. Soon pregnant, I was hugely relieved when the principal of the American School in London hired me as a substitute teacher.

We had two children, Dan first and four years later Amy, and moved to a large house in a boring London suburb. I felt like an alien. In the morning, I pushed a pram down to the one main street and pushed it back at lunchtime. I was utterly desperate. Deep inside, I felt an impulse to communicate things that mattered — I didn't know what, I didn't know how, but I did know that I was on the wrong course.

Kathy might have felt her world closing in on her, just as her mother had thirty years earlier. Louise Knapp was trained to be a journalist and had joined the United Nations Association in Iowa. But the Depression hit, and jobs were impossible to find, the journalists all men. Still full of aspiration, she became a tireless volunteer and devoted herself to her four children, nourishing their creativity at every turn. "I was so blessed by that," Kathy told me. "My mother concentrated her efforts on me because I was the youngest. I think she was pouring into me much of what she would have liked to have done herself." She impressed on Kathy that one day she would write books. She stirred dreams in her daughter.

⊙

In the suburbs, the yearnings of my soul grow louder. I suspect that many women experience a similar feeling when they have young children and are either working way too hard or not at all, with a husband who is gone too much. Mike is a salesman at a computer company and works his tail off to support us. He commutes three hours a day, and by the time he gets home, he's spent. As for me, I fill my time with writing and home-tutoring the children, but I feel like a caged bird.

Seven years later, when Mike is given the opportunity to run International Computers Limited in Kenya, I push him to take it. That little bird of mine wants to fly. It flies all the way to Africa and starts anew. Leaving the gray streets of suburban London for the riotous, untamed color of Nairobi, I feel my life explode. The children flourish, riding their bikes everywhere, exploring, having adventures, making friends with the Masai children. They're living life firsthand, instead of through television or videos or computer games.

We're in a land of possibilities, with few constraints and larger-than-life people who, when they want to do something, simply do it. They want to start a company, build a wing on the house, have a lover, they just do it — although not without consequences. One might build the wing on the house and, without a foundation, it falls over.

In the beginning, the freedom is intoxicating. I seize every possibility and devour it. Anything to be done, I volunteer to do. Anything to be explored, I explore. The passion for life brewing inside me bubbles over in ways that ultimately become rather dangerous for me. The heat gets turned up when Mike and I are invited to go up to Kitich Camp in northern Kenya to spend time with a man named Miles and his wife.

Miles is a great white hunter, a safari guy, a gorgeous and wonderful man. I'm enthralled with him, his wife, their life. They fascinate me. Just before leaving for Kitich, we get a call that Miles, who has been working with a camera crew making a film, has been killed in a plane crash. I'm stunned, utterly.

Miles's death easily could have made me cautious, pushing me acutely against mortality: Live on the edge and tomorrow you could be dead. But instead, I'm all the more desirous of life. If I could be dead tomorrow, I want to live more fully today. I move that much faster. I pack my life with more activities. I start writing books, I write for the newspaper, I become a consultant for a company in Kenya, I jam my life with so many activities that I hardly ever see Mike, and when I do, there's less and less left between us.

The inevitability of this wild, crazy life in Africa, with everything so vivid and exciting and possible and enticing, is that I step too far over the edge. I fall in love with someone else. I'm living with a recklessness of spirit that is both my discovery and my downfall, because it's born of a lack of center, something that to this day is hard for me to articulate. Something inside me wants out, and I'm running, running, running, trying to release it.

Inescapably, I have to stand still and face the consequences and examine what matters to me. The affair isn't about a man. It's about finding myself, and that quest will take me to the depths of depression, guilt, and despair over what I've done. How did I become a person who, so desperate to find herself, would cause such hurt? Grappling to understand, I move back to London alone and share a little flat with a friend. I grieve for what I've done, for the pain I've caused. I develop an autoimmune disease that affects the spleen, which I'm sure is caused by my emotional state. Antibiotics don't help, I start to hemorrhage, and I nearly die. It is the darkest time of my life.

Starting completely over, I plunge into the belly of the beast on a spiritual journey that is agonizing. Who am I, really? My redemption is a different kind of passion — a passion to understand destiny. Why am I here, who am I meant to be, what am I meant to do in the world? I believe each of us is here with a purpose, and we find that purpose by listening to a voice deep within us that speaks the truth. When other people's voices — those of our spouse, our parents, our children, society — become too loud, we can't hear our own.

Women easily, naturally, become selfless. We're brought up that way, maybe less so today, but when I was growing up in the Midwest in the 1950s, what we strived for was selflessness. The Protestant ethic is God first, everybody else second, and you third. A counselor once said to me, "If you look at the word *selfless*, it actually means without a self." I will come to believe that service and the divine are critical in our lives, yet the core of who we are, self, is utterly important.

At the same time that I'm exploring purpose, self, and service, my son, Dan, is grappling with his own questions about himself and leaves Africa for New York, where he has a design internship at *Mademoiselle*. Now seventeen, he flirts with danger, photographing homeless kids, street people, and gang members in the rougher parts of the city. The images in his journals — which he's been creating for three years — reflect the cold, the cynical, the hard-edged, and are starkly different from the journals he's created up to now. New York has him for three months before Africa reclaims him.

As Dan is returning to Africa, I'm discovering Shakti Gawain, one of the pioneers in the field of personal growth and consciousness. I read her books, *Creative Visualization* and *Living in the Light,* and start using her techniques to formulate with purpose what I want to create. I learn about manifestation and affirmations and all the ways that we can access the power within and around us.

For Dan and me, this is a hard time because we don't get to see much of each other, and he's sad and confused and angry about what I've done. He attends one college after another, learning what he wants to learn but never alighting long enough to get a degree. I press him: "I really think you should take the math classes and get your degree." Dyslexic and afraid of math, he counters, "Mom, I want to learn for the sake of learning, not because I'm supposed to." He quotes Emerson from "The Great American Scholar": "The one thing in the world of value is the active soul. . . . This every man is entitled to; this every man contains within him, although in almost all men, obstructed and as yet unborn."

It's about the quest of the soul, not about doing the math so that you can get a degree. Dan and I are both on a quest of the soul, and for several years I struggle to know myself, seeking spiritual tools for living a life of integrity and inner truth, not simply for surviving. It's especially hard to claim myself, to listen to myself, and to believe that I can go for what I want, because what I wanted before ended so badly.

Doggedly, I grow stronger, both emotionally and spiritually. And perhaps not surprisingly, I come back around to that desire to communicate things that matter, using the power of media — of film and television. I still don't have a clue how or what, but I'm fueled by the words of W. H. Murray in his book, *The Scottish Himalayan Expedition*. He wrote about definitive commitment and how, once made, it attracts all kinds of assistance, that Providence moves in unexpected ways to support that commitment. "Whatever you can do or dream you can, begin it," wrote Goethe. "Boldness has genius, power and magic in it."

I concentrate on what I want, and quite miraculously — or is it coincidentally? — I meet a film producer who is making a movie in Africa, and I spend the next five years working with him and learning exactly what I need to know. During this time, Dan, always restless, creates a charity to help refugees fleeing Mozambique, plots and leads safaris, and goes to Russia and Japan. People wonder why he always seems to be in such a hurry, as though he's afraid to miss even a moment. He documents everything, and his journals multiply, filled with images of and questions about humanity, violence, war. In April 1992, he joins me as third assistant director on the family adventure film I'm making in Kenya, *Lost in Africa*.

And then comes Somalia. Dan and a journalist friend follow rumors of a famine in southern Somalia. What they discover there irrevocably changes my son by putting him up close to a famine more horrifying than any of us knows. His photographs of dead babies and emaciated children, of hundreds of starving men and women, bring the world shocking images that are run in newspapers and magazines everywhere. Within months, the International Red Cross determines that one-fourth of the six million Somalis are starving, and the United States begins delivering emergency food supplies. When relief workers are attacked by Somalia's warring factions, international peacekeeping forces are sent in to help.

"After my first trip to Somalia," Dan writes, "the terror of being surrounded by violence and the horrors of the famine threw me into a dark depression. Even journalists who had covered many conflicts were moved to tears. But for me, this was my first experience with war. Before Somalia, I had only seen two dead bodies in my life. I have now seen hundreds, tossed into ditches like sacks."

He continues going back and forth to Somalia, growing closer to the people even as the conflict worsens. I know that it's dangerous. I was a journalist, not a war correspondent, but I'd been in dicey situations and lived through the coup in Kenya. And I'm more and more uneasy.

In an article entitled "Photography in Danger Zones" for *Executive* magazine in Kenya, Dan writes, "The hardest situation to deal with is a frenzied mob, because they cannot be reasoned with. I try to appeal to one or two of the most sympathetic and restrained-looking people with the most effective-looking assault rifles, but I have realized that no photograph is worth my life." The article is published in November 1992.

Seven months later, Dan calls me on my birthday. I learn later that he's confessed to friends that he's tired, weary of all the violence and killing. He's in Nairobi but soon to return to Mogadishu, where eighteen Pakistani peacekeepers have recently been murdered. Worried, I ask, "Don't you think it's time you left?"

"Mom, don't ask me to do that. I can't leave, not until the story is over."

I remember how he had supported me when I left Africa. "You're so brave," he had said. "I hate what you've done, but you're incredibly brave to have done it." I had sat down with him and told him the message of Delphi — "Know thyself and to thy own self be true" — and I had encouraged him to follow his heart. Now he's asking me to support him in doing just that. I can say, "No, that's ridiculous, you mustn't." Or I can validate what he's doing and support him in doing it. "No matter what," I finally say to him, "you're leading the life of your choice, and I'm proud of you."

Seventeen days later, Dan is killed. Three colleagues are murdered with him: Hansi Krauss of the Associated Press and Anthony Macharia and Hos Maina of Reuters.

I ask myself endlessly: If I had said something different, would he perhaps not have returned to Somalia? If I had not left my husband, would he have gone to college in a more conventional manner, would he have ended up someplace other than Somalia? If I hadn't been a journalist and encouraged him to come along with me and take photographs, would he have not become a photojournalist? All these questions . . . what if, what if, what if, blaming myself for Dan's death.

"For God's sake, Kathy, that's ridiculous," Mike says to me. "Dan was living exactly the life he wanted to lead. Be proud of the fact that he was able to do something that mattered so much. He died trying to tell a tragic story the world needed to hear."

Dan's is a very public, a very noisy death. He is stoned to death in the twentieth century. The *Times of London* runs a picture of him surrounded by smiling children. A wail goes up around the world about the injustice and tragedy of these young journalists dying to tell a story.

I cannot bear it. I must give his death purpose. And so I begin a quest to do just that, and in this quest, I am guided by Dan.


I believe that spirit remains, that the active soul continues after death. We are all souls inhabiting bodies, and our purpose may not be finished when we die. Over the years, Dan has helped me to use his life as a source of inspiration for others who are trying to live purposeful lives, passionate lives, lives of choice that have meaning not only for themselves but for others, lives of service.

What matters is that we each have a purpose. We are interconnected, and we have to work with one another and with the world of spirit to achieve the greatest good for ourselves and for the earth. I've seen too many people who are too constrained by the impossibility of things, by helplessness and hopelessness. They lose themselves. Dan's gift was helping people find and believe in themselves.

Dan was on a quest to find himself, to find his purpose in life and to live it. That's what we're all here for, to live and learn and evolve and grow and to experience the joy and the pain of loving. We can't be afraid of that journey. After the breakup of my marriage, after Dan was killed, I was afraid to love because I didn't want to go through the pain of loss or death. But if we keep our hearts closed, we become constipated and sad. We've got to go forth with an open heart, and, yes, love will come and it will hurt and make us and break us, but that's okay.

When I was first leaving Africa, sad beyond measure, Dan gave me a Cat Stevens recording of the song "You're Only Dancing on This Earth for a Short Time." It reminded me of how precious life is. At the Ceremony of Life held for Dan when he was killed, I told those gathered, "I believe that Dan would have said to kids all over the world, you may only dance for a short time — his dance was very short indeed — so choose your dance, choose your music, and dance proudly. Dance with incredible spirit and vigor and creativity and life and joy, and, especially, dance with love."

⊙

Shortly after Dan's death, the work of the photographers killed in Somalia was featured in an exhibition that traveled to eight countries. *Images of Conflict* was supported by Reuters and the Associated Press. Opening nights were hosted by such luminaries as Dan Rather and Tom Brokaw and the presidents of Kenya, Cyprus, and Ireland.

*Dying to Tell the Story* was nominated for an Emmy and has been aired around the world on CNN every year. It was shown again when Danny Pearl was killed. Schools of journalism around the country incorporate it into their curriculum. Kathy and Amy also produced a film about the effects of war on children. Made for CNN, *Soldiers of Peace: A Children's Crusade* is about the children's peace movement in Colombia. UNICEF is distributing the film to show what can happen when children are given the tools of peace.

Books have also come from Kathy and her daughter. First came *Angel Catcher: A Journal of Loss and Remembrance,* to help people mourning the loss of someone they love. Their next book, *Soul Catcher: A Journal to Help You Become Who You Really Are,* embodied everything Kathy had learned in her quest to find herself, a book about being the biggest self you can be. *Love Catcher: A Journal to Invite More Love into Your Life* followed.

Throughout her journey, Kathy's guide and teacher has been Mahatma Gandhi, who encouraged people to be the change they wished to see in the world, saying, "My life is my message."

# FIVE

## Standing Up for What's Right

Our lives begin to end the day we become silent about things that matter.

—*Martin Luther King Jr.*

## Fear and the elephant in the room

I used to be a big fan of the rallying cry "Be fearless!" I thought of it as the quintessential mantra of the daring. But now I cringe when I hear it because, around courage, it's the eight-hundred-pound elephant in the room. Guaranteed, when we do something courageous, we will feel fear. And we need to be able to engage it, rather than disconnecting from what's going on inside.

"We are very rarely told to move closer, to just be there, to become familiar with fear," writes Western Buddhist nun Pema Chödrön in her book *When Things Fall Apart*. We are, she says, in a kind of perpetual flight from fear, as though we could outrun it. "The advice we usually get is to sweeten it up, smooth it over, take a pill, or distract ourselves, but by all means make it go away."

Maybe we're fearless in certain areas of our lives, and that freedom and sense of abandon are exhilarating. But when we think about doing something courageous or daring, our stomach knots. Truth is, if our stomach doesn't knot, what we're thinking about doing doesn't take courage but something else altogether.

The way I see it, fear is either instinctual or imagined. One type of fear keeps us alive. The other keeps us from really living. Instinctual fear is the primal fight-or-flight mechanism that kicks in when we react to danger or crisis. It enables a mother to act beyond her strength when her child's safety is in jeopardy. It warns us when we are in potentially life-threatening situations.

Sometimes we face this instinctual fear and refuse to back down even though our lives are threatened, the way Bill Wassmuth and Debbie Williams, whom we will meet in this chapter, refused to be cowed. We make an excruciatingly conscious choice to put ourselves in harm's way because of the bigness of what we're doing.

Other fears arise not out of instinct, but out of our dark imagination, where they fester. I call them "sucker fears." Here's why: I grew up in Minnesota, and every summer we packed into the station wagon the day school got out, headed for the north woods, and didn't return until the day before school started. We summered on Ten Mile Lake, where the water was pure, the bottom sandy, and the days long. We spent more time in the water than out. Invariably, someone got the unlucky attention of a leech. They were big and slimy and grayish, and when one attached itself to you, you felt it and a commotion followed. Parents usually pried them off, poured salt on them, and sat them in the sun. End of story. They were icky but part of the summer culture.

And then there were the suckers, another kind of leech altogether. A sucker was small and dark green and took to sucking your blood without notice until you got out of the lake and someone gasped. They could be murder to get off.

Contrived fears remind me of suckers because they can attach themselves without notice and drain the life out of us metaphorically, and they can be murder to get rid of, especially if they've burrowed into our subconscious. Sucker fears keep us from fully being who we can be, from doing what we can do. They can paralyze us with caution and warnings of dire consequences, make us doubt ourselves, color our judgment.

"Fear defeats more people than any other one thing in the world," said Ralph Waldo Emerson.

Too often we're afraid to be afraid. And yet fear can be our ally. It grabs our attention and pulls us acutely into the moment, into focus. When we don't run from it, fear can sharpen our clarity of purpose, empower our choices, fortify our will and character — essential elements of crafting a courageous life.

Working *with* our fear — rather than against it — helps us to build an abiding trust in ourselves and in our confidence to act courageously. Rather than striving to be fearless, we develop the art of being afraid and acting anyway. If you're convinced that you cannot be courageous or make a difference until you're fearless, you'll miss out on the full-bodied, out-loud living that passes by as you prepare or work on being fearless. Don't wait. Don't cheerlead your way around it. Enter fear.

Don't be afraid to be afraid, and your life will expand exponentially.

⊙

When we're willing to work with our fear, it can show us underlying emotions and beliefs, the intangibles of what's holding us back, why we're stuck, as well as the natural way out. Knowing our fears intimately, we're not defeated by them or knocked off course. "What is needed, rather than running away or controlling or suppressing or any other resistance, is understanding fear," said Krishnamurti, one of the great philosophers of the twentieth century. "That means watch it, learn about it, come directly into contact with it. We are to learn about fear, not how to escape from it."

When fear sets itself upon you, you may want to run and hide. You may instantly drop whatever you had planned to do. You may deny that you're afraid and find some perfectly plausible reason why you don't really want to do that thing after all. You may convince yourself that you're not really afraid — oh, no, it's simply that some unexpected project at work has taken priority, but you'll definitely be ready next week . . . next month . . . next year. You may pull back, buying yourself time to work on becoming fearless.

If you make it through this stage, you may plunge into your fear, eyes shut tightly and hoping for the best. Once inside, you'll probably experience confusion, doubt, or a slow numbing that takes hold of your mind and makes you wonder whatever possessed you and why on God's green earth you ended up *here*. You may freeze up entirely.

The key to getting *through* fear is to go into it with your eyes wide open, to know it intimately, to understand it, to study it. What is this fear made of? It may be the fear of making a mistake, of being wrong, of being embarrassed. It may be the fear of losing control, of being alone, of being hurt, of being visible. What is this fear's function? It may protect you, keep you safe from humiliation. It may keep you small enough that no one criticizes you. It may dismiss you from responsibility.

Where did this fear come from? Who gave it to you? Sometimes our fears are handed down from parents or mentors or family, and we take them on without examination. At other times, they are generated by the media. What is the origin of this particular fear?

What's the worst-case scenario? If your worst fears were to come true, how would you deal with that? Are you bigger than the worst-case scenario? Are you willing to accept the consequences? At times, the choice *not* to do something is scarier than the choice *to* do it. And sometimes, it's just the other way around.

How can you use the fear instead of being used *by* it? How can you work with or dismantle your fear? What can you learn from it?

Who do you have to be to move through your fear?

When you move into fear with your eyes open, you can transform it. It becomes a resource rather than a drain. As much as fear foils you, it can fuel you. Nothing catches your attention quite like it: The adrenaline pumps. The heart races. The throat catches. Fear won't be ignored. *Pay attention,* fear says. *Wake up.*

Before starting *Women of Courage,* I would do just about anything not to feel afraid or nervous. Now I periodically go in hunt of fear. *Have I done something lately that I'm afraid of, that makes me nervous? Have I been uncomfortable?* That's where I stretch myself and find more of what I can do, who I can be. That's where I pick up pieces of myself that I've set down, where I reclaim myself. That's where the adventure is, where life is vibrant, juicy, and full of meaning.

Bill Wassmuth

# A Priest, a Bomb, and the Killing of Hate
## *Taking Down Racism*

In all our conversations, Bill Wassmuth never spoke with me about his childhood, of growing up as one of nine on a farm outside Greencreek, Idaho, population thirty. At first blush, it seemed an unlikely place for the forging of his incessant drive to effect change and to fight racism. And yet traces of that drive can be found in Greencreek, on a winter's day, at the knee of his father, Henry.

Now, Henry Wassmuth was not without his faults, *rigid* and *controlling* being two of the words Bill used to describe him. But what happened at the skating rink was Henry at his best. He managed that rink and got people up in arms when he let in young black boys. Why, they were fraternizing with white girls! Actually, as Bill recalls later in his book, *Hate Is My Neighbor,* co-authored with Tom Alibrandi, "The girls had pursued the black boys, but the people of Greencreek were not satisfied to let facts stand in the way of them acting on their racism." In the face of pressure from his friends and neighbors, Henry stood his ground. For that Bill admired his father. It was his "innate sense of social justice, an instinctive knowledge of what was right and wrong" that Bill would carry, with ferocious conviction, into his adult life. "Henry Wassmuth operated under the ethic that one person could make a difference," writes Alibrandi. "He believed that if you wanted to make a change, you 'got off your butt' and got into action. Henry passed along to his children that basic sense of fairness, along with the belief that one person could effect changes in their community."

And so young Bill grew up to be "possessed by some driving, unconscious need to rock the boat" — even as a Catholic priest. Tacked to the wall of his office at St. Pius X Catholic Church was this sign:

THINGS TO DO TODAY:

1. STOP NUCLEAR WAR.

2. FLOSS.

In Coeur d'Alene, the charismatic young priest insisted that people call him by his first name rather than "Father." He was a man of the people, and the size of his parish doubled. I didn't learn that from Bill, not directly.

⊙

In 1985 I was pastor of a church in northern Idaho, Coeur d'Alene. Over a period of a year, I faced the startling realizations that I had become an alcoholic, that my lifelong service as a priest was about to end, and that I was the target of an assassination plot.

It all started when I was on my annual summer vacation in Oregon with my sister and brother-in-law and a couple of friends. A fair amount of alcohol flowed during vacations, and this particular year, my friend said to me,

"You know, Bill, when we go on these vacations, you always say, 'Rats, I'm drinking more this year than I did last year, I gotta slow down.' You say that every year, and every year it strikes me that you drink just a little bit more." From my own work with alcoholic support groups, I knew this was a bad sign. If you're drinking more and wanting to drink less, you've got a problem. And mine had been growing for ten years.

During that time, I had worked in Coeur d'Alene with an alcohol counselor, a woman named Sam, who had asked me to do the Fifth Step with her clients. A person in an alcohol treatment program does the Fifth Step when coming to grips with and seeking forgiveness for some of the things that he or she has done. It's what the Catholic Church calls confession and so is a very natural thing for a priest to do. Because she asked me, I did the Fifth Step with Sam's clients, but somewhere in the back of my mind, I must have known that I needed to be connected with an alcohol program, that sooner or later I'd need it myself.

The summer ended with my friend's sage observation, and when I returned home, I called Sam — this time for me. She met with me twice, and then she said, "Bill, you've got to fix this dilemma in your life."

*What was she talking about?*

"You want to be a priest, but you don't want to be single the rest of your life." On the surface, I was shocked. The only life I had known was that of a priest; I had been ordained at twenty-six. It was the only thing I had ever wanted to do. And yet for all the strength of my commitment and the love of my work, I knew that deep inside, if I told the truth, she was right — I did not want to be single all my life. It was a conflict that had haunted me for a long time, and for a long time, I had shoved it down where I wouldn't have to face it. Now there was no way around it. In retrospect, I see that this fundamental dilemma was tearing me up at a very deep level and I was covering it with alcohol.

Later, Sam would tell me that, from her perspective, I made the decision right then and there to leave the priesthood. But it was much too scary for me to grasp instantly. It took four months for me to come to grips with the thought, and during that time, I felt immensely alone. Although I had a close group of clergy friends, I couldn't bring myself to talk with them. I was pretty certain what their response would be, that they wouldn't really be dealing with my struggle, but with their own reactions. And that wasn't going to be helpful.

In December, I quit drinking.

In January, I decided to leave the priesthood.

Trauma set in when I started to grapple with a time line for leaving, because then the reality of my decision hit me hard. I remember very clearly, one afternoon in the back of our church, pacing back and forth for a couple of hours, just back and forth, back and forth. I can still see myself doing it, wrestling with *If I am going to do this, I need to implement a time line.* I came up with all kinds of ways to leave, but they all depended on somebody else. For example, I could talk to my bishop and say I wanted to go to school for a while, and then I could leave for school and simply see what happened. Or I could ask for a sabbatical and not come back. But these were stall moves, ways to avoid making the decision myself, to cling to the hope that somebody else would make it for me. As I paced in the back of the chapel that day, I had to face the fact that this was my decision and I had to be the one to make it.

It was the hardest decision of my life, and I have never felt more alone.

Setting up a sequence of events was the defining moment for me and the one that took the most courage. *This is when I will leave. I will spend the time between now and then putting things in order. I will tell my mother on this date, I will tell my bishop on this date, I will announce it to the parish on this date, and on this date I will leave.*

I started with my mother. While my father would have taken it very hard had he been alive, my mother's first question was "What took you so long?" I knew that my bishop wouldn't take it so easily. He had a lot of confidence in me, we had a good relationship, and I didn't want to hurt him. Knowing how hard it would be for him, I planned to tell him one year before leaving. In the meantime, I needed to focus on my work.

When I first arrived in Coeur d'Alene, I knew that I was in territory with a strong Aryan presence. I knew about Richard Butler, the head of the Aryan Nations, and I knew that dealing with his white supremacist group was going to be a challenge. I had no idea how big a challenge it would prove to be.

Aryan Nations activity in Coeur d'Alene is on the rise. Like a number of other ministers in our community, I'm deeply disturbed that they're preaching racism in the name of Christianity. Racism is bad enough, but when they use Christianity to justify it, a number of us are compelled to speak out at a press conference. Several of us also help form a group called the Kootenani County Task Force on Human Relations. Our mandate is to address the Aryan threat by challenging their message. We have some successes, including a law prohibiting malicious harassment that we lobby for and get passed in the state legislature.

My role changes when our chairman moves out of state and the task force flounders. The director of the chamber of commerce and a local real estate agent come to my office. As I recall, the meeting goes something like this: The real estate agent opens with, "We need to keep this task force alive," and then we all talk about how important it is, until the director of the chamber of commerce blurts out, "We think you ought to chair it."

"Me? I'm not qualified."

That doesn't dissuade them. "You're the one to do it."

"But why?"

"You don't have a wife or children for the Aryans to harass, and your church is made out of brick, so it won't burn easily if they attack you."

He means it as a joke, and we all laugh. "With such affirmation of my leadership skills, I should take this job." And so I do.

Shortly thereafter, we start hearing about the arrests of members of Order One, an offshoot of the Aryan Nations. They've gone on a terrorist spree around the Northwest, killing Alan Berg, the Jewish radio talk show host in Denver, robbing banks up and down the West Coast, and bombing a synagogue in Boise. Their inspiration is *The Turner Diaries,* a blueprint of terrorism to overthrow the U.S. government. Those diaries were also Timothy McVeigh's codebook.

It becomes apparent to us and everybody else that the Aryan Nations is more of a problem than we thought, that it's spinning off a more dangerous kind of violence and terrorism than we'd seen from it before. The task force steps up its activities and, over the following months, does many things to highlight human rights, culminating in a human rights rally in Coeur d'Alene held at the same time the Aryan Nations holds its annual gathering of white supremacists in the summer of 1986. We've timed it this way intentionally, to offset their message.

The press takes to the notion of the counter-rally with a great deal of interest. Normally, reporters attending city council meetings are bored to tears, but when the issue of the rally arises, they light up. For weeks before the rally, we're covered by the local press and media around the Northwest. By July, it's become an event: Eleven television cameras and a horde of reporters from across the country are there.

We've written to every city council and county commissioner throughout the five northwestern states, saying, "Please join us in this effort, because the Aryans want to make the entire five-state area into a white Aryan homeland." Two hundred cities and counties send statements of reaffirmation of their commitment to human rights. A thousand people come to the rally. It's a great celebration of human dignity.

A number of things happen as a result of that rally. For one, the media and people around the country see a very different way of responding to the Aryans. Rather than focusing on the hate that they promote, we focus on the promotion of human rights, dignity, and justice. For another, the rally gets the attention of Richard Butler, who starts preaching against the Coeur d'Alene task force and me specifically because I'm the chair and was the spokesperson during the rally. Three of his followers, part of an Order Two offshoot, begin making plans.

The FBI — who have already warned me that the Aryan Nations' new security chief has talked about "whacking" me — have the three guys under surveillance. Originally, they numbered four, but they killed one of their own because they suspected him of being an informant. Concerned about their activities, an agent targets the most vulnerable of the remaining three and at a fast-food place one day walks up to him while another undercover agent takes his picture standing right next to the guy. A few days later, he shows the guy the photo and says, "What do you think your leader will say when I show him this picture of you with an FBI agent?" The guy knows he could be the next one hanging from a tree.

So when they come to the parish house with a pipe bomb on the night of September 15, knowing that I live alone, the guy in the FBI photo has a change of heart. He plants the bomb outside the back door rather than throwing it through the window of the living room where I'm sitting, talking on the phone.

The blast is huge. It blows the garbage can and other debris onto the roof of the house across the street. It blows windows out next door. And if the kitchen stove hadn't been between the bomb and me, I would have been killed. The kitchen is sprayed with shrapnel, as if someone had stood at the back door with a machine gun and shot the whole place up. Had I not been on the phone, had I heard them and stood up and taken just two steps, I would have caught the shrapnel that ended up in the kitchen ceiling.

Law enforcement and federal and state agents swarm the area. Everyone knows right away that some arm of the Aryan Nations is responsible, and FBI agents drive straight out to where the head of an Order Two group lives to try to catch him driving back. At the parish house, police light up the backyard and start searching for evidence. The whole thing is strange, surreal, and somehow so macabre that I'm not aware of being frightened right away.

I'm not quite sure why, but I go over to the chapel. Being there alone, in the utter quiet, I start to shake. Nobody has trained me for this. I've never dealt with anything like it before. In my entire life, I've never so much as had a hand raised against me. As far as I know, nobody has ever hated me enough to want to do that. And now to have somebody hate me so much that they want to kill me, I don't know how to cope with it.

I spend a couple hours in the chapel by myself. I know it's the only time I'll have to be alone with what's happened, because, come morning, the media will be all over the place and I'll have to be a community and church leader again. By morning, it isn't going to be just me dealing with what's happened, but the whole community. And I'll need to be ready to respond as a member of that community, not as somebody who has just been bombed. I'll need to have my head on straight.

During those hours in the chapel, I pace in back just as I had done nine months earlier, facing the decision to leave the priesthood. I'm panicked and traumatized. "All right, God, I don't know what the heck this is all about, I don't know what to do, so You've got to help me." I don't hear voices from the skies, but I do gain clarity: This isn't an attack against me personally as much as it is an attack against the task force and the whole community. It isn't mine, it's ours, and we need to make sure that we turn it positively rather than negatively. It has the potential to make people so angry that it could escalate into violence from our side. I'm very popular in the community. I'm seen as a leader and, if I want to, I can make this a personal issue. People will rally to my defense and literally go hurt folks for me. I simply cannot let that happen.

When I return to the house, the police are still looking for evidence. I'm exhausted and head for my bedroom. One wall is shredded, broken glass and splintered wood cover my bed, and a shard of glass the size of a hunting knife has sliced through my pillow. Had I read just a little less of the newspaper that night, watched a little less of the news, not remembered that I needed to make a call to a friend in Seattle, I would have gone to bed earlier. . . . I yank off the bedspread, throw the pillow on the floor, and lie back on the bed in my clothes. A deep, welling loneliness engulfs me.

The next morning, the media, from *Life* magazine to the *New York Times* to national television, are there in droves. And the community is there. By eight o'clock, people are already showing up with hammers and saws, ready to start repairing the damage. The governor calls. My bishop calls. A steady stream of people comes by, flowers and food are left at my door, offers are made to put me up at hotels, to take me into people's homes.

And, all the while, I have this surreal feeling, like it isn't me somehow; it's a play, a page out of a book. And yet it is real, very real. People are looking to me and to what I do, what I say. How I respond is going to shape how the whole community responds. It's an onerous responsibility. And it isn't until I'm alone in the house trying to clean up the rubble that I get mad: This is really stupid, this thing they've done. The whole community will go through a terrible struggle because of it, and that makes me furious.

In our conversations, Bill didn't talk about the fear that plagued him for days after the bombing, and it wasn't until his book came out the following year that I understood how deep it went. Walking down the street, he'd find himself looking over his shoulder. When he came out of a building, he'd look right and left. He no longer jogged late at night, and never alone. He told no one how scared he was.

"It was not until the solidarity reception at North Idaho College that he truly stepped out of the fog and shadow of fear and shock," writes Alibrandi. More than seven hundred people came, and the sight of them, all crammed into the room, standing and applauding him, acted on Bill Wassmuth like a healing balm. He fought to hold it together. "So tired and emotional from the past week and a half, he was not sure he would be able to stop if he started crying."

The governor was there and took the stage, praising Bill. The pastor of Trinity Lutheran Church spoke about the need to transcend the urge to retaliate and called on the community to hold tightly to their principles of nonviolence. And then it was Bill's turn to speak. As he stepped up to the microphone, the audience came to their feet and started clapping. Bill tried to untangle the knot in his throat, his eyes sweeping across the rows and rows of folks he knew. But it wasn't until he locked onto a figure at the back of the room that the pressure in his throat sprang loose. Richard Butler was thirty feet from the podium, staring at Bill with the intensity and heat of hate.

Bill's heart exploded in his chest and, with it, all the pent-up fear and anger. "We will go after our goals from a different perspective now" — his voice was suddenly clear and impassioned — "knowing what it means to be vulnerable — what Jews and people of color have known all along. We feel it now, and we continue to stand alongside others who know it all the time. We say yes! to the dignity of each person and no! to racism and prejudice; yes! to nonviolence and peace, no! to violence; yes! to unity and no!, to division." Toward the end of his speech, he leveled a chilling look at Butler.

"Whoever bombed my house made a very big mistake... they reawakened our community to the task of confronting hate."

⊙

Not long after the solidarity rally, bombs go off at the federal building downtown, at a mercantile store, and in a parking lot, all within twenty-three minutes. Nobody is hurt, more by luck than by planning. The bomb is placed in the federal building so that it blows out the windows, but the people who would have been right on the other side just happen to be across the hall singing happy birthday to somebody. The second bomb is on the roof of a mercantile store right over the spot where a guy usually sits at his desk. He gets to work late that day.

After those bombings, the police have enough evidence to make arrests; the guys they pick up are the same Order Two guys who bombed the parish house. During the trial, it comes out that their plan was to set off the three bombs back to back to throw off the police so that they could rob a bank and steal weapons from the National Guard Armory. They're convicted and sent to prison.

In 1988 I finally leave the parish. It's hard, but the community and the parish rally around me, and I leave with the wind at my back.

People warn me that the transition is going to be difficult. When you leave the priesthood, you can be riddled with guilt because you've been told for so long that you simply can't do it. And you struggle with self-image. For a priest like me who went to seminary out of the eighth grade, it's the only life I've known. I went to the Benedictine Monastery for high school, two years of college, and then six years of theology. At age forty-seven, to let go of the only life, the only career I've ever known and to be in the job market with a theology degree that isn't terribly marketable and say, "Okay, world, here I am"... that's a scary thought.

When I leave Coeur d'Alene, I have ten thousand dollars saved up, a five-year-old car, and a few clothes. No furniture. No house. No property. In the priesthood, you don't build financial security. But leaving in a public way makes a big difference in how I'm able to adjust. Too often, priests simply go on sabbatical and never come back and by doing so deprive themselves of the support of the people around them. I've decided to move to Seattle, Washington, and the transition to civilian life there is unexpectedly wonderful. I get an apartment on Alki Beach and plan on doing absolutely nothing for three to six months. I'm going to use that time solely as a buffer, to deal with whatever struggles surface. I sit on the beach for three months and read books. Nothing happens, so finally I say to myself, "Okay, that's enough of that, let's move on."

My years as a priest were very good and rewarding, and the transition is easy. I'm blessed with a lot of self-confidence, and I know that I can find my way. I also have pretty modest living needs, so I can get by on very little money. If I end up flipping burgers in a hamburger stand, I'll be okay.

Instead, I end up being director of the Northwest Coalition against Malicious Harassment, which I run out of the spare bedroom in my apartment for the first year. Among other things, we monitor hate groups, identify their agendas, organize against them, and call them what they are — racists. In return, they come after us verbally and, in a couple of their newsletters, name me personally, using some pretty aggressive language.

Because they're not real fond of us, we take precautions, like listing post office boxes rather than street addresses and making it hard for people to find out where our offices are located. In some towns in the Northwest, if we're going into the community for a publicly announced meeting, we make sure that the police are there for everybody's safety. We take normal security measures and then do our jobs, because if we live in fear, they win. It's kind of like saying, *I'm going to live in my house; you're not going to scare me out of here by putting a bomb at the back door.*

I got involved in fighting the racism of white supremacists in Idaho for the same reason that I was drawn to the Coalition: I believe there's a right way and a wrong way to treat people. Social justice is at the core of my spirituality and faith. It can be a dangerous road to travel, but the difference now is that I'll never again have to pace the back of a church alone, because of Mary Frances, my wife.

⊙

Between the time that I interviewed Bill and the time this book was published, he learned that he had Lou Gehrig's disease. I spoke with him a couple of times after he'd been diagnosed, and he was indefatigable, as one would expect him to be, his spirit ever strong. I felt a sudden urgency about the book, wanting him to hold it in his hands and wanting others to know him before the disease claimed too much of him. I was too late.

*Seattle Times* reporter Florangela Davila visited Bill and wrote several pieces about him for the paper. "I'm very happy," he told her. "Very peaceful. I have led a very full life. I don't feel cheated. The only thing I regret is that I won't be there for Mary Frances."

He and Mary Frances, who is an artist, had been married thirteen years by then, and he had moved out of the limelight to sunny Ellensburg, Washington, "anticipating a gloriously mellow future," he told Florangela.

Bill never mentioned to me the awards he'd been given: the Citizen of the Year Award from Idaho's largest newspaper, the *Idaho Statesman;* the Citizen Activist Award from the Alan Gleitsman Foundation; the National Education Association Martin Luther King Jr. Memorial Award; and the American Civil Liberties Union William O. Douglas Award. As part of his ongoing focus on social justice, he chaired a state advisory committee of the U.S. Civil Rights Commission and sat on the board of the Institute for Action against Hate at Gonzaga University in Spokane.

As a tenacious leader in the fight against hate groups, Bill had the gratification of seeing the demise of Richard Butler's group, which lost control of its twenty-acre compound in 2000 as the result of a historic 6.2 million-dollar judgment against the Aryan Nations that bankrupted the group and forced it to abandon its Hayden Lake compound. Bill was there when the verdict was read. And he toured the compound after it had been purchased by a human rights organization that wanted to turn it into a peace park.

The city of Coeur d'Alene was awarded the Raoul Wallenberg Award for its relentless work to protect the human rights of its citizens. The award is given in the name of the Swedish diplomat who saved the lives of thousands of Jews by smuggling them out of Hungary during World War II. Fittingly, the mayor of Coeur d'Alene, who traveled to New York with Bill to accept the award, was a soldier in the first unit to liberate the Dachau concentration camp.

On September 3, 2002, some four hundred people attended a memorial service for Bill. On the back of the program was this, from a man who had indeed made a very big difference and left a very large footprint: "When we enlist our own humanity in combination with others, we make an indelible impression on *all* of humanity, and we uplift our world in the process. To ensure and enhance our survival, it is not only noble, but necessary, to act upon the voice within."

## Anna Smith

# Trouble in a Small Town
### *Uncovering the Truth and Speaking Out*

Courage can be intimidating, not a concept that many of us sit next to easily, much less try to embody. As I first started writing about courage, few people I interviewed owned up to it. They had friends I should talk to, mothers, aunts, sisters, daughters, grandmothers, great-grandmothers ...anybody but themselves. They were "just common folk" doing what anybody else surely would do.

One woman was oddly agitated by the letter I sent inviting her to be in *Women of Courage.* Anna Smith wasted no time calling me to set things straight. "Why did you send me this? Who are you? What do you want with me?" I reminded her that she had single-handedly fought for the cleanup of a toxic dump in her rural Pennsylvania town. Some folks didn't like her finding out about that dump in the first place. It was an embarrassment, a nuisance, something a small town could easily keep secret. People told her to hush up, sit down, leave it alone. *Don't make waves, Anna.* She was called names, laughed at, chided. But did she stop? You bet she didn't. Yet here she was, seemingly angry with me for suggesting that she was courageous. "You don't understand," she said. "I'm just a housewife in a small town." Click, she hung up on me.

*That's an interesting response.*

The next day, she called back. "Thank you for reminding me of what I'm doing," she started, and then came the tears. "It gets kinda lonely out here."

Talking with Anna gave me pause. Acknowledging our courage can pull loose a thread of deep emotion. *Is that why we avoid it?* Anna hadn't gone looking for this role as an environmental activist, but she wasn't about to turn away from it. "What else was I going to do?"

A full year and a half passed between that first letter to Anna and what came to me later through the mail. She had sat down to tell her story, which looked as though it had been typed on an old manual typewriter, the pages hand numbered and circled, and her signature in the lower right at the end. "Life is still chaotic here," she wrote in her cover letter. "My husband is scheduled for back surgery this Friday, and so, naturally, we are rather concerned. My youngest son, Sean, has just moved to Alabama to begin a new job there, and we expect that we shall be helping his wife with moving arrangements, etc., in the next two weeks." She remained grateful to me for thinking her story would be of interest to others.

Even though I had decided to write all the stories in this book from interviews and research, rather than accepting stories sent to me, I couldn't let Anna's sit on the shelf.

⊙

It was a dry, hot, windy day in Perkasie, Pennsylvania, as I stood with my two friends Mary and Shirley, and my granddaughters, Erin and Carly, in front of the town's South Junior High School.

I'd asked them to accompany me to an appointment with the state inspector. I hoped the meeting on that June day would resolve a series of events that had begun in the spring three years earlier when I walked across the wooded area behind the school with my dogs, Jethro and Daisy, and saw a dump truck parked against the back wall of the school.

Some men were on the roof shoveling old asphalt roofing down a chute and into the bed of the truck. I watched as the driver hauled away the debris in an unmarked company truck to the small wetland ravine behind the school, dumped it, and covered it with fill dirt. The dumping went on for several days.

My curiosity aroused, I decided to walk along the small tributary flowing through the rear of the school property. A bunch of stuff had been dumped back there — a duplicating machine, a crumpled metal shed, a large television, and venetian blinds, plus now-empty tar containers and old roofing, which had been tossed into the stream. Greatly disturbed by this lack of regard for the wetlands, I called the Pennsylvania Department of Environmental Resources. Not only is dumping in wetlands illegal, but the asphalt should have been recycled.

I filed a complaint with the Solid Waste Division of the Department of Resources. An inspector visited the site that summer but, of course, could see only the surface debris, which he ordered removed. The buried material remained.

This was the state of affairs three years later when a school-expansion project started. I wondered how the contractor would handle the illegal dump on the property, so after the initial earthmoving had taken place, my husband and I visited the site. All the beautiful mature trees to the rear of the school had been felled, although construction would not actually affect this area. Great care, however, had been taken to skirt the dump area, where roofing material now jutted out of the earth like a flag.

Once again, I made a call, to the Southeast Regional Office of the Department of Environmental Resources. The inspector scheduled an appointment to meet me outside the school at noon. The workers were at lunch when my friends, my granddaughters, and I walked the site with him to show him what I'd found. Suddenly, an extremely coarse individual approached and began cursing at us. He claimed we were trespassing and tried to get us off the site. I thought this person must be a laborer on the job and tried — to no avail — to ascertain his identity. He likened my face to an illegal dump and said he was going to call the police. I don't know why he was so extreme in his reaction or why he singled me out to yell at, unless he knew that I had filed other environmental complaints, for abuse or noncompliance with regulations.

We walked to the front of the school, where three police cruisers showed up awfully fast. "It's Mrs. Smith causing trouble again," said one of the officers, which apparently amused the others. The trouble he was referring to, I guess, was exposing environmental abuse, which, for the most part, I had discovered quite by accident.

The school principal came out but quickly retreated, citing pressing matters that required his attention. The crude man seemed to be taking cover behind the police. I kept asking for his name, but no one would tell me. I informed the police that I wished to file a complaint against this person for his conduct on school property, and that I would be coming by the police station to see a copy of their report. A few days later, I went to the police station and asked both the officers for their report of the complaint. It hadn't been filed yet, I was told.

Two weeks later, I learned that the offensive man was the general contractor for the school project. My husband spoke with the police chief and insisted that he charge the contractor with disorderly conduct. The chief reluctantly agreed, provided that I appear as a witness. And so I waited for a hearing date. After one continuance, it was finally set for October 30. Four of us showed up that morning, Mary, Erin, Carly, and I, to find a rather crowded district courtroom. When our turn came, the contractor's attorney asked for another continuance because of the criminal complaint filed against me by his client.

*What?*

When the district justice asked me what I had to say in response to the charges, I told him that I had no knowledge of any complaint. A short recess was called so that I could see a copy of the complaint. I had only a few minutes to read it and defend myself. I tried to digest the lengthy text while simultaneously being talked at by one of the police officers, who was bent on telling me that he couldn't act as my lawyer. Two terms in the text jumped out at me: *defiant trespass* and *harassment.* I realized that this accusation was a ploy to gain time and dissuade me from continuing with my own complaint. I decided to play out the charade.

I resumed my seat in the courtroom next to my six-year-old granddaughter, Erin. She tugged at my sleeve and handed me a tiny folded piece of paper. I opened it to find a message accompanied by a wobbly heart: "I love you, Grandma." It was all I needed to steady myself.

The district justice reconvened the hearing. I took the witness stand

and was sworn in. I was not allowed to state why I was present behind the school, or that a state official had also been present. Instead, I was directed to repeat, in full, the filthy language the contractor had used. That was that. I could step down.

Then the contractor was questioned. For some reason, he didn't have to sit in the witness stand but was allowed to testify sitting beside his attorney. Also, he wasn't sworn in but simply started talking. He accused me of having run in front of earthmoving equipment, trying to disrupt on-site activities. Now, it took no more than simple logic to know this was fabricated, since I had been at the site during lunchtime, when no one was working or operating the equipment in front of which I supposedly threw myself. He concluded his tale by referring to me, my granddaughters, and friends as "clowns."

Justice was swift. I was found not guilty of defiant trespass but guilty of harassment and fined a hundred dollars. The criminal complaint had been in my possession for approximately ten minutes. The contractor was found guilty of disorderly conduct and also fined a hundred dollars. Averse to paying a fine for something I didn't do, I found a lawyer and filed an appeal.

After I received notice of my appeal hearing at the Bucks County Courthouse in Doylestown, I contacted my lawyer to let him know the date. He couldn't remember what the charges were but didn't forget to bill me for services rendered. I ignored the bills and looked for another lawyer.

In the three years preceding this case, I had become more and more involved with environmental matters and discovered that people tend to ignore Pennsylvania's environmental rules and regulations. To get them to pay attention, I complained, but complaints often were not well received.

Thankfully, someone with the Army Corps of Engineers did listen — and did not argue — about a "dead zone" to which my two dogs had led me a year earlier. It was in a wetland only half a mile from the school and an obvious dumping ground for industrial waste. The state ended up paying 6.3 million dollars to clean it up. Among other things, it was contaminated by a radium extraction plant around 1916, leading to a poisoned municipal water supply downstream. Local authorities had known about this dumping ground and had done nothing about it, instead approving housing developments on adjacent grounds, so that youngsters ended up playing in and around a radioactive hazardous waste site — digging holes and tunnels, mounding the dirt, unearthing metal drums and barrels, and making an obstacle course for their trail bikes. I guess my taking photographs of the site and making it my business to expose it led people to think I was a troublemaker. A friend of mine lives quite close to the site; she has two young sons and is a nurse at the local hospital. We both worry for her children. We worry about the high levels of radioactivity at the site. We worry about leukemia and bone diseases and plan to petition for identification and health monitoring of children who used this place as a playground.

As a result of getting involved in these kinds of issues, I had met an attorney connected to an environmental group active in Bucks County. After I fired my other lawyer, he took over my appeal of the harassment charges, and things seemed to improve. After one continuance, the hearing was set for May 1.

The day dawned sunny and fair. My husband, Bryan, and I set out for Doylestown with Mary and Shirley. We met up with the lawyer and the state inspector, who would be my witness. The courthouse was a hive of activity, with a large group of schoolchildren in the hallways. Apparently, it was Law Day at the courthouse, and students were there to observe the workings of the judicial system.

Finally, my docket was called, and we trooped into the courtroom. Just as my hearing began, a whole crowd of children spilled in, at least sixty of them, all elementary-school age. The contractor had to take the witness stand this time and swear the oath. He hoped to impress the judge by emphasizing that he was a man of great importance and means. The judge wasn't interested in idle chitchat and instructed the contractor to get on with his story. No filthy language this time. Still seeming to enjoy himself, the contractor spiritedly concocted a tale that was only partially true. He had, in fact, called us clowns. And, as he now repeated, "I told that woman, if she wanted to see an illegal dump, to look in the mirror." The children in the courtroom gasped.

The judge asked the bailiff to bring in a copy of the legal definition of harassment. Apparently, nothing I had done even came close to meeting the definition. The charges were dismissed. The contractor stomped out of the room, his face burning.

Although I was vindicated that day, the dump is still there. Somehow, the school's consultants managed to convince the state's soil scientists — with anecdotal rather than scientific evidence — that it would be better to leave the material where it is than to remove it. No citations for dumping the roofing material were issued. The expansion project cost ten million dollars, but we couldn't spend a few more to ensure that deadly methane gas doesn't creep into the school basement, to collect there and, perhaps, one day explode.

This is not the only illegal dump by any stretch of the imagination. We have poisoned municipal wells, a plastics dump in the wetlands, and more. We have massive tire dumps, again in wetlands — always in the sensitive areas. These are the threats to our water resource.

We do not live in the city, but in beautiful Bucks County. I have lived here in Perkasie since 1972 and have watched its population almost double in that time. I fell in love with the natural beauty of the town and thought that those in authority cared the way I did. I was wrong. I found only love for money, reputation, and power. I couldn't understand, and still don't, how anyone who worked at the school could have seen what was going on and kept quiet. When I asked people why they hadn't said anything, I got responses like "Oh, so-and-so is a friend of mine, I couldn't do that," or "Gosh, that company has been here so long," or "We don't want to look bad."

I wasn't surprised to read that our superintendent thought that local residents were to blame for the dumping, not the contractor or construction company. Of course, it wasn't mentioned that the dump was covered over with fill dirt and that to accomplish that would require heavy equipment — machinery I'm sure many of our residents keep in their backyards. What an insult. Here in Perkasie, we have a wonderful recycling program, and yet supposedly we skulk about at night burying waste on school property.

As I grow older and become more involved in the difficult task of conservation, helping friends and sometimes strangers tackle the chemical pollution of streams, the potential destruction of wetlands, the failure of sewage systems, and other environmental threats, I find that the creed of the polluter is often "forgiveness is easier than permission." And anyone who dares to complain, criticize, or voice a concern is vilified.

I can't afford to be an environmental volunteer, but I can't afford not to be. What will my grandchildren do when they grow up? Will they stand by and say nothing when something is wrong? Or will they speak out and stand up for what's right? I feel I have to show the way, like my four-foot-six-inch Welsh grandmother who faced down even the biggest of men in her time. "Never back down," she would tell my mother. "If something needs to be said, say it."

And so I try to set an example for my granddaughters and hope they will remember that hot, dry day behind the school.

⊙

*If something needs to be said, say it.* If something needs to be done, do it. Courage is doing what we know we must even when we don't know how, because to not do it compromises our deeply seated principles and values. Courage is refusing to be cowed by the status quo. Anna isn't the most popular person in town. "I'm not very diplomatic," she laughs. "I'm blunt. Some town officials would probably like me to move."

When I caught up with Anna several years after that initial letter, not surprisingly, she had been busy. She was the conservation chair of the Sierra Club in Bucks County and had been named Activist of the Year in 2001. At the same time, she was the Pennsylvania chapter's hazardous waste chair and pesticide chair. "I consider them to be the same thing; I don't see any difference between hazardous waste and pesticides." She was also working part-time at the local library — which seemed just right, since Anna is a woman keen on knowledge and devoted to the power of information to produce proof and to force change.

With no legal training and a formal education that ended in a British grammar school, she has a hawk's eye for detail and is voracious for legal documents, finding truth in the darndest places. A few years back, some folks were worried about a landfill and hired a reputable environmental lawyer with money they'd raised at a roadside rug sale. He got the file on the dump, reviewed it, and came back with a thumbs-up appraisal. That landfill had been given a clean bill of health by the EPA eighteen years earlier. Everything was okeydokey. Well, Anna got ahold of that file and wrapped her tenacious mind around all that legal jargon until she discovered the most remarkable thing: The EPA had inspected the wrong site. Nobody had taken a look at the unlined landfill where thirty-two hundred tons of chemical waste had been dumped more than thirty years earlier. "The town's crawling with people from the EPA now," she told me. "They've designated it a Superfund site."

She had also been involved in an edgy borough election that, with the help of the Sierra Club, unseated four incumbents indifferent to environmental issues. She was proud of that. And then there was the case she hadn't yet spoken about publicly: a natural resource specialist at a national park who had been "dousing the woodlands with pesticides." Talk about not getting your job description. "The best thing is that it's harmful to dogs, and the Philadelphia police train in that area with their dogs . . . so maybe folks will pay attention. Sometimes, people are more interested in dogs than in people."

Anna gets involved when people are at their wit's end and call her. By now she's got enough of a reputation that folks end up at her door through referral. "I just do what I can do. I'm not a rich woman; I'm quite poor, actually. But I do what I can with what I've got and try to pass that on to other people. I'm committed to a clean, healthy environment for everybody."

When Anna takes on an issue, she doesn't always end up where she thought she would. The Superfund site came about because a woman who lived a few miles from her was concerned about a proposed development in wetlands behind her home and had gotten Anna's name from the Sierra Club. She just happened to mention that big old dump on the farm nearby and, boy, did that prick up Anna's ears.

"By the time somebody talks to me, they're scraping the bottom of the barrel, they've gone through the mill. I tell them, 'You're truly on your own in all this, but there are ways and means of achieving what you want; you just have to find them.'" She's accustomed to people rolling their eyes at her. When she finally got a state inspector to come out to what would become the Superfund site, he reported that a truckload of harmless debris needed to be carted away. It took the testing of neighborhood wells to uncover a level of arsenic that was, in one case, seven hundred times higher than the federal cancer-risk standard. "What I do doesn't always work for everybody, but there are ways to find out what works for you instead of banging your head against that same old brick wall."

In the background, Bryan says, "She's the Erin Brockovich of Perkasie." She laughs. "No, I'm the Pariah of Park Avenue. A hundred years ago, I'd be swinging from the local lamppost."

Debbie Williams

# The Prison Cover-Up
*A Nurse and Her Unbending Principles*

When we do something courageous, it doesn't always end up the way we want it to. Sometimes really crappy things happen when we stick our necks out and do something daring. Whistle-blowers know this all too well. They can be vilified; they can lose friends, lose work. Under relentless stress, their health may tank. They may watch helplessly as loved ones suffer under the weight of what they're doing.

I have never met Debbie Williams, but I spoke with her at length over several years. She had first come to my attention through the Giraffe Project, which had honored her with an award for sticking her neck out for the common good. She had also won a Cavallo Award for Moral Courage and sent me the video of the ceremony. There she was, a petite, pretty thing. To look at her, you'd never guess she'd taken on such a rough opponent as a Midwestern prison. Debbie was a nurse. She saw firsthand the medical malpractice in the prison where she worked. She witnessed the cover-up. And she blew the whistle.

Why would someone risk their safety and security, their life as they knew it, for the sake of criminals? "I simply did what was right," she told me.

I don't know what would have happened to Debbie had she not taken up this banner. I don't know how her life would have unfolded. Maybe it would have been filled with other forms of angst and misfortune. She filed a lawsuit to try to get her life back, but she never really fully recovered her work or her health or her relationship. Maybe these things would have happened anyway.

Maybe not.

⊙

*All my life, I've been fiercely proud of my country and believed in our justice system. But that's all shattered now, and I wonder if what I have done will resurrect any of my faith in our government.* These are my thoughts as I sit waiting for the courtroom to open, waiting for the jury to return, waiting for a verdict. I can still feel the cold fear that gripped me when I first realized that I had witnessed a cover-up.

I'm a registered nurse. I went into nursing because it felt important to do something worthwhile with my life. I wanted to be able to look back and know that I had given something to the world. I was very good at my job. I loved it. Being a nurse wasn't what I did for a living, it was who I was. So when I witnessed the medical mistreatment of prisoners at the correctional center where I worked, when I overheard conversations about protecting the doctors who were being negligent, I had to speak up, even though others wouldn't. I told the truth without any idea that I would be slandered and threatened as a result, that I would lose my job and end up in court bringing my own lawsuit against the prison for wrongful and retaliatory termination.

Except for a brief stint in a pediatric intensive care ward, I had always worked in emergency rooms. When my partner, Mike, and I moved from Texas to be close to his family, the town we lived in was rural and economically depressed. As a nurse, I had two choices: to work at the small community hospital or at the state correctional center. Eventually, I was hired as the healthcare supervisor at the prison, maintaining an as-needed status with the hospital so that I could pick up extra work when they needed a shift covered.

When I assumed my responsibilities, the town depended heavily on the prison for employment. On a scale of one to five — with five being maximum security — the prison was rated a four. Medically, it was rated a five, meaning it got the sickest of the inmates within the correctional system. The problems in the medical unit were severe. Everything was in disarray: There were no guidelines and no organization. The unit had a long history of insufficient participatory management. Staff morale was low. There was a tremendous lack of supplies, training, and functional equipment. I was told to go in and clean house, to get the place shipshape, to get it up and running.

I put my heart and soul into the job. I supervised nineteen positions that had a history of heavy turnover. Going in, I was told which employees to expect problems from and which to watch, but I decided that everyone would be evaluated on their work alone from that point forward.

Steadily, I started putting organizational pieces into place and procuring medical equipment and medicine. Paperwork was reduced. Morale climbed. People made more of an effort and took better care of medications and supplies, and services improved. I went in early, stayed late, worked weekends, and felt my staff becoming a team. The medical unit was turning around, and I got positive feedback and support for my efforts, including praise from the superintendent (the official name for the warden). During this time, officials at the central office continued to tell me what a great job I was doing, that I was the best healthcare supervisor they'd had, and that I would probably be promoted to the central office, which was the overseer of the four divisions within the Department of Corrections. Medical fell within the division of Classification and Treatment.

One problem remained at the prison: the two physicians who took care of around twelve hundred and fifty inmates. The central office knew about the trouble with the doctors. Starting years before I arrived, complaints had been made about medical misdiagnoses, mishandling of cases, and drinking. Multiple incidents predating my employment had been documented, and the personnel files on one doctor in particular were thick with official reprimands. I was told by my immediate supervisor, the chief of nursing services, to report any problems I saw, because when the file got big enough, his superiors would no longer be able to ignore it.

Over the radio of a custody officer assigned to the medical unit, I hear that there's a fight in progress: "We've got a stabbing."

Within minutes, a prisoner walks through the door into the emergency room covered in blood. "I'm hurt real bad. Please don't let me die." He has multiple stab wounds to his head and torso, including an open chest wound. Quickly, I get him onto a table and grab a dressing for the wound on his left side as the doctor on duty is summoned. Across from me, one of the licensed practical nurses (LPNs) tends the right wound. I can hear an audible air exchange when he breathes, which tells me he has a sucking chest wound;

this is serious because as more and more air gets into the chest cavity, it compresses the lungs and can start shifting the contents of the chest toward the heart. If enough pressure builds up, the heart is unable to keep beating.

I ask an LPN to listen for breath sounds. She looks at me and says she doesn't hear much. Another LPN listens and shakes her head. I'm holding pressure on his wound, so my hands aren't free. "Put the stethoscope in my ears!" The LPN presses the stethoscope to his upper back. Barely anything. The doctor arrives and checks the prisoner, then contradicts us by saying he can hear good breath sounds.

I don't want to excite the prisoner, and I don't want to offend the doctor, but at the same time I realize that we aren't equipped to handle his injuries. I tell the doctor that we need to send the prisoner out for emergency treatment, that he needs an X-ray, which we're not set up to take that day. The doctor wants to sew him back up first. I keep persisting — this man is critical and won't last through the process of being sewn up. I can't stand by and watch him die. I turn to an LPN: "Call the prison's control center and tell them we have an emergency outcount, we've got a sucking chest wound and need an ambulance!"

I look at the doctor. "We're sending him out." I need to get an IV and oxygen started. The prisoner is becoming agitated and complains of stomach pain. Suddenly, he sits bolt upright. "I can't breathe!" The doctor, who seems frustrated and annoyed, presses his hand against the prisoner's chest and forcefully pushes him back down into a prone position. Doesn't he understand that this man can't tolerate lying down, that he's not getting enough oxygen? If we had the right equipment, he'd be placed on a stretcher in a sitting position.

At the hospital, the initial X-ray shows that both the prisoner's lungs have been punctured and that one is filled with blood. Enough pressure had built up that the contents of his chest were already compressing his heart. If another ten to fifteen minutes had been spent debating what to do at the prison, his heart would have stopped by the time he got to the hospital. We saved his life by acting quickly, no thanks to the doctor on duty. The prisoner will make a full recovery.

My supervisor tells me to document this incident for the central office. I'm also told to continue reporting any problems and to file complaints about the other doctor if he arbitrarily cancels sick call (an inmate's request for medical attention), refuses to treat prisoners with whom he has personal problems, or comes in with alcohol on his breath. I'm incredibly concerned about all this.

At times I break down in tears out of sheer frustration over situations in which people could have died if I hadn't stepped in. The unofficial, off-the-record attitude within the institution is "They're just inmates." From my point of view as a nurse, I'm there to provide the best medical treatment possible. I'm not there to judge them; they've already been judged. I have legal and ethical responsibilities and am doing everything in my power to uphold them. Again and again, I'm promised that the situation will be remedied. The assistant director of our division tells me he wants to get rid of one of the doctors, wants to see him fired.

In midwinter on a Saturday night, an inmate serving a twenty-year sentence for possession of PCP comes to the medical unit. For more than four months, he's been coming in regularly, complaining of blurred vision, excruciating headaches, and numbness on his left side. The doctor thinks he's "malingering" and refuses to treat him unless he takes a psychological test.

Prison authorities order him to take the Minnesota Multiple Personality Inventory, but he says he can't see well enough to take the test, so they put him in isolation on medical hold to be observed and tell his lawyer that it's all in his head.

I get the call from the evening-shift supervisor that the inmate is in the medical unit again, numb on his left side. The doctor, who is required to be on call twenty-four hours a day but doesn't wear a pager, can't be found, and she's uncomfortable returning the prisoner to his housing unit. I tell her to keep calling the doctor every hour on the hour and to admit the prisoner to the infirmary, to check hourly on his blood pressure and pulse, and to do neurological checks, pupil response to light, grip strength in his hands, numbness, anything that will indicate whether he's getting worse.

The doctor isn't reached until Sunday and doesn't go in to see the prisoner until Monday, at which time he writes, "Patient has complained of left arm and left leg weakness, speech slightly slurred due to repeat episode. Patient was referred out despite no apparent neurological defect." I arrive shortly after the doctor, take one look at the prisoner, and know he needs to be sent out immediately. I have him brought up to the emergency treatment room and start an IV and oxygen. He has facial drooping on the left side, slurred speech, and decreased motor use of his left side, symptoms that a layperson would recognize as pointing to a stroke.

This prisoner is later called to testify in a lawsuit alleging inadequate medical care at the prison. He's paralyzed from the waist down and testifies while shackled in a wheelchair. The lawyer calls his treatment at the prison "unbelievably horrible" and "simply indefensible in a civilized society." During a two-year period, nine inmates died. Several of the deaths were due to poor medical care. One prisoner who had gone to the doctor with stomach pain, swollen genitals, and blood in his urine testified that the doctor "sat at his desk and told me I had kidney stones without examining me." He was given antibiotics that didn't help. Finally sent out to a hospital, he was diagnosed with an aortic aneurysm.

All this information is starting to come out in testimony because the state has applied for a two-hundred-and-fifty-bed increase at the prison, and attorneys for the inmates have filed a lawsuit to keep the expansion from occurring, citing insufficient medical care. When the lead attorney and a lawyer from the Legal Aid Society tour the prison, I'm told by my superiors that it's no big deal; they're just coming to look around, which they do, and I answer their questions and show them the medical unit.

At the conclusion of the tour, while the lawyers are reviewing medical charts, the assistant attorney general assigned to represent the Department of Corrections in this case asks to speak with me. We leave the prison so we won't be interrupted and go to lunch, where we discuss the medical unit and changes I've made. She tells me that I'll be asked to give testimony about the improvements I've made, the new equipment I've gotten, the in-service training I've run for staff, new procedures, things I've done to make the medical unit better. During our conversation, I make it clear to her that, in regard to certain questions, she might not like my answers. That's probably pretty naive and stupid on my part, but I tell her I won't lie. Her demeanor shifts subtly, and from that moment, I'm concerned that the department might have an agenda in conflict with the testimony I'm going to give.

With the help of a staff person from the correctional center, I'm assigned the task of gathering and preparing documents for the attorney general's office. The superintendent offers, then insists, that we do our work in his conference room, which connects directly to his office. He leaves the door open and periodically wanders in to see how things are going. He makes odd comments that I don't understand. At one point, he tells me that if the doctor loses, "we all lose." At another, he says, "You know, Debbie, you could testify for either side."

In spite of the shortcomings of the facility, in spite of the problems, I'm still a dedicated employee. I work hard for the prison and want to see things resolved. To this end, I write my supervisor affirming my loyalty to the department, to the correctional center, to the medical unit. But I also tell her that I feel I'm being placed in the untenable position of having to choose between my loyalty and my personal and professional ethics; I beseech her to provide me with some intervention. I don't hear back from her, but I do get a call rather quickly from the assistant attorney general, who poses a hypothetical question: If I were asked whether my problem with one of the doctors in particular was a "personality" problem, an administrative issue, or an issue that affected inmate care, what would I answer? I tell her, "An issue with inmate care." She says that's not what she wanted to hear.

Within minutes of that phone call, I receive another, informing me that a meeting has been called at the central office for 2:30 that afternoon. Relieved, I think, *Well, finally they're going to do something.* I feel secure in my job because I've recently been complimented by the director of Classification and Treatment, who told me that he'd heard I was doing a fine job up there at the prison and to keep up the good work; he also reassured me that, as far as the most worrisome doctor was concerned, he planned to get everybody together in the near future to take care of the situation.

The meeting is held in the office of the assistant division director, with the key players present. The assistant director says that we aren't there for discussion, that our medical unit has caused more problems than the other combined thirteen medical units within the Department of Corrections, and that there are to be no more complaints about the doctor regarding either his personal or professional conduct. Any future complaints made against any person will result in immediate termination of both people. It's gone too far, he said, all the way to the newspapers and federal court depositions. The federal case has been used to air personal complaints. Then he says that we're not to discuss this meeting with anyone at the institution or any other Department of Corrections employee, or to make reference to it in any deposition or trial testimony involving any federal cases. He is, he says, speaking for the division director.

The chief of medical services then says that he's reviewed the charts that the opposing counsel went through and chose to use in the upcoming case, and that he can find no evidence of incompetence or indifference on the part of the doctor. I find this a disturbing comment because the chief had come to the prison the day after the sudden death of an inmate and expressed to me his deep concern that the doctor had abandoned the patient.

To say that I'm in a state of shock and confusion at the end of this meeting is an understatement. I take notes at every meeting, and this one is no different. The pressure at work becomes intense. I'm busy trying to hire people and to fill empty positions. I'm away for training sessions. Routine, everyday matters usually handled by a phone call are now coming to me in written form. I'm being smothered in paperwork.

And then the threats begin. One morning, while the correctional officers are changing shifts, the hallway to the medical unit is full of people, the inmates lined up at the window for their morning medications. As I pass through a large group of them, I hear a voice behind me: "You'd better watch your back. An inmate will do anything for money." When I turn around, I'm looking at a sea of faces, with no way to identify the voice. Similar incidents occur that month. Every time I come into or leave the institution, my briefcase is searched.

Another meeting is held in the central office, this one in the office of the division director and, once again, with all the major players attending. But this time, it's the assistant attorney general who has called the meeting. She explains what each of us should be prepared to testify about, and, as usual, I take notes. At this point, I really get scared. She says that the lead attorney has filed a motion to obtain one doctor's personnel file and that she has filed objections. Everyone in the room knows about the reprimands in that file, that the problems are documented there in black and white.

During the meeting, other comments made about this doctor disturb me — for example, that he normally comes to work early. I myself get to work early, and I have never seen him in the medical unit at the times he claimed to be there. Someone expresses concern about how to deal with a disciplinary action taken when the doctor arrived at the institution under the influence of alcohol. This predated my employment but was no less disturbing. The chief of nursing services says she never witnessed a correctional physician with alcohol on his breath. The division director says no one ever came into the institution in an impaired condition. And the chief of medical services says that this doctor takes responsibility for himself to be on call above and beyond what's expected of him . . . and besides, everyone has one beer after work.

The most chilling thing I hear, however, is said quietly as the meeting is coming to a close. People are talking among themselves when I overhear the division director say to the assistant attorney general that if the doctor's personnel file is subpoenaed, they'll remove the last two letters of reprimand, especially the most recent one. At the formal close of the meeting, he says, "We are all in agreement about what we will say. We'll win this case. All these little write-ups, they're just family matters. No need for them to go to court. Just things you deal with within the family. Like your kids, when you spank them, you don't tell the neighbors. These family letters are not relevant. We will all support each other in court, there will be no shooting at each other."

I have just witnessed a potential conspiracy to withhold evidence in a federal court case. And I've taken notes during the entire meeting. As I weave my way through the screened-off offices to the front door of the central office, I expect that at any moment someone will put a hand on my shoulder and demand my notes. By the time I reach my car, I'm shaking. I drive as far as the parking lot of the grocery store around the corner before pulling over to calm down.

I'm scheduled to be deposed on June 4 and know that the repercussions from telling the truth will probably be severe. The first part of my deposition is taken under subpoena that afternoon and evening, with the assistant attorney general present. The lead attorney and the Legal Aid lawyer are there on behalf of the inmates as plaintiffs. I answer all the questions as honestly and as matter-of-factly as I can. The lead attorney will become one of my greatest allies and later tells me, "I knew you had something to say. I knew you were trying to tell me something. I just had to find the right questions to ask to get to the truth."

He does find the right questions, and I answer them truthfully. Before long, the assistant attorney general asks for a break, and all parties agree. When we're in the women's restroom, she confronts me: "What are you doing?" She's quite agitated. I tell her that I've sworn under oath to tell the truth, the whole truth, and nothing but the truth, not the truth as the Department of Corrections wishes me to tell it.

Shortly after returning to the conference room, she terminates the deposition because of the late hour, with the intention that it will continue the following day. After the lawyers leave, she takes me back into her office and explains that she has a conflict of interest as a result of my testimony, which is adverse to the interests of the defendants, and she can no longer represent me at the deposition. But, she informs me, the attorney general's office will appoint alternate counsel from within or retain outside counsel at their expense to represent me. From that point on, I'm never provided with legal representation.

Several days later, the deposition continues and lasts thirteen grueling hours. The legal counsel for the Department of Corrections makes every attempt to inflame me, accuse me, and question my competency and credibility. Calmly and clearly, I answer their questions. One thing about telling the truth, you never have to remember what you've said because your story doesn't change. The events that preceded the deposition were so intense, were so indelibly etched in my mind that I can repeat conversations that took place without referring to my notes.

The worst is yet to come.

Unbeknownst to me, on June 9 a letter of termination is written, typed, and signed by the division director but not sent, because the Department of Corrections and their legal counsel decide it won't look good to fire me so soon after my testimony. Naively, I still think that everything will blow over once the testimony is complete, although I might never get the promotion to the central office.

The enormous pressure and strain I've been under have taken a toll, though, and I apply for vacation time. I need time to regroup, to get my second wind. Oddly, I'm suddenly inundated at home with certified letters from the central office, all of which need to be responded to, since it's important for me to follow policy and procedure to the letter so that nothing can be used against me. The task of responding to them is arduous and overwhelming.

Around this time the anonymous phone calls start. First hang-ups, then heavy breathing, then the one-liners: "You're not going to make it." And "I'm going to get you." Frightening things begin happening around our house. Glass is broken in the driveway. Dead animals are left on the porch. We have prowlers. Windows are shot out. It is a terrifying time.

And the vilification begins. I'm still doing as-needed shifts at the community hospital, and before one of my shifts, I'm informed that the director of nurses has decided it's best if I not work there until "this thing with the prison has blown over." After numerous attempts to reach her by phone, I finally get her and am told that I'll have to provide a physician's letter certifying that I'm capable and stable enough to perform my duties in the emergency room. The Department of Corrections has started their witch hunt, saying that I'm incompetent. Even though I provide a letter, I never again am allowed to work at the community hospital.

I receive a lot of verbal support from workers at the hospital who say things like "I really admire what you did," "It's about time somebody did something about things out there," and "I really wish I could help, but I've got a family to take care of." Everyone has to do what they feel is best for them, best for their family. But I sure get tired of being admired.

Although I receive a partial paycheck from the prison, all the funds for accumulated vacation time and compensatory time owed me are withheld for four months. Now Mike and I are under financial pressure, which will be alleviated only when I return from time off and resume my duties as healthcare supervisor at the correctional facility on Tuesday, September 29. On Friday, September 25, I receive a letter postmarked September 25 and delivered September 25, informing me that, as of 5:00 P.M. on that date, I've been terminated.

Jobs are hard to find in the small town where we live. I send out more than a hundred résumés over the months that follow and receive several job offers, but always at the last minute, I'm informed that someone more qualified has been hired. At times I go on interviews only to have someone say to me, "I didn't really want to offer you a job, but I read about you in the newspaper" or "I saw you on television and just wanted to meet you."

Finally, I retain legal counsel with the intent of filing a suit against the department concerning my discharge. A few months later, I'm informed that the lawyer handling my case has left the office for health reasons and that the firm can no longer continue to represent me. I call dozens upon dozens of other attorneys. Many have heard of the case. I get benign refusals like "It's not my area of expertise" or "My caseload is full" or "Why don't you call so-and-so?" I call so-and-so, and he refers me to someone else. One lawyer actually charges me ninety dollars to tell me that she won't take my case without ten thousand dollars cash up-front.

Unable to pay bills, with ends increasingly harder to meet, and suffering through one of the area's coldest winters, Mike and I put our house on the market. I start selling off personal items and apply for jobs from Kansas to Kentucky, Missouri to Arkansas. Obviously, my credibility and competency have been so maligned that we'll have to move.

In February I fly to Maryland, where my family lives. A week's worth of interviews brings an offer from a hospital emergency room in Maryland.

Just short weeks before relocating, I finally secure legal representation. The case is taken on contingency, and I'm able to leave with the knowledge that at least I have representation. A lawsuit is filed on my behalf against the division director, the assistant director of our division, and the chief of nursing services, alleging a violation of my right to free speech under the U.S. Constitution, that the defendants retaliated against me for testifying in a lawsuit against the Department of Corrections, and that I have been wrongfully and illegally discharged as a result of exercising my right to free speech.

During a Midwest blizzard nearly a year later, I drive back for the trial.

Final arguments are on a Wednesday afternoon. The jury doesn't come back at the end of the day but continues deliberating, arriving early Thursday morning. Out of a jury of seven, one is on the fence. At lunchtime, the judge asks the attorneys if they're willing to accept a verdict of the six who are in agreement. Because we don't know whether they're for or against me, we debate over lunch and I tell my attorneys that I'm confident they've put on the best possible case. I got up and told the truth, and the jurors would see that. I was willing.

I return to the courtroom and wait outside for it to open. *Will any of this matter, will what I have done truly resurrect my faith in our government?*

I wonder as we wait. Thoughts of my father, who died years ago, fill my mind. He was career navy, retired as a lieutenant commander. He gave me a lot of advice as I was growing up, like take care of your teeth, buy good shoes, and get an education. But what I took to heart was the way he lived his life: he believed in doing the right thing, living by the Golden Rule, believing in yourself and your ability to be a part of the American Dream. He gave me the greatest gift any parent can give their child. In this moment, I miss him.

Abruptly, the court clerk comes out and announces that the jury has returned. We have a verdict.

We return to the courtroom, and I sit with my lawyers as the jury's findings are read: "By jury verdict...on plaintiff Debra Williams's claim against defendant...the jury finds in favor of Debra Williams." I barely hear the rest. A great weight slides off my back as the verdicts against two of the plaintiffs are read separately. The juror who was on the fence found in my favor, making it a unanimous judgment against the division director and the assistant director of the division. No judgment is found against the chief of nursing services.

After the courtroom clears, my attorneys pat me on the shoulder. "Debbie, you won! You won!" All I know is that I've been vindicated. I didn't even hear the amount of the award. "A hundred thousand dollars in damages," says my lawyer.

I go back to the motel. It takes three hours to absorb what has happened, and then I start making phone calls to let people know that it's over, it's really over. Justice has finally been served. My reputation — my credibility and competency — has been cleared. I've been vindicated in a court of law, it's a matter of public record. It's over.

I never considered myself a banner carrier. I never considered myself someone who took up causes. But with this, I couldn't give up. The lead attorney in the prison case told me that I was the most tenacious person he had ever met, that I had made a dent. But we all have that inner strength. We just test it in different ways. My test came, and I reached down deep inside, I reached up to my higher power, and I prevailed. Like anyone can.

⊙

In addition to the Cavallo Award for Moral Courage and the Giraffe Project Award, Debbie was honored with the Emergency Nurses Association's Ethics Award. In addition, one of the attorneys on the lawsuit for the prisoners told me, "There is no doubt that Debra Williams's courage and professional integrity — both in documenting medical care problems as they occurred and in providing truthful testimony in depositions — was key to the successful outcome of the federal court case, which resulted in major changes to the way health care was delivered at that prison."

"Some people called me a hero," Debbie told me, "but I flinched when they said that, because I'm not a hero. I simply did what any person would do. I simply did what was right." Nevertheless, the awards and recognition were restorative on many levels. "One of my greatest losses," she said, "the thing that hurt me most was that, for nearly a year, the thing I loved, the thing that makes me who I am — nursing — was taken from me."

PART

# SIX

Keys to a Daring Life

## Making courage real

It is not so much what people do in this world as their reasons for doing it which really makes a difference.

— *Eleanor Roosevelt*

Even as we admire the courage of people in this book or others in our lives, it's important to remember that the term *courageous people* is an oxymoron. Sometimes we're courageous. Sometimes we're not. We all have shadow sides. We all are imperfect. I've learned things about people I interviewed that I don't especially like. I've been warned to pull stories from books.

Must we be beyond reproach in our daring? Does an act of ferocious courage become null if one later does something unworthy? I want to believe that we all do the best with what we've got in the moment, but even that may not be true. We don't always do the best. Sometimes we take the easy way; we settle or get apathetic, lazy. We feel afraid and protect ourselves.

We are complex beings, and it follows that our courage is also complex. It ebbs and flows within us. It is not a constant, not always a straight line. But it lives in all of us, and all of us can access it. All of us can have our *courageous moments* and build on those moments so that they happen more frequently.

As the French philosopher Jean-Paul Sartre describes, "A crowd of small metamorphoses accumulate in me . . . and then, one fine day, a veritable revolution takes place."

## Owning Up

Several years ago, when Joan Borysenko and I settled in to talk about courage, one of the first things she said was, "This is difficult for me because I don't consider myself a particularly courageous person. It's hard to look through the threads of my life and decide what on earth we'll talk about. It sounds so terribly . . . wimpy, narcissistic, and self-centered." This from a woman whose life has been scribed time and again by daring leaps, from prestigious Harvard medical scientist and psychologist to pioneer in the field of mind-body research and to author of a whole slew of books, including *Fire in the Soul, Inner Peace for Busy People,* and *Minding the Body, Mending the Mind.*

Speaking with Joan, I wondered, *Why do so many people not see themselves as courageous?* You may squirm at the mere suggestion. It may not seem right, although you can't articulate why. I felt this way when a woman introducing me to a group I was about to address called me "courageous." My face flushed. I wanted to lunge forward and grab the microphone out of her hand. "Oh, no, no, that's wrong, *I'm* not courageous. I write *about* courageous people." The more she spoke, the hotter around the collar I got. I felt like an imposter. *I'm just a writer . . . why is she saying that?*

Our culture reserves courage for remarkably special people, and those we call heroes are elevated in a way that can make daring seem beyond the reach of us common folk. Aware of our weaknesses and flaws, do we feel unworthy?

Or do we avoid courage because of the responsibility, the demands it will make of us? Do we fear that it will possess us, rattle us, and ultimately separate us from others? Are we afraid that courage will plunge us into roiling emotions and forever change us? If we step up, if we make our voices heard, if we are visible, if we become more of who we really are, will we lose the love of those around us?

## Going Places We Never Thought We Could Go

Making waves in our lives, challenging the status quo, is risky business. Courage takes us beyond the edge where we're comfortable, where we know what to expect. It takes us places we've never been, where things are messy, not so predictable. Sometimes, it's pure raw instinct or intuition that pushes us forward. Sometimes, an issue — political, environmental, spiritual, or cultural — has been rumbling around inside us and suddenly demands that we not sit still any longer, that we stand up, speak out, do something. It may be something at work that we've been reluctant to tackle, even though it's the right thing to do. It may be a community issue that we know we can do something about, or a health issue that challenges us or someone we love. Courage may be a dream, an adventure, a thrill that calls us, and rather than turning away, we say yes!

But there's more. Every time we deepen the intimacy in our marriage or primary relationship, we must dare to open ourselves and be vulnerable. With courage, we break addictions — behavioral or chemical. We face uncomfortable truths and constricting beliefs and dismantle them, making way for change. Whatever the circumstance of our courage, with heart pounding and breath catching, we push off the comfortable, the familiar, the known. That moment can be frightening. It can be exhilarating. It can take our breath away.

Our courage is not only loud and dramatic. It may come in a fragile, vulnerable, quiet moment. It may be a deep look into our souls, a stillness with our divinity. It may be found in the exhalation of love. In the speaking of truth. In forgiving and in making peace. Our courage can be found in our hope, our dignity, our call to freedom. Our courage is being true to who we are at the bone, not bending to what others think we should be or do. It's refusing to live a life that does not reflect who we really are, our unique strengths, talents, and gifts... honoring those, bringing them fully to the table.

## Our Courage Muscle

Courage is like a muscle. The more you use it, the stronger it gets. The stronger it gets, the more you can rely on it. The idea of being courageous may feel huge to you because you link it metaphorically to climbing Mount Everest. That's how I saw it in the beginning. Intimidated by the bigness of courage, I didn't see the practical ways in which I could develop it, that I could encourage it to grow in me.

Think of it this way: If you're out of shape physically and you go to the gym, you don't start working out with hundred-pound weights. You start with pound-and-a-halfers. Gradually, you build muscle. When you're stronger, you move to the two-pound weights, then three, then five, and on you go, building a foundation for a strong body.

As you strengthen your courage muscle, it's important to honor your own rhythm of growth, your own cadence. Do not be distracted by how you think you *should* do this work, how your best friend would go about it, how your father or mother or aunt or uncle would have you do it. Instead, be in the allure of yourself and the person you are becoming. Pay attention to *how* you're growing and changing and becoming more daring, more authentic.

*Courage is a journey, not an end result.*

Taking small steps on that journey — ordinary, everyday ways in which you witness yourself changing — can be exhilarating. Let's say that, on any given day at work, you hang out with your co-workers around the water cooler, listening to them talk, periodically nodding whether you agree with what's being said or not. Maybe you walk away thinking, "I can't believe he said that" or "What a stupid idea" or "Boy, would I ever do that differently." But on this day, working your pound-and-a-half courage weights, you speak up: "You know, I don't agree with what you're saying. Here's what I think..."

Simply speaking your mind may be hard. It is for many people. It certainly was for me. I was a real people pleaser. Daring to say what I thought and what I felt — to my husband, to friends, to colleagues — was difficult. What if they thought I was stupid? What if they got angry? What if they didn't like me?

*Beyond heroism, courage infuses the everyday with meaning and possibility.*

Suppose I were to ask you, "Are you courageous?" Does the question make you laugh? Does it make you smile nervously? Does it carve a pit in your stomach? Does it make you feel cynical, angry, embarrassed? Do you feel like a phony? Would it feel arrogant to say such a thing about yourself?

Perhaps you take risks all the time at work or in your public life, but you break into a cold sweat at the thought of saying to your friend, "I want us to be more real with each other. I want to let down my guard with you, so you can know more of who I really am." Maybe you dare to be real in your relationships but can't find your voice at work and always downplay your insights, your strengths, your contributions. Where in your life would you most like to start building courage and being more real?

As you strengthen your courage muscle, take time to assimilate the changes in yourself. Pause and let yourself catch up to the bigger you whom you're becoming. Let it settle. You're growing into a larger skin, and if you don't take the time to stretch that skin, you may snap back into the old you.

Periodically work with your image. How do you see yourself? If you were writing a descriptive narrative about yourself, how would it read? How would you distill that narrative down to a paragraph that captures who you are? What's the one sentence that captures you? The one word? Then think about who you want to be as you stretch and become more, as you live a life that matters more and more, and find the word that captures that essence. It may well be the opposite of the word you've just distilled. Begin to flesh out that word, giving it breath in a sentence and adding sinew in a paragraph and finally imagining a full-bodied narrative about who you're becoming, who you want to be.

Consciously keep that new image as a focus. Before you get out of bed in the morning, spend time inside that new image. Fill your body, your heart, and your mind with it. Feel it taking up all the space left vacant by the old image. Inhale it into every cell of your being. Imagine yourself stepping into it, like a new skin, as you get out of bed, and live in that skin throughout the day. In the evening as you drift off to sleep, take a moment to sink into that new image and let it occupy you through the night, dreaming on it. By taking time to assimilate, to appreciate your progress, to alter your image of yourself, you'll ensure that the changes you're making aren't lost but, rather, settle into you at a deep level. You'll be giving yourself the strong message that you're putting down your Little Story and picking up your Big Story. Your Little Story is riddled with patterns of behavior and beliefs that keep you small. Your Big Story is who you really are, what your life is really all about, why you're here. It's your life purpose.

As you grow into your Big Story, keep in mind that this work is fluid, always new, changing you and demanding that you be fully present, responding uniquely to the moment. When you peel away preconceptions and expectations, as you forgive yourself for the times you've settled instead of stretched, when you step away from self-judgment, you'll find the freedom to redefine yourself, not as perfect but as good enough to be courageous.

Self-growth is tender; it's holy ground. There's no greater investment.

—*Stephen Covey*

From the people I've talked with over the past ten years, I've gleaned some essential elements that constitute a daring life. Using these can help us to steadily build a stronger and stronger foundation of courage in our lives.

## The Cornerstones of Courage

What I call the Cornerstones of Courage don't fit neatly into a sensible, four-cornered structure. As much as I've tried to reconfigure them, to make them more reasonable and thus more accessible to the logical mind, they'll have nothing of it. I've come to see the perfection of this, to appreciate that it's fitting for the Cornerstones of Courage *not* to sensibly fit the norm. Comprising a seven-sided structure instead, the Cornerstones of Courage are:

*Clarity*

*Choice*

*Confidence*

*Character*

*Conviction*

*Compassion*

*Connection*

No matter what courageous things you want to do or be — whether at work or at home, or anyplace in between — working with these Cornerstones will strengthen and steady you. Start with Clarity, sussing out what you want to accomplish and why, finding your luminous intent. Keep asking yourself why, so that you really understand what's motivating you. "Why do I want to do this?" Whatever answer you get, ask again, "And why do I want that? What does it get me?" Your first answers will be the most apparent, but the more you dig, the closer you'll get to the essence of why, and that essence is the bigger picture, the grander purpose that will sustain you as you go forward. If your Conviction softens at any point, this Bigger Why is what you'll want to remember to keep yourself going. When you get to the Bigger Why, you'll feel it in your gut: it will go *ka-chink*.

With Clarity in hand, make an empowered Choice, recognizing consequences, aware of what you'll accept and what you won't, recognizing that even compromise, when authored by you, is a Choice, *your* Choice. Then step into a new kind of Confidence, willing to act even if you're insecure or unsure or shy. Assess where your Character needs bolstering — are you aligned with your principles and values? are you paying attention to your intuitions, instincts, gut feelings? — and then fire your Conviction, steep it in Compassion, and Connect with a force greater than you. After you have built this firm foundation, then, with humility and presence, do the thing you know to be right.

Periodically, do a mental scan to see if you are out of balance, needing more Compassion or more Clarity, for example. If so, take the time to focus on those particular Cornerstones.

## When the Inner Critic Gets Loose

As you set out to live a daring life, a life that matters, you will rile up your inner critic — guaranteed. There is a part of you — your Dark Shadow, your Negative Ego, your Rapacious Inner Critic, call it what you will — that does not want the best for you. Being aware of that, you can run interference.

As I began this book, my inner critics had a field day. *Big mistake,* they warned. Unlike the other books, this one would include more of my own thoughts and insights. It took an inordinate amount of time to get under way. *You can't write a book this way,* they scolded. *Tell stories, be happy, who cares what* you *think?* I procrastinated. Maybe they were right. I got distracted with other "priorities." *You should write a cookbook! Or how about a rewrite of that last screenplay?* I wrote and rewrote without becoming any clearer about the structure of the book. *Didn't we tell you? You're good with other people's stories, honey, but the narrative has got to go . . . and the personal stuff, well, you know where that leads, people will excoriate you!* The day I sat down to write and ended up logging random corrections in my database, I couldn't pretend any longer. *But wait! You have more address changes to make!*

Straight up, I was nervous. Writing the first books, I had endeavored to capture authentically the voices of others. This time, I wanted my voice, what I had learned to be in the book as well.

*And just what was my voice?*

I had spent almost ten years getting outside my voice; I had "disappeared" myself, moved myself aside to allow others' voices to come through with authenticity. Now it was time to retrieve my voice and come out from behind other people's stories, a challenge of some proportion. Getting free of my critics was critical. They were tenacious. *All right, if you must, but take out the personal stuff!*

You may have a whole party of critics, as SARK did. When we sat down to talk about courage for the second courage book, she said, "Suddenly, the room fills with all my inner critics. They crowd around me: 'You're such a coward that when you couldn't figure out how to use the rowing machine at the gym, you didn't have the guts to ask for help. Your butt was going back and forth but your arms weren't going anywhere, and you were convinced the woman behind you was laughing at you . . . so you pretended to be done, got up, and walked away.' Then another elbows in to remind me that I'm an even bigger chicken when it comes to the dentist: 'You're so afraid that he had to send you a letter saying he wouldn't work on you if you didn't get the treatment done . . . and you burst into tears and vowed never to go to that dentist again.' And then there's the perfectionist. And the angry mother. And the kids, about eight of them. They get all excited. They want to be involved. 'Let me play, let me play.'"

Instead of a raucous group, your critic may take the form of one unrelenting tyrant. A woman on my iVillage.com courage board told me, "I hate feeling like I have to justify and defend almost everything I say or think. It's like I have some sort of Grand Inquisitor writing secret judgments to which I'm not privy." You may have a Grand Inquisitor who metes out all kinds of

START NOW | 339

opinions and verdicts and, even as you're reading this, demands that you attend to more important things like washing the car or cleaning the toilet or weeding the garden or checking your email.

Whatever your inner critics say, escort them out of the room. If they're reluctant to go, talk to them. Conjure them up in your mind's eye. See them one by one having at it with you; listen to their judgments and criticisms. Let them rant until they have nothing left to say. Then imagine yourself herding them all into a soundproof room called "The Critic's Room." Shut the door and lock it. They're sure to get out at times, but you're in charge and can handle them.

## Starting with What Matters

With your inner critics at bay, take a look at what matters to you and where you want to be more courageous. Give yourself time to daydream about this, to be quiet with it, to ponder. What really matters to you down at the bone — at home, at work, in friendships, with causes or volunteer work, spiritually, financially, with politics or education or adventure? How do you want to be courageous? Take this inquiry on a walk in the park, on a drive in the country. Run with it. Walk with it. Swim with it. Take it into a moving meditation or into a still prayer, in the deep silence inside you. Let thoughts and images swirl. Don't censor them. Let them flow, paying attention, being mindful, fully in the moment. Some thoughts may surprise you.

In a journal or on your computer, record what you discover. Include your thoughts and feelings about what comes to you. If your critics get loose, on a separate page, write down what they're saying:

"Oh, sure, like you'll ever really *do* that."

"Silly, silly."

"You'll never have the guts to do *that.*"

"Ha! What a pipedream!"

"Oh, boy, is that ever going to make people mad."

Keep those one-liners handy to remind you that they came from your critics' lips. You'll get good at anticipating what they're going to say, so you can have a laugh, move on, and not get stuck.

Your courage comes from the heart and stirs your soul. What really matters to you is sacred. Start your day by taking time with it.

What is my next step in being courageous?

What will get in the way? What am I avoiding?

How do I want to handle that?

Who do I have to be to live this courage?

## The Keys to Daring

The Keys to Daring, which I've listed on pages 342–343, can show you where you need to focus when you're about to do something specifically daring or when you want to be generally more courageous in your life. You can use them in a few different ways.

The first way is simply to sit with this book open on your lap, close your eyes gently, ask for help in seeing where you need to focus, and then let your fingers run lightly across the pages until you intuitively stop. Read that Key and let it be your focus, let it speak to you. Or instead you may want to write the Keys on small pieces of paper, fold each two times, and put all of them in a beautiful box or bowl near a door you routinely pass. As you leave the house first thing in the morning, let your fingers lightly ruffle the papers, pondering what your focus should be that day or that week, or what will help you handle a challenging situation, or what will give you insight into a risk you're taking, or whatever way you want guidance. Then pick out one of the papers and let that Key speak to you.

Some of the Keys may take you aback. "Have fun," for example. What does that have to do with living a daring and courageous life? At times, we need levity, to hold things lightly, in order to clear our perspective and renew our energy. We need the healing medicine of laughter to sustain us.

Using the Cornerstones of Courage and the Keys to Daring, with your inner critics at bay, with inspiration culled from the women and men you've met here and perhaps thoughts stirred by lessons I learned on this journey, you can set out on a grand adventure. You can begin an expedition of a truer life, a life replete with courage, infused with authenticity and love, a life tender and holy, a life that astounds, a life uncommon in its impact, engaged in what matters, leaving a trail where there is no path and making all the difference.

*Make your own choices, lots of them, even if they're wrong; don't let anyone make them for you.*

*Be responsible, 150 percent.*

*Do what's right.*

*Live with soul.*

*Speak up.*

*Have interesting failures.*

*Face the truth about your weaknesses and about your strengths.*

*Be willing to make mistakes.*

*Be willing to change course.*

*Challenge yourself.*

*Be a little messy.*

*Be imperfect.*

*Listen to the whispers, the intuitive clues.*

*Don't be afraid to be afraid.*

*Believe in yourself.*

*Champion yourself as you would a friend.*

*Know you are enough.*

*Trust yourself.*

*Be tenacious and willful but know when to let go or bend.*

*Listen beyond the words.*

*Change the beliefs that hold you back.*

*Listen to your intuitions, even if they seem irrational and illogical.*

*Stand by your principles, even when no one is looking.*

*Do not live smaller than who you truly are.*

*Be content but not complacent.*

*Speak from your heart.*

*Make time for those you love, including yourself.*

*Nourish your spirit in whatever way is right and meaningful to you.*
*Champion your dreams as though they were your children.*
*Think outside the box.*
*Have a vision, and don't worry if you don't completely understand it.*
*Be passionate about your life.*
*Be curious.*
*Be real.*
*Honor your emotional intelligence.*
*Nourish hope.*
*Work hard; be restless.*
*Know when to break the rules.*
*Be unique.*
*Be willing to be surprised.*
*Have a sense of humor about yourself.*
*Live with purpose.*
*Have fun.*
*Honor freedom with responsibility.*
*Be true to who you are at the bone.*
*Be compassionate — with yourself especially, and with others.*
*Allow for change.*
*Be flexible and fluid.*
*Give of yourself.*
*Be always on your way, present in your journey.*
*Let your limitations be illusions.*
*Feed your integrity.*
*Spend time daydreaming and imagining the future.*
*Assume nothing.*
*Beware of wanting to want.*
*Cherish and live your core values.*
*Do the unexpected.*
*Challenge the status quo.*

# Epilogue
*The legacy of our courage*

Our courage is a legacy we give. Not only does it enrich our lives, but it also shows the way to, gives permission to, and affects those we love, our family and friends, our colleagues, acquaintances in our community. Through six degrees of separation, the courageous step we take today, however small or large, may inspire someone halfway around the world. Don't hold back. Give that gift.

# Resources and Links

If we all did the things we are capable of doing, we would literally astound ourselves.

— *Thomas Edison*

## People and Organizations

So that you can get involved with the people in this book and their organizations or foundations or groups relevant to the issues in their stories, this directory provides contact information. From the first story to the last, here are addresses, phone numbers, email addresses, and websites. To reach me at People Who Dare, LLC, email katherine.martin@peoplewhodare.com or visit the website www.peoplewhodare.com.

### Part One. Pushing the Envelope

Nichelle Nichols

Website: www.uhura.com


NASA

Website: www.nasa.gov/home/index.html

## Hugh Herr

The Media Laboratory focuses on how electronic information overlaps with the everyday physical world. The Laboratory pioneered collaboration between academia and industry and provides a unique environment in which to explore basic research and applications without regard to traditional divisions among disciplines.

Email: hherr@media.mit.edu
Media Laboratory
Building E15, Room 419
77 Massachusetts Ave.
Cambridge, MA 02139-4307
617.258.6574

## Shannon Meehan

Refugees International generates lifesaving humanitarian assistance and protection for displaced people around the world and works to end the conditions that create displacement. The year 2004 marks the twenty-fifth anniversary of RI, which has expanded its areas of interest to include the issues that cause and surround displacement — landmines, HIV/AIDS, peacekeeping, conflict resolution, famine, and women's access to reproductive health services.

Website: www.refugeesinternational.org
Refugees International
1705 N St. N.W.
Washington, D.C. 20036
202.828.0110

The American Refugee Committee provides assistance to almost a million uprooted people around the world through primary healthcare delivery, improved water and sanitation, shelter reconstruction, microcredit projects, environmental rehabilitation, and psychosocial services.

Website: www.archq.org
American Refugee Committee International Headquarters
430 Oak Grove St., Suite 204
Minneapolis, MN 55403
612.872.7060

## Mark Nyberg

Email: Mbnyberg@aol.com

## Part Two. Leaving the Reasoned Path

## Adonal Foyle

Website: www.adonalfoyle.com

Democracy Matters informs and engages college students and communities in efforts to strengthen democracy, encouraging the emergence of a new generation of reform-minded leaders.

Website: www.democracymatters.org
The Democracy Matters Institute
2600 Johnny Cake Hill Rd.
Hamilton, NY 13346

## Janet Yang

Manifest Films
Email: manifilm@aol.com

## Jim Garrison

State of the World Forum is a global network of leaders dedicated to discerning and implementing the principles, values, and actions necessary to guide humanity toward a more sustainable global civilization.

Website: www.worldforum.org
State of the World Forum
The Presidio, Building 992
P.O. Box 29434
San Francisco, CA 94129
415.561.2345
415.561.2323 (fax)

## John Perkins

Website: www.JohnPerkins.org

The Dream Change Coalition is a grassroots movement of people from many cultures who are dedicated to creating new values and ways of living. Dream Change programs include trips to visit, work with, and learn from indigenous teachers; workshops and training courses in the United States and Europe; films, videos, and television presentations; and POLE (Pollution Offset Lease for Earth).

Website: www.dreamchange.org
Dream Change Coalition
P.O. Box 31357
Palm Beach Gardens, FL 33410
561.622.6064

## Part Three. Loving beyond All Measure

Karen Murray

The National Marfan Foundation disseminates accurate and timely information about Marfan syndrome to patients, family members, and the healthcare community. It also provides a network of communication for patients and relatives to share experiences, support one another, and improve their medical care. The Foundation supports and fosters research about Marfan syndrome, which is an inheritable disorder of the connective tissue that affects many organ systems, including the skeleton, lungs, eyes, heart, and blood vessels.

Website: www.marfan.org
National Marfan Foundation
22 Manhasset Ave.
Port Washington, NY 11050
800.8.MARFAN

Robert Lewis

The National Conference for Community and Justice is a human relations organization dedicated to fighting bias, racism, and bigotry. NCCJ promotes respect and understanding among all races, religions, and cultures through advocacy, conflict resolution, and education.

Website: www.nccj.org
National Conference for Community and Justice
38 Chauncy St., Suite 812
Boston, MA 02111
617.451.5010
617.451.9495 (fax)

City Year is an "action tank" for national service, seeking to demonstrate, improve, and promote the concept of national service as a way to build a stronger democracy. An action tank combines theory and practice to advance new policy ideas, to make programmatic breakthroughs, and to bring about major changes in society.

Website: www.cityyear.org
City Year Boston
285 Columbus Ave.
Boston, MA 02116
617.927.2500

## Paul Cox

Seacology is a nonprofit nongovernmental organization with the sole and unique purpose of preserving the environments and cultures of islands across the globe.

Website: www.seacology.org
Seacology
2009 Hopkins St.
Berkeley, CA 94707
510.559.3505
510.559.3506 (fax)

The AIDS ReSearch Alliance's research agenda includes developing more effective and less toxic direct anti-HIV therapies, including therapies outside the three main drug classes to which all currently available therapies belong; determining how best to eradicate the HIV viral reservoirs that "fly beneath the radar" of currently available drugs; developing vaccines and microbicides that prevent the spread of the virus; and helping to prevent the loss of immune function in recently infected people, to restore immune function in those who are more compromised, and to address questions of long-term disease management.

Website: www.aidsresearch.org
AIDS ReSearch Alliance
621-A North San Vicente Blvd.
West Hollywood, CA 90069
310.358.2423 (administration)
310.358.2429 (clinic)
310.358.2431 (fax)

The National Tropical Botanical Garden is dedicated to the conservation of tropical plant diversity, particularly rare and endangered species.

Under its congressional charter, the privately funded NTBG administers gardens of extraordinary beauty and historical significance, advancing scientific research, public education, and plant conservation.

Website: www.ntbg.org
National Tropical Botanical Garden
3530 Papalina Rd.
Kalaheo, HI 96741
808.332.7324

### Part Four. Living Replete

### Nelly Rodriguez

Cita Con Nelly Productions
Todd Gang, Executive Producer
Email: citaconnelly@msn.com
503.936.5944

### George McLaird

Website: www.mclaird.com
Email: gmpersonal@cs.com

### Karen Gaffney

The Karen Gaffney Foundation champions full inclusion in families, schools, communities, and the workplace of those with Down syndrome and other learning disabilities.

Website: www.karengaffneyfoundation.com
Karen Gaffney Foundation
1328 N.W. Kearney
Portland, OR 97209
503.973.5130

The National Down Syndrome Congress is the chief advocacy organization for those with Down syndrome and their families.

Website: www.ndsccenter.org
National Down Syndrome Congress
1370 Center Dr., Suite 102
Atlanta, GA 30338
770.604.9500

The National Association for Down Syndrome works to foster understanding and acceptance of people with Down syndrome.

Website: www.nads.org
National Association for Down Syndrome
P.O. Box 4542
Oak Brook, IL 60522
630.325.9112

The National Down Syndrome Society benefits people with Down syndrome and their families through national leadership in education, research, and advocacy. It is committed to enhancing the quality of life and realizing the potential of all people with Down syndrome.

Website: www.ndss.org

The ARC of the United States, through education, research, and advocacy, works to include all children and adults with cognitive, intellectual, and developmental disabilities in their communities.

Website: www.thearc.org
The ARC
1010 Wayne Ave., Suite 650
Silver Spring, MD 20910
301.565.3842
301.565.3843 (fax)

## Kathy Eldon

Creative Visions uses the power of the media and the limitless creativity of the human spirit to empower, inspire, and enable individuals to act on behalf of global issues — to achieve their own potential both for themselves and for the planet.

Website: www.creativevisions.org
Creative Visions
8539 Sunset Blvd., Suite 4-122
West Hollywood, CA 90069
310.289.5037 (fax)

To learn more about Dan Eldon, his work, his journals, and how educators around the world are using Dan's art and story for inspiration in the classroom, go to www.daneldon.org.

*Global Tribe* is a PBS series that combines the spirit of travel with a meaningful exploration of the global issues that affect us all, from healing racial wounds to saving the environment to improving the lives of the poorest among us. The quest is to find solutions and to meet the unsung heroes in every country who offer us hope and a path to a better tomorrow.

Website: www.pbs.org/globaltribe

## Part Five. Standing Up for What's Right
### Bill Wassmuth

The Gonzaga University Institute for Action against Hate was founded as a positive and enduring vehicle for combating hate and hate crimes on campuses and in communities throughout the nation.

Website: www.gonzaga.edu/againsthate
Gonzaga University Institute for Action against Hate
AD Box 43
502 E. Boon Ave.
Spokane, WA 99258-0043
509.323.3665

### Anna Smith

Email: cas25@netcarrier.com

## Debbie Williams

The Giraffe Project fosters active citizenship and recognizes people who stick their necks out for the common good and who display the kind of courage and commitment that inspires others to action.

Website: www.giraffe.org
The Giraffe Project
P.O. Box 759
Langley, WA 98260
360.221.7989

The Cavallo Foundation Awards for Moral Courage gave awards annually to three people in the country who spoke out against an injustice when it would have been easier to remain silent. The selection criteria were taking action against government or corporate wrongdoing by exposing it to the public view; doing so to save lives, to prevent harm to public health, the environment, or civil liberties, or to promote social justice; and doing so in spite of risk to one's life, career, or economic welfare. The recipients were chosen by a selection committee that included experts from academia, law, business, and public interest groups.

The Project on Government Oversight is committed to exposing waste, fraud, and corruption in the following areas: defense, energy and environment, contract oversight, and open government.

Website: www.pogo.org
Project on Government Oversight
666 Eleventh St. N.W., Suite 500
Washington, D.C. 20001
202.347.1122

The Government Accountability Project's mission is to protect the public interest by promoting government and corporate accountability through advancing occupational free speech and ethical conduct, defending whistle-blowers, and empowering citizen activists. It is the nation's leading whistle-blower organization, litigating whistle-blower cases, publicizing whistle-blower concerns, and developing policy and legal reforms of whistle-blower laws.

Website: www.whistleblower.org
Government Accountability Project
1612 K St. N.W., Suite 400
Washington, D.C. 20006
202.408.0034

## Further Reading

Alibrandi, Tom, with Bill Wassmuth. *Hate Is My Neighbor* (Coeur d'Alene, ID: University of Idaho Press, 2001).

Cox, Paul. *Nafanua: Saving the Samoan Rain Forest* (New York: W. H. Freeman and Company, 1997).

Cox, Paul, and Sandra Anne Banack. *Islands, Plants, and Polynesians: An*

*Introduction to Polynesian Ethnobotany* (Portland, OR: Timber Press, 1991).

Eldon, Dan, and Kathy Eldon. *The Journey Is the Destination: The Journals of Dan Eldon* (San Francisco: Chronicle, 1997).

Eldon, Kathy, and Amy Eldon. *Love Catcher: Inviting Love into Your Life* (San Francisco: Chronicle Books, 2001).

Eldon, Kathy, Amy Eldon, and Michelle Barnes. *Soul Catcher: A Journal to Help You Become Who You Really Are* (San Francisco: Chronicle Books, 1999).

Eldon, Kathy, Amy Eldon, and Elisabeth Zeilon. *Angel Catcher* (San Francisco: Chronicle Books, 1998).

Garrison, Jim. *America as Empire: Global Leader or Rogue Power?* (San Francisco: Berrett-Koehler Publishers, 2004).

———. *Civilization and the Transformation of Power* (New York: Paraview Press, 2000).

———. *The Darkness of God: Theology after Hiroshima* (Grand Rapids, MI: Eerdmans Publishing Company, 1983).

———. *The Plutonium Culture: From Hiroshima to Harrisburg* (New York: Continuum, 1981).

Garrison, Jim, and John-Francis Phipps. *The New Diplomats: Citizens As Ambassadors for Peace* (Devon: U.K.: Green Books, 1991).

Garrison, Jim, and Pyare Shivpuri. *The Russian Threat: Its Myths and Realities* (Nevada City, CA: Gateways Books, 1985).

Mandle, Jay R., and Joan D. Mandle, *Caribbean Hoops: The Development of West Indian Basketball* (Langhorne, PA: Gordon and Breach, 1994).

———. *Grass Roots Commitment: Basketball and Society in Trinidad and Tobago* (Parkersburg, IA: Caribbean Books, 1988).

McLaird, George. *Marriage Maze: McLaird's Field Guide for the Journey* (Mill Valley, CA: Malcomb Morrow Publishing House, 1995).

———. *Transformation Is an Inside Job: A Primer for Transformation* (Camarillo, CA: DeVorss Publications, 1982).

Nichols, Nichelle. *Beyond Uhura: Star Trek and Other Memories* (New York: Putnam, 1994).

Osius, Alison. *Second Ascent: The Story of Hugh Herr* (New York: Dell, 1993).

Perkins, John. *Confessions of an Economic Hit Man.* (San Francisco: Berrett-Koehler Publishers, 2004).

———. *Psychonavigation: Techniques for Travel Beyond Time* (Rochester, VT: Destiny Books, 1990).

———. *Shapeshifting: Shamanic Techniques for Global and Personal Transformation* (Rochester, VT: Destiny Books, 1997).

———. *The World Is As You Dream It: Shamanic Teachings from the Amazon and Andes* (Rochester, VT: Destiny Books, 1994).

Perkins, John, and Shakaim Mariano Shakaim Ijisam Chumpi. *Spirit of the Shuar: Wisdom from the Last Unconquered People of the Amazon* (Rochester, VT: Destiny Books, 2001).

## Recommended Viewing

Videos available from the Karen Gaffney Foundation, Portland, Oregon:

*Journey of a Lifetime... Beginning with the End in Mind*
*Opening Doors of Tomorrow, Today*
*Imagine the Possibilities: Navigating the English Channel and Life's Other Currents*

# Photo Credits

Photo direction by Robin Damore (www.robindamore.com).

Photos on pages 9, 27, 43, 61, 181, 215, 243, and 257 by Robin Damore.

Photo on page 93 provided by Adonal Foyle.

Photo on page 113 provided by Janet Yang.

Photo on page 131 provided by Jim Garrison.

Photo on page 143 provided by John Perkins.

Photo on page 167 provided by Karen Murray.

Photo on page 195 by David Littschwager and Susan Middleton.

Photo on page 229 provided by George McLaird.

Photo on page 279 by Chris Nordfors.

Photo on page 295 by Bryan Smith.

Photo on page 307 provided by the Giraffe Project.

## About the Author

Katherine Martin is the author of *Women of Courage* and *Women of Spirit*. Please visit her website at www.peoplewhodare.com.